MAD FRANK AND FRIENDS

Frank Fraser and James Morton

WARNER BOOKS

A *Warner* Book

First published in Great Britain in 1998
by Little, Brown and Company
This edition published by Warner Books in 1999
Reprinted 2001

Copyright © Francis Fraser and James Morton 1998

The moral right of the author has been asserted.

A CIP catalogue record for this book
is available from the British Library.

ISBN 0 7515 2464 6

Typeset by Palimpsest Book Production Limited,
Polmont, Stirlingshire
Printed and bound in Great Britain by
Clays Ltd, St Ives plc

Warner Books
A Division of
Little, Brown and Company (UK)
Brettenham House
Lancaster Place
London WC2E 7EN

www.littlebrown.co.uk

Contents

Reviews for *Mad Frank and Friends*

'Fraser can still use his name to see things are right. So any critic tempted to pen a less than glowing review might end up going for a dip in a pair of concrete wellies. With that in mind, I'd like it to be known that this is a work of unfettered genius. And doesn't Frank look good for his age'
Daily Mirror

'There are few big names in the London underworld he has not met'
The Times

'More jolly yarns from the loveable retired gangland figure'
The Bookseller

'What intelligent reader would fail to be intrigued ... perversely entertaining'
Manchester Evening News

'... brings home a forgotten era of underworld Britain'
Parklife

'Frank's new book evokes a vanished world'
South London Press

'... very readable ...'
Oxford Mail

'... his second extraordinary volume of memoirs ... Fascinating in their own right, Fraser's recollections also provide a compelling portrait of growing up in poverty in South East London'
Tangled Web

'fascinating'
Ireland on Sunday

Reviews for *Mad Frank*

'One of the most feared villains in London's underworld'
Time Out

'a chillingly unrepentant story'
The Times

'… evokes a vanished era'
Independent on Sunday

'… colourful … chilling'
Sunday Express

'… fascinating, it reads like a Who's Who of the British criminal class.'
Coventry Evening News

'… pulls no punches … compelling reading.'
Kent Today

'… the full, violent story. Read it if you have the stomach.'
Glasgow Evening Times

'Macabre, malignant and malevolent, Mad Frank is an incredible phenomenon … fascinating.'
Scallywag

'… horrific account of his life and crimes.'
South Wales Echo

'vivid and brutally honest account of a life revolving around crime'
Bolton Evening News

'In this compelling memoir Fraser recounts his past in the gangs: the killings, the revenge and the dealings with notorious names such as the Krays and the Richardsons'
Newtownards Chronicle

For Marilyn
with my thanks and love

Introduction

The call was on my answering machine that night when I arrived home: 'A Mr Francis Fraser has telephoned and wants to speak to you urgently.' He had left a number. There was only one Francis Fraser I knew. There couldn't possibly be two of them who wished to speak with me urgently.

In 1992 I had just written a history of London's Gangland in which I had offended some players who had been remonstrating with me over what they saw as unjustified comments on their behaviour. That little problem had more or less been smoothed over, but the prospect of dealing with the formidable Fraser seemed a wholly different proposition.

I hadn't spoken to him for over twenty years since the time I had defended him in the so-called Parkhurst riot of 1969, after he had been charged with incitement to murder and a string of charges of grievous bodily harm. Then prison officers at Parkhurst had placed me in the doctor's room when I went to interview this man who had been certified insane three times. There was a special button they pointed out on the inside of the desk: 'Press it with your knee,' they advised, 'and we'll try and get in before he gets to you.' He never tried and now, with hindsight, I suspect they were playing an elaborate charade. Defence lawyers in the trial were not popular. I found on more than one occasion that two of my tyres had been let down while my car was parked in the side road leading to the prison gates – and no, they hadn't any equipment which would help me reinflate them. I took to parking further away and walking.

Apart from Fraser's insistence that I see him before any other prisoners I was down to interview during a session, I never had the slightest trouble with him. It was not an unreasonable request. He was, without doubt, the senior prisoner and so needed respect shown. The others did not mind. They had the afternoon out of their cells or the workshop to chat and smoke with their friends while waiting their turn, which would be delayed as long as Fraser and – to a much lesser extent – I chose. The trial had been as satisfactory as could be expected in the circumstances. He was acquitted of the main charges and received a further five years, to add to the fifteen he was already serving, for the more minor ones.

He could not be holding a grudge against me for that trial, so what had I written which had offended him? I could not ignore the call, there would only be another, and so it was a question of swallowing a glass of unpleasant medicine. However, when I telephoned it was immediately apparent I had not offended him.

'I read your book,' he said. 'Not bad, some things you had wrong.'

I said nothing. 'Now I want you to write my book.'

My agent did not approve. I am not sure she approved of true crime books as a concept, let alone the autobiography of a criminal, particularly this one, but I agreed to meet him. He turned up slightly late and very apologetic. He had broken his arm and had been delayed at the hospital. 'You could have cancelled,' I said. 'No,' he said. 'I had an appointment with you and I had to keep it.'

Over the years I had seen snips in the newspapers about him. His most recent exploit had been when he was shot outside a club in Clerkenwell Green. Drugs, said the newspapers. The police, said Fraser. I prevaricated. I was writing another book which would not be finished until the spring. He would wait. He said he had a publisher lined up but, when it came to it, that deal failed to materialise. I prepared an outline for him for Little, Brown and started seeing him every Friday morning.

Fraser was born in South London in 1922, of poor but completely honest parents, and was the youngest of five children. Three of his siblings have no criminal convictions. One, his sister Eva, was a top-class shoplifter in her younger days but, apart from a conviction when she tried to assist her brother in what was known as the Torture trial in 1965, she has had no convictions for fifty years. On the other hand, from just before the War until the end of the 1980s Fraser had rarely been out of prison. Apart from working in his own right, although physically small he has been an enforcer and strong man for the leaders of the Underworld over the years; in the 1940s and 1950s for Billy Hill, and in the 1960s for the Richardson brothers. His major sentences included seven years for slashing Hill's rival Jack Spot, five for an affray at Mr Smith's Club in which Richard Hart was killed and of whose murder Fraser was acquitted. This was followed by ten years' consecutive for his part in the so-called Torture trial following which the Richardson brothers were convicted and Charles, the elder, was sentenced to twenty-five years. The five years for the Parkhurst riot made a total of twenty for that particular spell alone. Because of his behaviour in prison over the years he forfeited almost every day of his remission, and his years in prison totalled something over forty served. During his sentences he received regular beatings in the prisons for his behaviour. He would seem to be one of those rare people, like bullfighters, who are simply impervious to pain, something which made him such a danger to those to whom he took a dislike. It was because of his violence in prison, rather than because he fancied he was Napoleon, that he was certified and sent to mental hospitals.

Once the book *Mad Frank* was published, a second career took off and Fraser became something of a media darling, a role to which he has applied himself with as much fervour as he showed in his younger days when he attacked rival criminals, prison officers and governors alike. It is interesting, if idle, to speculate as to what he might have achieved had he not embarked on his first occupation.

James Morton, 1998

One

At the time when I was born in 1923, there was no great villains who ran south-east London. In north London and Soho, the Italians – the Sabini brothers led by Darby – were the governors. They had a bit of a quarrel with the Cortesi brothers which ended in a shooting in the Fratellanza Club in Little Italy and with Enrico Cortesi getting four years. Some people thought he was the real brains behind the Sabinis, and there's no question that Darby lost his touch as things went on. But he more or less had things under control until Alf White from King's Cross and his boys, who'd been great friends with them in the 1920s, took them on in 1935. That was something that ended with a pitched battle at Lewes racecourse. That copper Ted Greeno said the Sabinis had tipped the police that something was going to go down that day, and as a result many good men went down for long sentences. After that the Sabinis and the Whites divided up Clerkenwell and King's Cross between them; and when the Sabinis got interned as undesirable aliens at the beginning of the War, that was just about the end of them. Then Darby got a spell for receiving down in Sussex where he was living.[1]

One of their men, Albert Dimes, whose real name was Dimeo,

[1] In June 1943 Darby Sabini was convicted in the name of Fred Sabini of receiving £383 worth of silver and wine which had been stolen by soldiers from the house of a retired Sussex magistrate in Uckfield. His defence was that he thought he was buying goods from an hotel which was being sold out. Sentencing him on 17 June to two years' hard labour the Recorder, Gilbert Paull, commented, 'It is men like you who lay temptation before soldiers. If there were none like you there would be no temptation to steal.' There are references in the court files to him by the name Darby. He was said to be aged 54 and to have no previous convictions. [QR/E/1344]. He died, a small-time racecourse bookmaker, in 1951.

survived and in the late 1940s he, Billy Hill and Jack Spot – who was Jewish and was really called Comer – pushed the Whites out of Soho. Billy and Spot ran the West End together for some years until Spot thought he was getting the thin end of things and started causing trouble. He picked on Albert Dimes in a fight in Frith Street; they both ended up at the Old Bailey, and both got chucked after Spot called a bent vicar to give evidence for him. But it was the end of Spot. Billy more or less retired and Albert more or less became respectable. For a time the Nash family from Islington had an interest in some of the London clubs, but they faded away in the early 1960s and from then on it was the Twins in east London and Charlie and Eddie Richardson and me over the water in Peckham.

When I say there was no villains in south-east London when I grew up, I mean in the sense that there was no one in overall control. There was what was called the Elephant and Castle Boys who had fought the Sabinis over the racecourse pitches in the 1920s. They'd been aligned with the Camden Town Mob and Fred Gilbert, and with Fred Kimber and his Brummagem Boys, but they didn't control the area. They were more thieves than anything else; that doesn't mean to say there weren't some good men amongst them though. I'm not sure that Fred Kimber was ever head of the Elephant Gang. You got rumours, but there might be as much truth in the cup on that table being the leader. I think Alf Hinds Snr, who was nicked with Johnnie Parker and Ben Bennett over the Portsmouth bank, he was as much head. Alf got five years and fifteen strokes of the cat in 1932,[2]

[2]On 25 April 1932 £23,477 was stolen from two Lloyds Bank clerks in Edinburgh Road, Portsmouth. Hinds, who called an alibi, was defended by G.L. Hardy who later defended Fraser. Before being sentenced one of his co-defendants, Parker, asked the judge Mr Justice Avory, whom he said had not given him a fair crack of the whip, if he could be flogged. 'If you can give me corporal punishment and so lighten my sentence so I can come out to my children, I hope you will.' Imposing fifteen strokes and five years Avory commented, 'The time has come when it is necessary that stern measures be taken to repress this class of offence for which you have been, in my opinion, rightly convicted by the jury.' One of the clerks, Robert Poor, received £5 for his bravery. His Lordship's words did not strike terror into the hearts of motor-car bandits. In the week following the trial there were what the local paper called four 'outrages' in as many days. Garage proprietors at lonely spots were said to be 'almost afraid to give night service' and, 'The police are unable to cope with the new menace.' [*Portsmouth Evening News* 16 August 1932].

and the others got more or less the same. He died a bit later from TB, and it was always said the cat had brought it on – that and being in Dartmoor. When Bennett come out he went bent. He wrote to the assessors saying his brother Harry had had the money and had put it into business, but there was no evidence and I'm glad to say Harry never even got charged. I can't say for sure, but it looked as though one brother had given the other the money to look after and he turned him over, and so Ben got wicked. It was a good job, that one – something like £23,000, and not a penny recovered. They got nicked through sheer folly. After the robbery, Hinds' mother was dressed up in furs in pubs round the Elephant. I know in them days a woman would almost prefer to have furs rather than jewellery, but to go on parade like that! Well, she was asking for it.

You could also say Alf and Ernie Gregory were heads. They were both older than me, Ernie about ten years older and Alf about five. One got twelve and the other seven in 1951 for doing the manager in the Alfred's Head at the Elephant. Paul Watkins got eight years in the same thing. Paddy O'Nione, known as Paddy Onions, was the one who actually did him and was found not guilty. When my mother died Ernie led the hearse down the street, which was a nice thing to do. Now, if anyone was nicked for a famous case the papers said they were the head of the Elephant Boys. It was kudos if you got your name mentioned as head of the gang.

Franny Daniels was another to look up to when I was young: a great thief, a great fellow. He came from the back of East Lane off the Walworth Road, and was another member of the Elephant Gang. He had three years' penal servitude in 1941 for a smash-and-grab, and when he came out in 1943 he started having an affair with one of the daughters of Johnny Jackson who was Alf White's right-hand man. The trouble was she was married to Fatty Cook, who was doing bird at the time.

Years earlier when Johnny Jackson had been having it off with Billy Hill's sister Maggie, he'd had a straightener on the cobbles with a bloke. Maggie was a good one with her hatpin – she put out a copper's eye once – and she stabbed the man in the face just to make sure Johnny come out on top.

Then in September 1944 Franny got three years along with Cherry Titmuss and Babsy Martin. They got nicked by Capstick – the man who liked to call himself 'Charlie Artful' and whose son is now a judge at the Old Bailey – over a ladies' clothing factory in Clerkenwell which had been done, in fact, by Jimmy and Lennie Garrett. Martin, who'd never done a day in his life, got three as well. He gave a Nazi-style salute as he was sentenced to show what he thought of things. When Fatty Cook come out Franny was inside over the factory job, and he'd left all his suits round the girl's house, so Fatty cut them all up and dumped what was left of them outside Franny's mother's house. He'd knocked on the door, found no one wasn't in and just left them.

Babsy Martin's father – along with Joey, one of the Sabinis – had a crooked screw fetching bottles in for him when he was in Maidstone. Eventually the screw got nine months.

When Franny came out in 1946 it was straight back to work, but after he got away on the London Airport bullion job he more or less give up thieving and went into racing and gambling. He realised he'd had a touch getting away and, knowing how you could be fitted up, he more or less turned it in.

The Murrays were big around the Elephant; so was Billy Howard, who joined the Army before the War. He was eight years older than me, so when I was 14 he was a man of 22. Later he owned the Beehive Club and he could have a good straightener with anybody. He had it in for Mikey Conners – cut him about three times, he did. Billy was always at funerals; there's a picture of him carrying Tommy Smithson's coffin. If he wasn't at a funeral everyone would be worried. Billy was nice, but he was a professional mourner.

He was having a straightener with 'Spindles' Jackson – Arthur Clawson was his real name – in Monkton Road off the New Kent Road over Spindles' wife, when an unexploded bomb went off in the next street and they stopped fighting to run round and see what they could do to help.

After his fight with Billy Howard, Spindles and Billy Hooper got twenty-one months each and the wife Spindles was with, she left him. In prison he went round the bend. By today's standards he'd have had to be certified, but then you had to be really uncontainable. He snapped out of it and come together, but the signs were already there then.

Then Spindles got two years with me in 1945 for a clothing coupon job at the Town Hall at Benfleet, when we ran out of petrol in the Rotherhithe tunnel and the coppers were waiting for us. That tunnel was never lucky for me. He got two years, I got twenty months and again he went a little bit funny. We had a whip-round for him after his two years and for a time he was with Nellie Harmon, who was a top shoplifter and a lovely girl, but he just went round the bend. She broke up with him; she couldn't take any more, and he went in a nut-house. As far as I know, he's still alive.

People say the best fight they ever saw after the War was between Billy Howard and Tony Mella. It was on the cobbles about 1 a.m. at the back of Leicester Square somewhere. I was in prison, so I missed it, but I'm told they were both still standing at the end. Tony Mella wasn't a bad fighter in his way. We fixed a couple for him to help him along, but then he ran into a really good boy. He had a terrific punch, and could take a bit, but by then he wasn't fast enough. As for fixing fights, it wasn't difficult. There was no inquisitive press or TV or radio then. There was only really *Boxing News* and, even if they knew, they might try and make sure it didn't happen again, but they'd never print it in those days. The boys were boxing for nothing. The betting on them fights lower down the scale would be non-existent. It was only the big fights that would have Mickey Duff running round as a gofer putting bets on for Solomons. For the others, bets would be private. Purses were nothing and a tenner would work wonders. The number of

5

times I was told the fight was hookey – you wouldn't believe it.[3] A lot of it was spread as propaganda to get back to the fighter's camp and upset him. You never knew when you were seeing a straight fight in the Thirties. Nowadays you don't have to bribe the opposition, you hand-pick the opponent, whereas in the old days the public wouldn't stand for it. Better they didn't know it was fixed.

After he left the ring Mella had clubs in Soho and he got topped by a friend of his, Alf Melvin, who shot him one afternoon in the Bus Stop Club. Then in turn Melvin went and topped himself: just sat on the pavement and put the gun in his mouth, by all accounts.

People haven't really heard of Jack Stanley, but he was a good thief and a muscle man as well, for whoever required him. If someone opened a little drinker, he was a handy man to have on their side. A publican would like to keep sweet with certain people and Jackie was one of those people. He was big. He died in a car crash coming home from the races in about 1948. Little Alec Robb was another who was in the Dartmoor prison mutiny. His real name was Jackson and he was a good thief and safe-blower. He was doing ten and got another six for the mutiny, so he wound up doing sixteen.

'Ruby' Sparks was in the mutiny as well; he came from Camberwell originally, where apparently he had led a gang called the Tiger Yard Boys when he was young. Jackie Hayes, who died not so long ago, was related to Timmy Hayes who carried a lot of clout in West Ham. Ruby was one of the first to do smash-and-grabs and he had a girl-friend Lilian Goldstein who went on them with him. She was known as the 'Bobbed-Haired Bandit', and when she was young she was something of a looker. Some people say she was Timmy Hayes' daughter and, as she was Jewish herself, she could have been. She really was a bit of a mystery. When they were trying

---

[3]Hook(e)y meaning dishonest, comes from the Australian sporting slang term to hook-up a horse to prevent it winning, and dates from the 1940s. To play hookey means to absent oneself without permission, usually from school.

to find Ruby after he finally escaped from the Moor she set up a really good smokescreen, getting a woman to write to the papers saying how she'd abandoned Ruby and begging him to give himself up – and all the while he was staying at her place in north London!

I was too young for the Dartmoor mutiny of 1932, which was just as well; but, as the years went on, I got to know a lot of the men who had been involved. Ruby Sparks was always telling me about it.

Ruby was a good man. His real name was Alfred Watson. He called himself Charles, but no one else ever called him that. He was known as Ruby because, when he was a young man, he did a Maharajah and came away with all these rubies. But he thought they were fake, and so he gave them away.

Ruby came from Camberwell originally, like I said. He'd had six months as far back as 1920 and he was one of the first prisoners at Portland Borstal in 1922–3 when it was changed from a security prison to a Borstal, and he escaped. That really set him on the road. It was a bit of a feat because it is on a peninsula, only one way off and one way on unless you're a Channel swimmer.

Lilian Goldstein – she nearly got Ruby out of Strangeways when he was nicked in 1927. He'd had three years' penal servitude for housebreaking. The police reckoned he was really the top man at the time. Before that he was wanted for murder in Birmingham when a woman got knocked down as they got away in a smash-and-grab, but no one picked him out on the ID.

So Lilian drove up and arranged to sit outside the prison until he got over the wall, but the trouble was that at the last minute he took another man along with him. By the time they were over they were so late she thought something had gone wrong inside and she'd driven off. He got caught within a couple of hours. He was found by some workmen and, what with having a cockney accent and being found shivering in a pond about five in the morning, it was obvious what he was.

Dartmoor was a dreadful place. Even when I was there in the 1950s, the walls were still running with water. It had been built at the time of the Napoleonic Wars and I don't think it had been modernised since. At the time of the mutiny, if you got penal servitude you either went to Parkhurst or to the Moor, and you were there within a month of starting your sentence. That was the worst thing about the sentence; you were so far away. You got a ticket-of-leave as well, which was a sort of licence and meant they could pull you back, but it was being in Dartmoor which was the thing. You stayed there for the whole of the sentence. No help with visits; the man was literally abandoned if his family lived some way away and couldn't afford to come.

The mutiny was over beatings down in the E wing, which then as now was the punishment block. Ruby used to say that they'd had a decent governor there but then he had been replaced by a Captain Roberts who more or less let the screws do what they liked.

Given that there was no real association time and all work was done in silence, it was a magnificent feat to get the mutiny organised. It was only as you got on with your sentence that you were allowed association. You got an hour after eighteen months, and you could talk a bit on exercise. Then when you'd done two and a half you got a little bit more, and when you done four you got a little bit more again. And the rest was done by word of mouth on exercise – passed on. You could get words in here and there, even though as late as my day you were only meant to speak with the man you was walking with.

Remember, the prison authorities weren't as alert in cultivating a grass as they have become. Grasses have always existed in prison and out, but it wasn't a vital thing. They couldn't believe there could even be such a mutiny. One had never taken place in modern history from 1895 – when a screw got killed – to 1932. They had also brought in one or two reforms after the First World War. The arrows on the uniform had gone and so had the ball and chain. They already thought they'd given the prisoners far more than they should have done. The other thing was that in 1932 the whole of life outside, let alone in prison, was extremely disciplined.

It was decided they would have a go, but then Tommy Speedles jumped the gun. He cut the prison officer a lovely stripe, which ran all the way down the right side of his face. He was still an officer when I went there and the cut still showed from his hairline right down his cheek to his chin. It was a blinder of a cut. That was on the day before the actual riot.

Speedles was doing ten years for slinging vitriol in the face of a West End brass – Fanny Simmonds, who was known as Polish Fanny – at Wimbledon dog track. She was in a terrible state. They'd been together for years and they'd been high on the hog when he was winning on the dogs, and when he wasn't then he'd had her on the game. She prosecuted him once for stealing a brooch off her in Pall Mall, but she'd dropped the charge. Then she'd gone and left him and was living somewhere off the Edgware Road, and he was in the Borough. He did her just as she left the track. It took off part of an ear and her nose, and she had what they call a wry neck for the rest of her life. What did for him was there was another woman who was with her who got splashed – her and a Jewish bloke who was a bookmaker. Judges were always more harsh when someone who wasn't involved got injured. Ruth Ellis might have been reprieved if one of the bullets hadn't hit a bystander, and a lot of fuss was kicked up over that.

Speedles, he was pretty wild when he was young. He'd shot another man in a card game and done time for that as well. He got another twelve consecutive for striping the screw, so that made twenty-two in all. His brief in the vitriol case said that he was mentally deficient, just as they used to put that fanny out for me when I needed a bit of help in the Spot case. 'Been made use of by others for a foul purpose,' said my brief. Speedles used to tell me they'd thrown him out of the Army after two months and marked him down as a mental defective, but I never noticed anything defective about him.

I think he came from Australia originally. I knew him well because he was always round the West End after he come out. He was chauffeur to Edgar Britt, the great jockey, who was also an Australian. Like most Aussies, Tommy was a great con-man. I think that's what he must have done – conned the Army he was defective, because in those days some of the doctors weren't too bright themselves. He stayed in England and died here. I last see him in Frith Street in 1965 just before I was arrested over Mr Smith's Club. Albert Dimes, who was with me, had his betting shop A. Barnett in the street, and we all went and had a coffee together.

Bert Wilkins, who'd been chucked for a murder at Wandsworth dogs himself and later did really well, was very good to Tommy, looking after him throughout his bird. So was another bookmaker, Hector MacDonald, who was great pals with Bert Wilkins' friend, Marsh. His real name was Pasqualino Papa, but he used to fight as Bert Marsh. He was a man who was very close to the Sabinis and he'd got acquitted over the same killing at Wandsworth dogs. It was all over who could work a pitch. Jim Wicks, who was later Henry Cooper's manager, was a witness.

Hector, who had done a Borstal, was 'Harry the Doctor's' great pal.[4] There was another South London bookmaker was very good to Tommy and all. After the Lewes racecourse battle a few years later, when Jimmy Spinks got sent down George Chandler looked after him throughout his time. It was a shame because after that sentence over the Lewes racecourse he became something of a drinker. He'd been a good man before, with a good reputation.

The reason why these bookmakers should help out? Anyone who was a rebel, he had the liking and respect of everyone. By

---

[4]Harry Bass, 'Harry the Doctor', specialised in pretending to be a medical man so that his partner, a brilliant locksmith known as 'Johnny No Legs', could obtain impressions of keys to the premises of chemists. *See Mad Frank pp. 50–52.*

and large the bookmakers had never been in prison, but they were by inclination quite favourable to the Underworld. After all, they gained from the Underworld's losses. Don't forget also that bookmaking was illegal then.

The day after Speedles cut the screw, 25 January 1932, the Dartmoor mutiny started properly. As I said, there hadn't been one for nearly forty years. It was a Sunday and it started when they were being marched over to the chapel about half-past nine. The Strangeways riot, a few years ago, was a bit the same. That started in the chapel too, and it spread from there. They got hold of some paving stones and started pelting the screws, who panicked. Apparently there'd been booing and jeering at breakfast, although it was meant to be silent, and someone threw the porridge back over the warder.

The first thing they went for was the prison officers' mess, through the second gate. You turned right and just along behind the wall was the mess. That's the first thing they went for, where all the booze was. And of course that was where they made their mistake. Instead of getting drunk, they should have got out while they could. They had a half-hour start and they didn't use it.

They came down to the punishment cells and unlocked Tommy Speedles and some others, and locked up the Governor and the Deputy Commissioner, a man called Turner; they call them Director nowadays. In those days the Commissioner was responsible for the whole country: one for Borstals and one for prisons. They took their wallets and watches off them, and these were never found.

It was magnificent, they set the prison alight. What Ruby wanted to do was get over the wall and just go off on to the Moor and take his chance. There was no way there could be outside help. How could you get anybody down from London? You'd have to get a message, then they'd have to have a car. You couldn't have a whole series of motors arriving in the village in those days; everyone would know something was up. To get them all the way down after it started – well, that would take a few hours. Speed had to be the thing. Over and out.

Then, of course, they didn't act fast enough. They called in the Army with machine guns. Ruby was shot as he got on top of the wall. He got a bullet in his collarbone, but he was lucky. Another was shot in the throat and, although he lived, he never spoke again. Every time someone got on the wall, he was shot down. The inquiry said the guy who got shot in the throat had fallen off the wall; well, in a way, I suppose he had done. Nearly ninety prisoners were shot or injured, but no screw had anything more than a few bruises. That was what the report said.

Ruby often used to say how disappointed he was when quite a lot of the prisoners let him down because they never took part in the planning. When the prisoners who did take part won through for a bit, then these others were 'Jack the Lad' for five minutes. But when it was over they crept back into their shells.

One of the ones who didn't take no part in the mutiny was a bit of a surprise. It was 'Dodger' Mullins, who was a hard man. He wasn't a thief, he was a fighter; he didn't take liberties, he could stand up on the cobbles and have a set-to with anyone. He might lean on a bookmaker here or there, and in fact he'd got nine years along with Timmy Hayes who got seven, when it was said they'd demanded money with menaces – protection – and the coppers got a couple of Jewish geezers to swear blind they did.[5]

But, in a way, Mullins was another Charlie Kray who wouldn't stand up for others in prison. In the mutiny, Mullins

[5]John 'Dodger' Mullins had a long-standing reputation in the East End. He was convicted of grievous bodily harm in 1908 and received five years for a stabbing for which he was, according to Arthur Harding, set up. He later tried to demand money with menaces from Harding and received six years. He had by this time become an associate of the Sabinis. He seems to have worked as a strike breaker during the General Strike of 1926 and also to have been awarded the DCM during the First World War. He was tried for his part in the Dartmoor mutiny and acquitted. In his twilight years he was a friend of the Krays. He died following a car accident.

just went in his cell and shut his door. When the prisoners opened it, he shut it again. To be fair, though, he did have a straight fight with a prison officer after the mutiny. Poor Wally Challis collected him after he came out and it was on the way back he knocked someone down and got five years himself. Wally also got ten, with Johnny Humphreys [no relation to the porn man Jimmy Humphreys] getting seven and Jimmy Hussey, who was later on the Train, who got five. I met them all when we were in Liverpool together. Wally was a big all-rounder before the War. He could look after himself, a good thief but, in fairness, not really into protection. I read in the papers a bit ago that in Devon a man named Walter Challis had killed his wife; he was about 88. Jimmy Hussey mentioned it at a funeral we went to recently and I wondered whether it was the same man. He'd have been about the right age.

The last time I saw Dodger Mullins was in 1948 when he was on a J.R.[6] in Wandsworth. He was standing at the end of A wing. Little did I know that forty years later I'd be on the same spot as Dodger and I could see people looking at me knowing I'd been there forty years previous. Between us, we went back eighty prison years.

As for the ringleaders, Ruby got four years. The reason he got off light was his nature got the better of him and he saved a couple of screws from getting a thrashing. Little Alec Robb got six. He was a good man, a mate of Ruby in the smash-and-grabs, and he was just starting ten years for robbery with violence. He'd had a six and the cat some years back, and I think he'd also shot at a copper. When he came out he had a garage in Brixton. He was a good thief, blew safes and everything. He's well dead now and so's most of the rest of them. Afterwards, some prisoner told the papers they'd got the idea from watching a film *The Big House*, but I never heard Ruby say it was.

There was still trouble in Dartmoor throughout the year,

---

[6]Judge's Remand, when a man was held for reports prior to being sentenced.

this time about the food, although the authorities did their best to hush things up. In the October the new Governor, a man called Parnell, got assaulted by a con who he was visiting in the punishment block, and went on sick leave. He was replaced by a Major Harvey who came from Pentonville, who was meant to be an iron disciplinary. Harvey let it be known that he had looked at the food himself, and that prisoners could either eat it or leave it. He also brought some screws in from Wakefield and said that not only must they make sure every rule was observed, but that if they talked to outsiders they'd get the sack at once. Things calmed down after that.

Overall, though, the mutiny changed the conditions for the next few years and things did get better. Then in 1941 the prison officers made another move and when everyone was locked up about 8 o'clock one night, leading lights who were seen as troublemakers were dragged down to the punishment cells and given a belting. From then until 1945, when it changed into a Borstal for about twenty-one months, it was the worst prison there's ever been here. Out of each batch of prisoners who came in once a month, they would dig out three, four or five and make an example to intimidate the rest. They'd really got it sewn up.

Ruby did a bit better later on. He got sent back to Dartmoor and Lilian sheltered him when he got clean off the Moor in January 1940. He got out over the wall with Alec Marsh and Paddy Dolan. They were both caught almost at once, but Ruby stayed out six months which was the longest anyone ever had done at the time. I suppose Frank Mitchell holds the record nowadays. The Krays got him off the Moor in 1966 and, since no one's been convicted for doing him, he may still be around but I would doubt it.

Conditions stayed bad until 1945, when for a few months it became a Borstal. The war had highlighted the prisoners-of-war and horror camps and Dartmoor had such a name that this was one of the first things the Labour government done. It was well-intentioned, but when so many boys who worked outside were escaping and some were even getting off the Moor and everything, it went back to being a prison in about 1947.

A few years later I came across the Church Army captain who'd been at the Moor at the time of the mutiny. He was called Baden Ball, and he'd been locked up in it. Later he wrote a book, *Prison was my Parish*. I'd come out of Feltham where I'd done a screw over mailbags, and I was sent to Wandsworth and down into the punishment cells. I got a bit of help there straight away from Ruby, who just came over and give me a bit of bread and cheese right out in front of the warders, but it was really Dicky Horne who give me the most help. I was on bread and water diet, but he was working in the library and had a bit more freedom than others. He used to manage to collect bits and pieces for me, take them back to his cell and send them down on a piece of string because his cell was on the landings directly above mine.

They had a big clock at Wandsworth which struck on the hour, and at ten at night he'd put together a bottle with cold tea and a bit of cheese and he would lower it down a line. There was no wire mesh outside the windows then and the screws never bothered to patrol the grounds. I'd climb up on my bed and get what I could in through the little window, drink the tea, and then I'd give a tug and he pulled the line straight back up. I'd keep the bit of cheese and bread and marge and try to space it out.

I'd have it in my shirt, but I was never searched. They wouldn't search the cell, there was no place to hide it. One day in the dinner hour when I got out me lump of bread the chaplain, Baden Ball, he came round on his daily routine.

I was spreading marg on the bread with me fingers when he came in the cell. I just shoved it all straight in me mouth. There was a little bit of cheese I'd been saving for tea. 'Morning,' he said, and I mumbled something. I was supposed to stand when the chaplain came in the cell, but I just shoved the food in my mouth. When he went I immediately finished every little last bit. Once I'd eaten it, it couldn't be taken away. For once

Baden Ball wasn't too bad. For an hour or so I had expected any minute I was going to be searched, but then instinct told me he might not shop me and he kept his mouth shut.

Dicky would also send down notes saying he'd got a message to my sister. I was in the strong cell at least three months, and then I got transferred to Leeds. I was meant to be allowed a visitor every eight weeks, but you were at their mercy over the time they sent out the visiting order and the time when you got your visit.

Dicky got killed at a party in the 1960s. It was a one-off thing. Two of the Hennessey brothers got done for it, but thankfully they were acquitted. Peter Hennessey was the man Eddie Richardson had the straightener with at Mr Smith's Club when Dickie Hart got shot, which is what did for us all. Peter got done a bit later at a boxing tournament in Kensington. Apparently he'd been going round a bit drunk asking people to give money to a charity other than the official one, and there was a fight between him and Paddy Onions. According to the doctor, Peter got stabbed sixty times. Anyway, they did Paddy and Jimmy Coleman, who was a brother-in-law of the Arif family from south-west London, and both were chucked.

Then in November 1982 Paddy Onions got killed outside a wine bar which his son owned in the Tower Bridge Road. Paddy'd been shot a few months earlier when he was sitting at home; he'd been hit in the face but he survived. I liked him. I'm not sure what it was all about. Some people said it was a revenge for Peter Hennessey, some said it was because he was a grass, and there were others who said it was something to do with drugs.

There was a funny sequel to it. About five months later Jimmy Davey, who'd been in Parkhurst with Mickey Hennessey and who was a real wild man, was arrested in Coventry over the killing. His real name was Bowman, but he'd changed it after his brother David had been knifed to death. He did six years in 1979 for cutting a copper, Brian Merry, and hadn't been out long. The story was that he'd been paid £5,000 to do Onions.

When some officers came up from London to take him back, they say he lunged out at an officer who put him in a choke-hold and he lost consciousness. Anyway, about a fortnight later they switched off the life-support machine. I don't think there's any doubt someone put the money up for him, but he'd never recovered consciousness so we'll never know for sure or, if it is right, what the real reason behind it was.

But of course all that was many years later.

Two

I've got a photograph of me as the school football captain in the 1936–7 season. I really do look like a Red Indian. There's Billy Murray in the picture – his father was the caretaker. Billy got Borstal, and then in about 1954 was working on the railways when he got a six months. He'd have probably had probation today. Then his son Bill Jnr got life up in Scotland, but he was a bit unlucky. He was a member of a team they called the Go Anywhere Gang, which did a series of raids at banks all over Scotland. Just before Christmas 1973 there was a robbery in Glasgow on a payroll at a railway and the security guard got shot. This one had been set up by a man called Robert Markey; he got nicked when they staked out his gaff, and then he went crooked on everyone. Billy was the last to get nicked and they got him down in Brighton in the New Year. Sidney Draper was another of the Go Anywheres who I was in the nick with over the years.[1]

Billy was released a year or so ago and then sent back for violating his parole. He hadn't done anything serious, just not reported or something. They fetch them back off parole like eyes are winking nowadays. Tony Burns is also in the photo. He got done during the War in the Army, when he had a row

[1] On 10 December 1987 Sid Draper escaped from Gartree prison along with Andrew Russell, the organiser, and John Kendall, a member of the so-called Hole-in-the-Wall gang known for its use of mechanical diggers, in a hi-jacked helicopter. Kendall and Russell were caught by the end of January 1988. Draper was not recaptured until he was found in Enfield in February 1989.

with another soldier and killed him. He was sentenced to death but he was reprieved. Of course I got acquitted of the murder of Dickie Hart, and a not guilty on incitement to murder in the Parkhurst riot, but still it's not a bad record for the school photo for them days. Three out of eleven, not counting the masters.

We couldn't get into St Patrick's, the Roman Catholic School in Cornwall Road near The Cut. Now it's some sort of factory, but the church next door is still there. So at first I went to St Peter's in Clerkenwell. Eva and I walked over Waterloo Bridge and instead of going left towards Soho, like we did when we went to get cheap second-day bread at Godden & Hanken in Great Newport Street, we turned right up Chancery Lane and across into what they call Little Italy. We were five and seven.

A bit later there was room at St Patrick's, and from then on we was at that school the whole of my school life. Just round the corner was St John's C. of E. church, and there was a playground football pitch where we played. But then for serious matches we went to Bishops Park, the other end of The Cut by Lambeth Palace, or to Bedlam Park by the Imperial War Museum.

We didn't have football boots; whose parents could afford them? We played in plimsolls. We did have shirts from the school. Ours were green and white like Celtic, being Roman Catholic, and black and white as well. They were so faded; they'd been used for years. Untold generations must have worn them. I was captain from about ten until I left. I was picked for Lambeth Schoolboys and South London Schoolboys. Then we played at Dulwich Hamlets ground. I was inside right, which was ideal for me. I wasn't big enough for any other position.

All the classes were mixed. Everybody – except them that were really docile who escaped it – got beaten regularly. It was very high in sport; one of the Irish teachers, Barry, was an Irish rugby international and the French master, Dapree, did the 100 yards in ten seconds. He always wore a medal hanging out of his top pocket. Barry loved to bet; he would give Billy Murray's father sixpence or a shilling and we would run down to the bookmaker in Wooton Street for him. Part of our reward was that he showed us the examination answers and that's how I come top and Billy come second, and they were big classes. Billy couldn't hardly read and write, and I wasn't much better.

At the school they were nearly all Italians or Irish. Religion was very strong and powerful then. It was a prop for people, whereas now there's television and things which have removed that prop to a large extent. All the planes going up in space and things like that has taken the myth away. Look at churches now, they're literally deserted. When I was young you could hardly get in for the main service. You were expected to be at church. My mother was the religious one. My father never interfered, but Mum had us all in church on a Sunday. It was when I was 12 or 13 I stopped going.

Of all the family of my generation, I've been closest to Eva. She's stood by me through everything and she'd had some problems of her own. She was just that bit older than me, and she started trying to protect me when I was at school.

There was one time when the headmaster of our school, he give Eva eight strokes on each hand because she steamed in when they were dragging me down to give me some and she thought she could stop them. They were full cracks with a cane and he never got a murmur out of her. She'd be about 12, and I'd be 11 or 10. He was a prison governor type; in fact he'd run an approved school before St Peter's. He was a sadistic man – another Governor Lawton – but, to be fair, he was a brilliant teacher. Life was so strict, particularly in his generation, that I don't suppose he even thought he was being brutal.

Not a word out of her – Eva never ran home and told our Mum or Gran. Even if she had, I don't suppose Mum would have gone round the school to complain. There again she might have done, for she was a bit of a rebel in her quiet way. Eva's hands were terribly swollen, but she could keep them hidden. You washed yourself, you didn't eat that often sitting round the table so there was a good chance neither my father nor mother would notice. I can't believe it when I hear kids call their teacher Richard or something nowadays. If you didn't call them 'sir' when I was young, then BAM! and a right-hander.

My father was strict as well. He was a good man and a fair one, but if Eva or me'd been beaten by a teacher then he'd have believed we deserved it. Anyway, Eva was living round our grandmother's mostly. At one time my mother's mother lived with us and had the room upstairs, but as we got older she moved back to Cornwall Road, just past the school. It's been knocked down now for the building of the Jubilee Line. We were all born there, but the family moved to Howley Terrace just round the corner. The street got bombed when I was in Borstal. They were after Waterloo Station or the railway. Numbers 1 to 5 were knocked flat, and No. 6 where we lived took a lot of damage but it was still upright. You couldn't live in it, of course, and then the family moved to the Elephant and when that copped it they went to the Borough.

I never knew how badly it had been bombed until I come home. I had a letter from the family whilst I was in Borstal, but it didn't say much. There was no notification by the authorities, and there was no counselling went on. You weren't called in front of the Governor or nothing, and there wasn't any home leave – even if you had a home to go to. The most you would get was just before you were due to go out, a couple of screws might take three or four of you down to the little local village for an hour or two. That was your rehabilitation into society. They were rigid, but they didn't even think they were being wicked; it was just how things were at the time.

If a member of a man's family died, a Church Army captain or the chaplain would come to the cell and tell him. The only experience I had was when my grandmother died. The Church Army captain come to the cell door and said she had. There was no big scene and he didn't lay the treacle on, so it was good in that sense. That's how it was. There were no welfare people in prison then. The prisoner himself accepted it. So far as he was concerned, that was life.

My father was very strict with the girls, but he wasn't daft strict – as long as they were in by ten o'clock, half-ten at the very latest. By today's standards you wouldn't even have gone out by then. You could go to the sixpenny hop, but I never went to any. It wasn't for me, but for girls it was really something. I was already going into pubs. That was more for me from the time I was 13 or 14, with a couple of pals. I never went to a dance in me life. Most real crooked ones never went dancing.

All your top hoisters[2] didn't go either; it was beneath them. They would go to the clubs and pubs. Who would they meet at some dance at the Town Hall or whatever? With their gear in clubs and pubs they would always find buyers or someone they could go out and shoplift for personally. At the sixpenny hops, the girls there couldn't afford the smart dresses which had been lifted.

It was only the expensive shops which sold clothes. Marks and Spencers didn't sell clothes then. These shops were so cheap. You wouldn't see unlimited women's clothes shops as you do now in any part of London. A lot of women got their gear off the tallyman, and I don't know anyone who didn't knock them. Everyone would start buttering them up, paying their sixpence regular because the gear they sold was cheap and cheerful. In no time it was falling off you, but it was handy. How many times did I have the ungrateful job (being the youngest) of going to the door saying, 'Mummy's not in' and that he would have to come back next week. Like so many kids must have said, one day I answered the knock with, 'Mummy's told me to say she's not in.' He said, 'What?' and Eva rushed out the front room and slammed the door shut. The tragedy was that my mother and father worked really hard, never unemployed. Dad worked all day long seven days a week,

---

[2]Shoplifters.

and they wasn't gamblers or drinkers. Every penny went on the home, and there just wasn't enough. They tried to give the girls and Jimmy decent clothes.

I know we had a tallyman over a few years later. Eva was married by now, and in 1951 he came round to her house. She was living at the Borough at the time and her flat looked out one side on Great Dover Street and the other on to the turning. When the tallyman come round, Eva always kept him sweet and ordered quite extensively and give him tea although he was a nasty sod. One day he boasted how he got some guys six months for trying to nick his van. 'Impossible to steal, Mrs Brindle. I've got all gadgets on it.' Eva told me about this and we decided this would be one occasion when his van would be nicked. So he comes this Friday, and she had him in and give him a cup of tea. God stone me, but who's round but my brother Jimmy who'd just popped in? Eva said, 'You can't go, Jim, something's going to happen.' In the meantime me and Billy Blythe – God rest his soul – were downstairs. The tallyman's parked in the side street. Eva told us she'd leave the light on and when he'd be leaving she'd turn it out to give us warning.

It was so sweet. He was right – it was impossible to steal. We had to tow his motor away, but we'd sold it and come back while the light was still on. That's how quick we was. He was up there nearly an hour. Then off goes the light and down he comes, and inside two minutes he's back up to Eva's. 'Me van's gone, Mrs Brindle.'

My brother hadn't even left. The man rushed to the police station saying his motor's been nicked, Then, betting shops wasn't legal but 'Tom Thumb' Brindle, the local bookmaker, who was Eva's brother-in-law, had some good street pitches and had the coppers straightened. As it was only a jump-up, the constable come and told him what happened. 'Who were you delivering to?' they had asked him and when he replied, 'Mrs Brindle,' they all fell about laughing. We had all the clothes and the van, and it came to a nice few quid. The only thing wrong was my poor old brother was late getting into work!

If a girl got pregnant even in a rough-and-ready atmosphere, the family had to go through something. That's where the illegal abortionists made their money. There would be three or four in every district, and they weren't cheap. The family had to get the money to go to them and most couldn't afford it. Remember, the abortionists got a lot of bird if they were caught. I remember one got five years; just before the War she was on bail. That was a really long time for a woman.

These women were regarded as a necessary evil, but in their own way they were respected. They were running big risks: the mother might shop her; the girl might die, and they wouldn't need the evidence they need today. It was almost a conspiracy of silence. The police must have been under orders not to raid them unless word got around that their work was messy: 'Oh, you don't want to go to that one. She slaughters you.'

You also knew who the moneylenders were. Even as a young boy you knew who they were, same as knowing the abortionists. There'd be two or three of them in every district, so you'd have to go to them if a girl got knocked up to get the price. The strange thing is, it was always women who were the moneylenders. The woman would have a husband, but you'd go to the woman. I remember there was a Mrs Whitelock in Commercial Road near Upper Ground, just round the corner from the Royal Festival Hall.

Anyway, it was from Mrs Whitelock that my mum borrowed, though my dad never knew. The interest was astronomical. Shylock would have been proud of them. Exorbitant! It would be at least six for five, if not more. If someone needed an abortion, there was no question of tick. That's where you went to get your money. Strangely enough, people all round were honest. Much as they hated the lenders, they still paid them. Eventually the tallyman'd get paid as well.

The abortionists didn't have to have protection. People were honest. If that was her game, then there was a need for it and so she didn't need protection. Husband maybe, but he wouldn't be there just for minding her. Like I said, if anything she was looked on with respect but in a fearsome way. After all, she did give a service. She saved many a girl's reputation, and many a wife who couldn't afford another baby. Contraception wasn't what it is today. You couldn't just go into the chemist's or up to a machine and buy a pack of things in different colours, like you can now. Women were always frightened, because there were deaths. If a woman died, somehow or other they'd cart her home and say she died in bed at her own home as if she'd tampered with herself. That would be one of the deals the abortionist would make with the woman's family. It would only be if someone screamed that she'd be nicked, or if the girl went into a hospital where they'd known what had happened and might pressure her. We needed the abortionists more than the local moneylender. Maybe the police would raid them now and again, looking for the utensils, and nick them for conspiracy, but in a way they were just confirming things. The news of the raid would get round the district and frighten people off going to her. She'd have to move to another house, if possible in the same area, and start up again.

Three or four streets in them days seemed miles away. You'd very rarely ever see a car or a van overnight. Cars were so rare, if you had one you had a garage to keep it in. In fact I grew up thinking it was illegal to leave a car or van in the street.

If you were in the crooked business you had to have a garage for your rung-in.[3] You couldn't dare leave it out overnight. If you did, you made the copper suspicious.

There was the City of London's Corporation's refuse dump where the barge was moored. Once a year the Corporation would sling a party for the kids to keep their parents sweet. The rest of the year it was a rubbish dump and then shovelled into the barges. The stink in the summer could be pretty terrible. Maybe the party would cost three or four hundred pounds – a lot

[3]A ringer is a stolen motor-car with the number plates changed.

of dough. There'd be an accordion player and a juggler, there'd be buns and cakes and ice cream. Maybe it wasn't just to keep families quiet. Maybe they recognised the distress the dump could cause.

Coming back to where the Royal Festival Hall complex is now, there was London Wastepaper Company, Wilmotts. Further down there was Belvedere Road. There was College Street with the local bookmaker; he'd have a pitch just standing in a doorway. College Street was great for bookmaking. One end of the street was the Thames, and the police couldn't come in that way. At the other there'd be two dog eyes.[4] If the police came in the vicinity, there would be a signal and the bookmaker would just go in the house. Nothing they could do about it. Anyway, the local sergeant would be getting money every week and he'd treat his inspector. Then, to make it look good, every three months or so there'd have to be a raid. Of course the bookmaker himself wouldn't get nicked. He would simply put up someone, probably somebody just out of prison, to stand up and get fined a few shillings. His fine would be paid and he'd be given a quid for his trouble.

Going up Waterloo Road where the Children's Hospital used to be, on the opposite side was the famous tattooist and little hotels and on the corner of Stamford Street was the hospital. I never had a tattoo, nor funnily enough did my dad, although since he'd been a seaman you'd have expected him to have one.

Further towards the bridge there were barbers and other little shops, and there was one which sold guns and ammunition. It didn't have any steel doors or shutters – this would be about 1937. Patsy Clarke and Terry Finch broke in from the roof and nicked the guns; that's how easy it was. Just before the War there was an IRA campaign going on, so when it was raided it was thought to be the IRA. But unfortunately they

---

[4]This is a strictly London term for a look-out, once used for a street bookmaker but now specifically meaning part of a three-card-trick team. It comes from a dog's keen sight. The verb is *to keep dog*.

soon got to Patsy and Terry, what with them coming from Irish backgrounds, so they both got Borstal.

In the part where we lived, the girls on the game were the half-a-crown touches, right down market, and I never knew a single local girl go on the game. These were really rough, otherwise they wouldn't have been in Waterloo Road. There you had the Union Jack Club – soldiers, sailors, airmen. All servicemen on leave could stay there overnight: it was incredibly cheap. This was before the War, and it continued long afterwards as well.

There was a great trade in rolling the sailors by the brasses and their Johnsons.[5] That would be their stock in trade, but it was something the local boys never touched. The brasses went in the Wellington pub and another named after a famous military general. In York Road, where me and Eva nicked a cigarette machine, all the way along it on the other side from the railway were little hotels, really case joints[6] for the brasses, and also up Waterloo Road. The Hole in the Wall was another brasses' pub in the old days. That was just at the back of Waterloo Road. Sometimes they'd fetch their punters down our terrace in the dark. If people heard them they'd chase them out, but otherwise they'd do it against the wall. Sometimes us kids would call out 'Dirty brasses' and they'd shout out and sling us a tanner to keep us quiet, but they'd be half laughing. My grandmother cooked in a hotel in the Waterloo Road which was not too bad by them standards. My grandmother would

[5]A Johnson is a prostitute's pimp and comes from the derisory reference to Jack Johnson, the first black heavyweight boxing champion of the world. Johnson was later convicted under the White Slave Traffic Act 1910, known as the Mann Act, when he took a white woman – whom he later married – over a state line for the purposes of sexual intercourse. The Act was intended to prevent the trade in women for prostitution, but was used to ensnare the unfortunate Johnson who was most unpopular because he had captured the title from a white man. He was sentenced to a year's imprisonment in 1912 and fled the country before returning in 1920 to serve his sentence.
[6]Case joint comes from case, a 17th-century English word meaning a brothel. Fraser uses it in the sense that the hotel was a place where prostitutes took clients rather than a brothel in the strict sense. The American equivalent would be hot pillow or hot sheet joint, from the fact that the bedding is still warm from the previous user.

cook and my mother would do a bit of cleaning and cooking in the afternoon before she went to her evening job. I don't think it was a case joint, but if it was they'd never know being in the kitchen.

There were whole families from the courtyard almost opposite the Lambeth Walk where the girls were shoplifters and the men were good fighters. It was still much as Dickens wrote about even in the 1930s. It was a lovely place. I shouldn't think a straight person had ever been born there in a hundred years. When I'd go round there, you never thought anything about it. There were many other little turnings round Lambeth. Modern flats hadn't started going up even then.

Waxwell Terrace was opposite Gatty's Cinema in Westminster Bridge Road, and on the corner was Siemens where they made the diving equipment – there'd be a dummy dressed in a diver's outfit in the window. That was 'kill 'em and eat 'em' street. They say coppers went down there in twos; not true, they never went down there at all. In the summer when it was warm, people brought their beds out on the pavement. I knew everyone from there.

A bit down the Westminster Bridge Road on the opposite side to Gatty's was the Canterbury. All the old music hall stars appeared there. It was all balconies, but where the posh people went was in the stalls. You call them posh, but they'd probably paid ninepence. In the galleries you could have a cup of tea. They had a famous ex-fighter as a doorman, done up in a uniform. Not Bombardier Billy Wells of course, but Gunner Moir; he was a good heavyweight in his day. He used to let us bunk in at the back door sometimes. Tod Slaughter used to play Sweeney Todd the Demon Barber of Fleet Street, and he was the villain in *Maria Marten* there. They were frightening, and when he gets hanged on stage at the end we loved it. You fought to get in when he was on.

The Canterbury was a bit posh and we used to go to the Central or Gatty's. The Central was called the bakehouse because it got so hot; it was the opposite side from the Ring on the way towards Blackfriars Bridge. Films never bothered my father, but sometimes my mother would take us as a treat. I saw all the films of Cagney, Bogart and Edward G. Robinson. In them there was bars in the cells through which prisoners could see one another and talk, and where there was two or three in the cell. I thought all prisons would be like that. I'd met enough prisoners before I actually went in, but somehow you didn't go into that sort of detail. I just presumed it was the same here. When I first went into Wormwood Scrubs I'll never forget it. I was locked in a cell and I couldn't see anyone – nothing. The door slammed shut and then it really hit me, because I thought you'd be able to see people and there'd be nice bunk beds like in the films. There was just a bedboard, mattress up against the wall: 'That don't go down until eight o'clock at night.' And there I was.

Later the Trocadero opened at the Elephant, which was the biggest theatre in Europe at the time when it was first built. There the stage things were absolutely brilliant – Ambrose, Vera Lynn when she was literally just a girl; all the top acts of the day. Even though it was only 6d to get in, it was so big they could get huge crowds and so they could afford it. Anne Shelton was there as well; Jack Payne and sometimes an American band of the period. Van Damm led the resident band, and Quentin McLean was on the organ. It was the first to rise up out of the auditorium, and it was magnificent. After the War they had the Inkspots, who were really top in their day.

I got a good living looking after the cars at The Ring, Blackfriars, where they had boxing and wrestling. If there was a big fight, people would come in cars and you would look after them. You'd get 2d and sometimes whilst they were going to see a show or after they come out a couple of you would have a fight so people would throw coppers at you. Sunday afternoon was terrific. You'd get all-in wrestling there and sometimes you got Bert Assirati, one of the Italians from the Angel. He was a hard man. He used to let you take a free swing at him on condition he had the next one. Years later he was the doorman at the dance hall where Ronnie Marwood got done after the copper was stabbed. It was well known he wasn't actually the one who had the knife, but he swung for it anyway.[7] I met Bert much later when he lived down near Seaford. He was crippled with arthritis and in a wheelchair by then. He was a great friend of my wife Doreen's uncle, Georgie Shillingford.

My father never took me to the boxing or the wrestling. What spare time did he have? He worked seven days a week and anyway, in a way, he was a Red Indian and he didn't like these things. He got the blood from my grandmother, who was a full-blooded Red Indian. My grandfather had married her when he went out to Canada in the last century.

One of the earliest touches Eva and me had was when I was about 10 and she'd be a year older. She was game for anything. It was in one of those little hotels in the York Road, half bed-and-breakfast and half case joint. Eva and I just went in to see if there was anything lying around, and there was a little foyer. No one heard us or came to the front desk and we saw the cigarette machine. It was big for us to handle with the cigarettes and money inside, but somehow we carried it out between us. It was dark, about six in the evening, and we carried and dragged it all the way to St John's Church in Waterloo Road. Either side of the church there was a clinic built on stilts with an open space underneath, and we dragged it under and opened it up there. Peter Daley, who was married to 'Dartmoor Annie' – the woman who could be relied on to give

---

[7]In December 1958 there was a fight between the so-called Finsbury and the Angel mobs outside Grays Dance Academy near Highbury Corner, Islington. P.C. Raymond Summers tried to break up the fight and was stabbed to death. Marwood was sheltered for a time by either the Nash or the Kray brothers, or possibly both, but surrendered in January 1959. He was hanged on 8 May 1959 after a prolonged campaign for a reprieve and scenes of great hostility towards the police. The reason was that the killer in another dance-hall fight had been reprieved. Reggie Kray later complained that the fact he and his brother had sheltered Marwood had brought them the unwelcome attentions of the police.

a handout to people come off the train after they'd been released from the Moor – was still selling his evening newspapers at his pitch on the corner of Alaska Street and we sold the cigarettes to him right away. Then we went home to Mum and told her our famous story once again that we'd found some money. She'd never have dreamed we'd nicked a cigarette machine and carried it along the street.

Before the War being a shoplifter – we called them hoisters – was top of the tree. They've been called hoisters as long as I've been born. Every sensible girl round the Elephant, and that included Eva, was a hoister. Something was wrong with them if they wasn't. You could make really good money: a hundred a week plus during the War. Money like that. It was all done to order. The girls had coats and bloomers. Alice Diamond, who was Billy Benstead's mother-in-law, was the head of the Forty Thieves team. Billy was in the London Bullion robbery in 1948. Joanie Warren was another who was very, very good. She was from Kennington and married Jimmy Frazer, who was no relation – different spelling. She came from around Lambeth Walk and I think, although I can't swear to it, her father was a copper. In 1946 or 1947 she got three or four years of penal servitude, which was quite a bit of bird for a hoister, a wicked sentence.

There were whole families of shoplifters. The Harmons were one. There was Jessie the mother, Nellie and Rosie and another daughter as well. All top hoisters. Nellie Waites, Billy Howard's girl-friend – he owned the Beehive in the 1950s – was another good one. After they split up, she got married and asked Billy to be the best man. Once the ceremony was over Billy just laid the bridegroom flat.

These girls were the cream. I know there weren't tabs and security guards in them days, but by comparison the shops were empty and there weren't the quality places there are today. The girls had to do the same shops week in week out and not get spotted, and the staff were both more dedicated and more long-serving. They took their jobs seriously.

Billy Howard – who as I said earlier was having a straightener with Spindles Jackson when an unexploded bomb suddenly went off – was a handsome face, extremely smart, about 5 foot 9 inches. He was known as the Guv'nor. He joined the Army when he was a boy of seventeen and after a year they kicked him out, but they called him up during the War like everyone else. Years later he was hookey. He had a row down Bruce Bracey's club, Winstons, for which he was on a pension.[8] A member of the family who had car showrooms on Brixton Hill kicked Billy in the cobblers and he nicked him. Before he died Billy married the daughter of Archie Macauley, the Arsenal football player, but she pissed off with the milkman. All this happened when I was doing the twenty. Billy went downhill and then, after a black cut him badly at a spiel he was running, he ended up almost destitute. But he'd nicked the guy long before he went downhill, and that went against him. In his day he really was good. A tragedy really.

Hoisting was mostly clothes. The girls would go out every day of the week and then sell the stuff very cheap. They'd employ a driver. In them days cars could pull up outside somewhere like Selfridges and the driver would just wait; there was no question of being moved on. There wasn't much risk for the drivers either. They'd be in straight cars, and if one was stopped it was only a question of saying someone asked him for a lift. Funnily enough, although the girls were well thought of, their drivers weren't well respected. They were regarded as half a ponce. In them days the girls wouldn't think of pickpocketing or rolling a drunk as they did later.

Eva went to Holloway when she was 17 or 18. She got six months for shoplifting. She'd only have been caught with a frock, something like that, but them days it was prison for a

---

[8]'On a pension' means to receive a weekly sum, often as a wage. This may be paid whether the recipient actually earns it or is simply on the books of a firm. He may even be in prison. The phrase can also mean receiving money by way of protection.

first offence; that would have been common. Prison was really hard and the judges and magistrates knew that themselves, so sentences were shorter. There were no open nicks then. Very few people got probation or fines. They might be lucky the first time but it was definitely prison the next. Guys I knew around Waterloo all had jobs on the railways, and as soon as they got nicked for stealing from the railways they got six months.

By the time Eva got her last half a stretch in 1944, she'd done two or three in quite a short time. She was in Holloway along with the fascist leader Sir Oswald Mosley and his wife, who were interned there. After she finished that last shoplifting sentence she was never again into crime, but she'd never turn away anyone who needed help. After Paddy Meehan, who got convicted of the murder in Ayrshire and was later given a pardon and compensation, escaped with a whole lot of others from Nottingham in the early 1960s where they were meant to have been watching a cricket match, they came round to Eva's and she helped them.[9]

One of them was a great pal of hers, which is why she did it. Little Joey Hogan, who was a Londoner who'd been out to work with me, came from Hoxton and that's how they come to go round to Eva's. She gave them food and clothes and her husband, Jimmy Brindle, who was in Borstal with me, went round for a whip for them. Paddy had been doing a sentence for a safe down in London. He was a very good man with the jelly, a friend of Arthur Thompson – the 'King of Glasgow' – who I knew well. Paddy had come down here to do the job and someone had just grassed him up.

Jimmy Brindle was one of a big family. One of his brothers, 'Tom Thumb' Brindle, was a big street bookmaker as I said earlier. When bookmaking became legal, the local licensing

[9]On the occasion he escaped Meehan was serving eight years under the name of Patrick Carson for a burglary at the Fore Street Co-op, Edmonton. He was later convicted of the murder on 8 July 1969 of Rachel Ross in Ayr. He maintained his innocence and through the efforts of his lawyer, Joe Beltrami, was eventually pardoned and received the sum of £50,500 in compensation. He died of throat cancer in August 1994.

authority said that they were going to give priority to local people who'd been in bookmaking whether legal or illegal, and so Tom got a licence.

A bit later, there was Shirley Pitts who was about the best hoister there was. She had her apprenticeship with the old-timers as she was quite a bit younger, but she was top grade and so was most of her family. They come from round the Elephant. The one I knew best was her father Harry, but I also knew her brother Adgie very well indeed. Adgie was a giant of a man, who had the birch for doing a hospital screw in Wandsworth. He got killed driving back to Brighton one night; just ran into the back of a lorry.

I'd done him a favour in the 1960s, when there was a classy club called Isows in London. The boxer Nosher Powell was the minder down there then. Jack Isow'd been in the nick with me when he got eighteen months for tax in 1942 and again in the 1950s. He and Terry Sansom, who'd got out of murder at Clapham when a bus taking money to the depot got raided, had a fight with two punters who were getting uppity and they went and squealed.[10] Adgie and Terry approached us to see if we could straighten it out. We saw the owner and of course he was sweet, but his son was a dead straight man and that was a bit difficult. I'm pleased to say that it got slung out at the magistrates' court.

For his size, Adgie wasn't a bully with it. Some of them are when they're great big guys. For example, Tony Mella was a bully if he could get away with it. If he was getting on top he was unbeatable, but like a bully he'd just give up if someone stood up to him. If he'd been handled properly he could have gone a long way in the ring. He cut Tommy Smithson in a club in Soho one night over nothing. Mind, most people had cut Tommy Smithson sooner or later. He'd been done really badly behind the Black Cat cigarette factory in Camden Town and nearly died from that one; he'd been interfering with a

[10]See Ch. 11, fn. 3.

club Billy Hill had an interest in. Eventually the Malts did for Tommy – shot him one morning. He was trying to put the arm on them, trying to raise money for his girl who was in the nick, and they weren't having it.

Billy had to straighten out Tony one night. In 1960 or 1961 there was a benefit in the Pigalle for Sulky, who'd only got one leg and who later managed the Astor. Tony Mella got very flash and Billy did him over the head with a whisky bottle. I was still doing the seven when it happened, but that reporter Arthur Helliwell wrote about it. They got quite a chunk of dough for Sulky.

There were some good robberies in those pre-War days. A couple of bullion thefts down Clerkenwell, one of around £9,000 in 1932 when no one was caught, and in the summer of 1936 when John Murray who was the planner got two years. This time he'd got away with £2,000 of gold ingots and some coins and dust off an L.N.E.R. lorry as well.[11] Charlie Barwick was in the frame for that and the earlier one, but he got away with it.

Charlie was a good man. He and Moishe Cohen, who came from the East End, were thick. Moishe Cohen became a famous bookmaker and opened a string of betting shops in the name of Major Collins. Jackie, his brother, was a big on-course bookmaker who was a big gambler. I think he won about £70,000 in one bet and it was all over the papers. Really large dough. Eventually Moishe turned it all in, but not before he'd started using Jack Spot as his man at the races and running spielers for him.

When they was young, Moishe and Charlie Barwick got a lot of tom in a smash-and-grab raid. They went to a fence, as you called them then, to sell it. He had a fire going in the grate and as he was looking at the stuff he kept saying, 'Rubbish, what are you doing fetching this round to me?' and slung it

---

[11]John Murray, aka James Francis aka Hoppy McCarthy of Packington Street, Islington, had first been sent to prison in 1902. In July 1910 he received a sentence in France for stealing 21,000 francs from a Paris bank.

in the bottom of the grate. They were happy enough to take a pittance for the rest, thinking it was all truly rubbish. Actually it was good gear and that was their lesson. The fence soon took it out when they'd gone.

In the early 1950s Jackie Cohen went to Spot to say his wife was having an affair and could he do something about the man? Spot took the problem to Billy Hill. Billy knew the woman wasn't all that, and if it wasn't that man it would have been someone else, and so he didn't exact the full penalty. He gave him a slap or two, told him to walk round Brighton all bandaged up and then disappear. He got £5,000 off Jackie Cohen, who really thought the man had been cut.

Moishe was good to me when I was on the Richardson trial. One thing I had to explain was how I came to be able to buy a small house in Hove. It only cost five and a half grand, but that was still money. All I could think of was to say that I was Moishe's chauffeur and I drove him to race meetings. It was true to an extent. I *did* drive him, but not all that regular. Moishe was dying and he only had a few days to live then, so Doreen, my wife, went to see him to ask for help. He was too ill to give evidence, so he made a statement that I was his regular chauffeur. He was a lovely man, very good. It shows that people who have been into crime have the decency to stand by people.

Me and Eddie Richardson went to a wedding anniversary for Jackie Cohen at the Savoy in around 1964. I don't know if it was the same wife, but I can't think so. Jackie was a brilliant businessman, but in affairs of the heart it's incredible how many like him get clobbered. He only died recently. He was in his nineties.

The best of the bullion robberies of the 1930s was the gold snatch at Croydon Airport. I was only a kid when it went off, but it was so clever it was the talk of the neighbourhood. What happened was that gold used to be shipped from Croydon Airport and on 6 March 1936 there were three boxes of gold bars, sovereigns and dollars which were meant to be sent by

Imperial Airways to Brussels and Paris when they disappeared. They'd been placed in a safe room and there was no forcing of the doors. Security was very lax in them days. People didn't think a robbery like this could happen. There was a man called Francis Johnson who was the only person on the aerodrome overnight, and he had to leave the actual building at 4.15 in the morning to receive a German airliner which was landing. Someone had got hold of the keys to the safe room and made an impression of them, and while Johnson was on the tarmac they got the gold out. They'd hired a cab from King's Cross and had it drive to the airport, where the boxes were loaded and brought back to Harringay. Three men got done eventually. There was a man called Cecil Swanland, a John O'Brien and Silvio Mazzardo, who was one of Darby Sabini's men and lived off Saffron Hill. He was known as Shonk, and he was the only one of the three I ever met. There had to be more, of course.

The police found wrappers and seals from the gold in Swanland's room but there wasn't a trace of the gold itself. There was all sorts of moody evidence from a grass in prison, and some sort of an ID, but Shonk and O'Brien got chucked and Swanland went down. His defence was that by the time the boxes arrived at his place they were empty. He'd got a lot of form, mainly for forgery, and had done a five and a six penal servitude, and this time he got a seven. Nothing was ever recovered, which was what made it so brilliant.

There was no doubt that Bert Marsh of the Sabinis was behind it, and I reckon that's why they all got interned at the start of the War. Nothing to do with being Italian, half of them couldn't speak a word. No, it was revenge for the bullion, and for the cheek they showed as well. What they did was, they went and set up a bookmaker in the ring under the name of Nick Gold.

Now if there was ever a Mr Big, it could well have been Bert Marsh. As I said, his real name was Pasqualino Papa but it wasn't fashionable for Italians to box under their own names and so he called himself Marsh in the ring. Of course I never saw him fight, but it was said he was a crowd pleaser at the Lime Grove Baths and Shepherds Bush.

He and his great friend Bert Wilkins, who was Joe's uncle, got done for murder over a man at the Wandsworth dogs when it started getting popular. Bert Marsh got himself work in the 2/6d ring, and he then got the Montecolumbo brothers jobs there. He then got Jim Wicks – who went on to be Henry Cooper's manager but was then just an ordinary bookmaker – to employ Camillo Montecolumbo. I'm not really sure what it was all about, but another bookmaker took on Bert Wilkins instead of another of the Montecolumbo brothers and the family objected. There was something about kickbacks, and they were also looking for more money from Marsh. Fighting broke out and Massimo Montecolumbo was stabbed in the neck.

At the Old Bailey the Berts had a good strong team out, including Norman Birkett. The fanny was that their defence was said to have been paid for by racing men, and the newspapers said that Bert Marsh's wife had pawned her jewellery and drawn out her savings to retain Birkett. In fact, the racing men who put up the money were Moishe and Jackie Cohen. There wasn't much need for that really because there was still plenty over from the Croydon job.

The other thing they did which went well for them was while in Brixton they went and 'saved' a screw who was being attacked. What the Berts did gave the idea to Billy Hill when years later he pulled Jackie Rosa (from the Elephant) off a screw and got himself remission. Jack got five grand for his trouble.

I'm glad to say the murder charge was chucked and Bert Marsh, who'd got a bit of form with assaults and unlawful wounding, received twelve months for manslaughter. Bert Wilkins got nine.

After he was interned at the beginning of the War, Bert Marsh kept up the links through Albert. He was really big although not physically – that way, he was only my size. Where he was very good was with the Montecolumbo brothers. Next to the Griffin pub in Clerkenwell there was the Central Club where all the Raddis[12] used to go. Not Bert. It wasn't fear; it was too much respect for the family of the man he'd done. Jim Wicks and Bert Marsh became partners; all their lives – maybe not on paper but by a handshake. Jim did a lot to help Bert both at that trial and afterwards. I was there on the day. Bert Marsh introduced Henry Cooper to the girl he married. She worked in Peter Mario's restaurant in Gerrard Street. When I was out Jim Wicks would always greet me, but he wouldn't go over the top.

Bert had fingers in many other little pies. You never saw him spending his money in the night-clubs; very low profile. Every penny he got he kept; from gambling, clubs, protection, bit of receiving. That's where he was sensible. He died during my twenty-year sentence around 1980. He had a heart attack while he was driving his car; he wouldn't be young. I was told on a visit, and Eva sent a wreath.

---

[12]The Sabinis in particular and the Italians in general were known as the Raddis, short for the Radicals. The name derives from the Garibaldi-Mazzini Radicals of the nineteenth century.

Three

The years after the War were really good for us. There was not much unemployment; everyone had his dough and they wanted the things which were on ration, so there was a thriving black market. Bobby Hedley, who was sentenced to death over the killing of Captain Binney, was known as Silver because of the number of times he did Silvers, the tailors at the Bermondsey end of the Tower Bridge Road. Suit lengths were better than jewellery in them days. They were rationed, and another tailor would bite your hand off for them. There was some doubt about something in Bobby's case and he was reprieved.[1] He did his life, and I heard he went to Australia. I think the doubt was that he was actually at the wheel. The story was that Charles Lilley had been.

He'd had a bit of a charmed life, had Lilley. He came from a good family. His father had done three years' penal servitude before the war and so Charles had a good reputation on the strength of his father. He'd been on the raid at the comedian Monty Modlyn's, dress shop in Lower Marsh, Lambeth in 1942 when a copper, P.C. Skeggs, came across

[1]Captain Ralph Binney was knocked down whilst trying to prevent a jewel robbery in the City of London. He was pulled underneath the getaway car and dragged for some distance, dying of his injuries. A medal was struck commemorating his gallantry. Also charged was Tommy Jenkins. His brother Harry Boy Jenkins avoided an identification parade. In 1947 'Harry Boy' was sentenced to death for the murder of Alec de Antiquis, who also tried to prevent a robbery; he was a posthumous recipient of the Binney Medal.

them in the black-out just as they was loading up the car and he got stabbed. Johnny Osborne got five years over it. Charles just got six months, but he was the one did the stabbing. Mind you, that's not to say he should have put himself in the frame as it were. It was just bad luck for Johnny on the face of it. Then he got pulled in over the Binney, but he was never charged. He pleaded guilty to some car in the City months before and got six months. People were wary of him after that. He was accepted, but it was a wary acceptance, and I did a bit of work with him myself and I never come to any harm. At least I don't think so.

Then he became a mate of Bobby Welch, who was on the Train. Bobby was from the Angel and so he never had a clue what Charles was like. There were rumours he had Bobby's money, but you hear so many things. If I say I've got a pencil in my hand you can see I'm telling the truth, but if you say he was driving the car which killed Captain Binney it's very hard to accept that as gospel. He died a few years back, so we'll never know.

Although I was on a lot of good paying jobs, I missed the three great robberies after the War: the London Airport bullion robbery – the one that went wrong – and the two of Billy Hill's that went right.

I was in Wandsworth with Billy Hill when the bullion robbery went off in July 1948. It was known it was going off – common knowledge amongst a certain few but not exactly every detail. I'd say maybe 20–30 knew about it, and that was about 10–20 too many.

We didn't hear at once what had happened. You couldn't in them days. We didn't have radios or newspapers, but we heard it through a visit or from people who'd been on bail and then come in after conviction. You'd get a rather cock-eyed version of a lot of it. You couldn't talk in the prison shops; there were no two in the cell, so you wouldn't get a clear-cut picture.

When you had a visit it was behind the glass, and if you got half an hour you did very well. You had to shout through the side of the glass, sort of air ducts. The prison officers – wherever they would be – would literally be able to hear every word that everyone was saying, but people who did have a visit would briefly tell whoever they visited when a gang of men had been arrested. Another visit from someone else the next day would give some names. Then someone who'd been on bail when it went off and got convicted later would tell you a bit more, but it was hit and miss and you didn't know if people had got it right.

What I heard over the years from Georgie Wood, Franny Daniels and the others was that someone had laid out the London Airport bullion job at Heathrow Airport – it was called London then. There was meant to be over £600,000 of diamonds and money. The target was the bonded warehouse which contained £388,000-worth of diamonds and was due to receive a further £250,000. The idea was that the coffee of the warehouse staff should be doped, but the man who was approached went hookey and talked to the security. So instead of there being doped warehouse staff, there was alive-and-well Flying Squad officers waiting for them. There was a terrific fight, and they all turned up in the dock the next day looking very battered.[2]

Teddy Hughes got twelve; he was 48 and the oldest of them. Sammy Ross had eleven; he came out of Marat Street in Brixton. Alfie Roome got ten; he was known as Donk and, when he came out, his wife was having an affair with a guy who sold newspapers. Roome was a rather sullen man, nice but sullen; people thought he was a bit of a loose cannon, but a good man to go on anything like that. He came from Ilford way. I had a drink with him but I never actually worked with him. He steamed into the man and his wife with a chopper. Then he killed himself. Six years eight months he'd be in,

---

[2]The attempted robbery was on 30 July 1948, and the men were sentenced on 17 September that year.

so he'd come out spring '55 and he did it almost straight after that.[3]

Jimmy Wood picked up nine; George Smith, George Wood (known as John Wallis at the time) and Sydney Cook all had eight. Ainsworth had five and Andrew Walsh was bound over for two years. The judge was the Common Serjeant at the Bailey, Gerald Dodson, who'd had the run-in with Maggie Hill. When once he'd sentenced her he said, 'Take her away,' and she called out, 'You didn't say that when you were making love to me last night.' He had one of those little speeches for the men who'd had a good beating from the coppers in the fight: 'You were prepared for violence and you got it. You got the worst of it, and you can hardly complain about that.'

Billy Benstead, Franny Daniels, Teddy Machin and Jock McQuillan were a bit more lucky. They all got away from the airport, with Franny holding on to the underside of a lorry which burned him. I say it was Franny, but the same story has been told about each of them. Jimmy and Georgie Wood came from Upton Park. They used to drink in the Queens pub in Upton Park which was run by Teddy and Billy Robins. Teddy got done for a murder along with Georgie at the Ranch House. It was over a fight at some party. Jimmy Fellowes, the brief who acted for me a lot, got struck off for talking to prosecution witnesses, but they had to reinstate him later when they found he'd done nothing wrong.

I always remember Billy Hill talking about the Airport job. I was walking with him in the exercise yard in Wandsworth and Bert Rogers, the comedian Ted Rogers' uncle, was with us. You could talk on exercise. There was only two of you

[3]On 20 January 1956, the day before his elder daughter's wedding, Roome attacked his wife and John Wirth, at their newspaper stall outside the main gate at Ford's Dagenham, with a knife and a hatchet. He then committed suicide by swallowing a potassium cyanide capsule. Mrs Roome told the inquest that after his release in June 1955 he had been moody and jealous as well as being violent to her. He had, apparently worked a few days on the newspaper stall but had then tried to persuade Wirth to sack Mrs Roome. He had already set fire to his daughter's wedding clothes.

together and the two in front or behind weren't allowed to talk, but you could get the odd word in. Billy Hill said if he'd been out no one would have been nicked, because he had that top copper straight who would have marked his card that the police would be waiting for them. So he did. He had a top superintendent straightened. He'd known him from way back. He'd have delegated someone to tell Bill.

Those men on the Airport robbery were such a good firm; really getting dough. They were organised and sensible and intelligent enough to be doing very well. When they were nicked and so many got such bird, it took the heart out of their organisation. Teddy Machin was never really the same after it. He was a Spot man. In 1948 he took a chopper to Jimmy Wooder at Ascot Races for Spotty. It was all part of a long feud. Before the War him and another beat Spot up and he nicked them, and both got some bird. That wasn't enough for Spot. In 1943 he cut Jimmy Wooder in a club in the East End, a very bad cut. Of course Jimmy didn't nick him, but from then on Jimmy could never stop talking about how Spot had given evidence.

That day at the races Jimmy was working on the bookmaker's box, and Teddy Machin just started cutting him off at the ankles. Jimmy never nicked him and he didn't retaliate neither. Spot was really above Billy at the time, and Jimmy Wooder just didn't have the power himself or anyone to go to for help. In 1952 Machin was in custody for a long time for leaning on a club which Sulky used to manage in Mayfair. He got out of it eventually when someone saw Sulky and explained things to him. Just before his death he was thought to have done Harry Barham, the bookmaker, who'd fenced the stuff for me years earlier and who had been going round collecting money he needed for his defence at the Bailey. Barham was seen in Holborn in a café, and then his body was found in a car over Hackney marshes without the money. But then it may just be convenient that Machin's dead and he's got the blame.[4]

Machin got killed in May 1973 when he was walking near his home. It wasn't the first time someone had a go at him, but it was the last. He'd been leaning on a woman, borrowing money from her and treating her badly.[5]

Billy Benstead, who was another on the Airport job, was in Billy Hill's Eastcastle Street job, and so was 'Taters' Chatham. He got his name because he was always complaining about the cold when he was on the Moor.[6] That was the one which showed how it could be done. Billy Benstead's wife was the daughter of Alice Diamond, and she was a great pal of Maggie Hill. Funnily, much earlier Maggie Hill did Lou Williams, who was the mother of Jimmy Wooder's girl-friend, Rosie. I used to work with her brother Charlie. Maggie stuck her in the eye with a hatpin. She was a girl with a hatpin, was Maggie. Did a policeman the same way, as I said earlier.

Billy Benstead was a terrific thief, but he was a terrible gambler. So was Taters. I reckon he was the best burglar I ever knew, better even than Peter Scott and the Welshman Ray Jones.

People have always said Jack Spot was behind the Airport, but I'm not so sure. Spot was never a thief. He would have a whack out of it though, same as Billy give him something out of the Eastcastle Street job. In fact he gave him £6,000, which was really big money then, but he was so frightened he wouldn't come and collect it. He sent his brother in a cab to

---

[4]The body of bookmaker Harry Barham was found in his car at 6.30 p.m. on 14 February 1972 in Windmill Lane, Stratford in East London. He had been shot in the back of the head. It was thought the motive was robbery. He had been losing heavily, and one suggestion is that the killing was to recoup money loaned to Barham before it was swallowed up in fines and compensation orders at the Old Bailey where he was facing charges of evading betting tax.

[5]Alan Mackenzie, the nephew of the woman, was charged with Machin's murder and pleaded self-defence, saying that the gun was Machin's and he was struggling with him when it had gone off. The first jury disagreed and on a retrial Mackenzie pleaded guilty to manslaughter and was sentenced to three years' imprisonment.

[6]From the Cockney rhyming slang: potatoes in the mould = cold.

Bill's place in the East End. I was inside then; that is a regret I have. I'm confident Bill would have had me on it if I'd been on the outside. In 1952 Bob Lee got looked at very closely over the Eastcastle Street robbery, but nothing came of it. Nor did anyone claim the reward money.

When Jimmy and Georgie Wood had finished their time for the bullion robbery, they worked with Billy Hill. Like me they missed the KLM robbery, but Billy made sure everyone got alibis when they nicked the platinum from a van in Lincoln's Inn Fields in September 1954. Billy Benstead was on it as well. The employees of KLM were due to unload when a smaller van backed up tailboard to tailboard, a man called out 'Hold on' and jumped on to the KLM van, threw two boxes of gold bullion on to the smaller van, hopped over again and was gone. It was a brilliant coup. What Bill had done was have a padlock cut at the Holborn end of Jockey's Fields which is really a small mews off the Theobald's Road. He'd replaced it with his own, so it looked as though there could be no entry from that end. So there was the KLM van with its tail towards Holborn because it had been backed in, and Bill's van also backed in because he has a guy to be there to open the padlock and lock it again after Billy's van got through. An old boy who people thought was passing by gave false descriptions; he was in the plot. One guy, the driver who's now got a club in the East End, was convicted of smelting the gold down, and so was a man called Jones who was some sort of dealer. But that's all. The real men behind it got clean away. The official scream was for £45,000, which was big money; but it was more than that, and anyway you'd get twice as much on the black market.

They pulled Bill in, of course, but he'd got an A1 alibi. He'd been in the offices of the *People* talking to his mate Duncan Webb, the crime reporter, and Hannen Swaffer. You couldn't do much better than that. Of course, everyone including the Old Bill knew who was behind it, but they could never prove it.

In between he'd organised his greatest coup, the Great Mailbag Robbery of 21 May 1952 when £287,000 in hard cash was stolen from a post office mailbag van. Billy had picked his men carefully. The night before the robbery they were all collected and taken to a flat in the West End where they were locked in before being fully briefed on the operation. It wasn't that he didn't trust them; it was just that Hilly wasn't taking any chances of a leak at that stage. What he did was teach the coppers. When that 'Nipper' Read swooped on the Krays and Bert Wickstead ran raids, they did exactly the same thing: had the coppers in a police gym or something before they were told what they were going to do, and then not let them out so they couldn't give someone a bell and let them know a raid's coming.

What Bill had done was have the mail-van followed every night for months as it left on its journey to Oxford Street. Cars had been stolen specifically for the raid. As the van turned into Eastcastle Street off Oxford Street, two cars blocked the driver's path. In the early hours of Wednesday morning they'd disconnected the alarm system on the van while the staff were on their tea-break. They had it watched as it went to Paddington Station. Once it left there there was a call to the flat. They'd also nicked a green Vanguard and a Riley, and off they went in them.

As the van turned into Eastcastle Street, the two cars blocked the driver's path. They did the three post-office workers, left them on the pavement and drove off. The van was driven to Augustus Street in the City where they moved the cash, transferring it into boxes on a fruiterer's lorry left there earlier. Only thirteen out of thirty-one bags had been taken. 'The thieves were surprised,' claimed the police, but Bill said that wasn't so. The remaining bags were left because there wasn't any more room in the lorry, which was then driven to Spitalfields market and parked there under observation for a further 24 hours before it was unloaded. The money got moved about quite a bit for the next few days. The nicked cars had been left in Covent Garden. The money was hidden in Jack Gyp's wholesale fruit and veg lorry – Sonny Sullivan was his minder. It then went to one of Gyp's big fruit lorries with sacks of potatoes and fruit all around it, and it went to Spitalfields and was parked with his other lorries before it was taken to the Borough, then Covent Garden, on to Stratford, and back to Spitalfields for six weeks. This was nothing unusual; it was right on show really. The police stormed in everywhere, but they found nothing. Really it was out in the open for everyone to see. There was no question of anyone saying anything. They were all good men who kept their mouths shut. Billy picked his people well.

There were big rewards totalling £25,000 put up by the insurance companies, but they never got near it. They had Billy in, of course, and that's when he said to the copper, 'Brixton Jock sends his regards,' and he was out in no time. That and the Lincoln's Inn Fields job more or less ended the investigating officer's career. He'd been a big riser but since he never really got anyone for either job, he more or less got pensioned off. He wasn't going anywhere.

Christmas 1955 I had a good touch which nearly led to a bigger one; one which would have ranked with the other three. We done a really good robbery in Victoria Park. Just before Christmas a thing was stuck up to us; one of the drivers of a private hire firm engaged to take the deputy manager and clerks with a load of money in Stratford to a bank in the City once a week come to me. In this particular period, as there'd been some robberies, the bank decided they'd have special bank sacks and the clerks would be handcuffed to them before they left the bank in Stratford and taken off when they got to the City. The guy said the clerks felt it wasn't dignified to be handcuffed, and sometimes the deputy manager would take the cuffs off and put them on again just before they got to the London bank. Brake lights had just come on cars then; it's almost unbelievable that there weren't any before the 1950s. The driver said if that happened he'd brake five times as he went round a corner and we'd know the cuffs were off. Every week he had to change the route, and he wouldn't know which roads he had to take until the night before or even that morning. He'd ring from one call-box to another. In those days you just put two pennies in and if there was no reply you pressed Button B and got your money back. That night he told us the route would be through Victoria Park, which suited us well. We had bolt cutters with us and since there was no lights we knew they'd kept the cuffs on. On the phone the driver did say, 'Don't hurt me, but take the ignition key so I can't chase you.'

We had two cars in Victoria Park and one stopped the car with the other straight behind. We dragged the clerks out, cut the handcuffs, slung the bags in our motor and I knocked the driver about. I knew what I was doing. When he was in hospital with about twenty-seven stitches in his nut, he was going to be questioned different from if he'd been untouched. In them days the police could browbeat the driver or the clerks even though they were respectable people: 'Come on, we know you done it.' When they saw him in hospital all stitched up they didn't even faintly suspect him. He was a streetwise, intelligent man and he saw the fuss they made of him. When he come out and I met him to give him his whack, he said what a good idea it had been. If there'd not been a scratch on him they'd have made life hell for him and he might not have stood up. As it was, it was a wonderful Christmas. Two of the guys was Alfie Allpress, who was uncle of the Danny Allpress who was grassed up by Bertie Smalls in the 1960s, and Cherry Titmuss. They're both dead now. Bill knew all about this, but he never had a cut.

Cherry was someone special. He was an unsung hero, dead game. I went to his funeral, me and 'Battles' Rossi. He was a terrific guy, come from Clerkenwell, grew up with the Italians, knew Bert Marsh, Albert, everybody. He done bird but nothing long. Dartmoor before the War. He was a very good thief. He just led a quiet life, but he worked quietly right up to the end; going out with the keys mostly.[7]

[7]Fraser means that he had false keys cut which would give him entrance to unoccupied flats.

Shortly after that Christmas, I read in the *South London Press* about how a factory in Kennington Lane had been broken into and some platinum had been stolen. I couldn't believe it. Apparently it hadn't been burglar alarmed up, so I went and had a look at the factory. With a bit of work we discovered that a van would come from the factory to an office building in Guildford Street, just near Russell Square, and go in with boxes full of platinum. It's almost unbelievable. About 5 o'clock in the evening a van would come in and take them or others back to the factory. We traced a garage where the van was parked so we could go in there without breaking in. The keys of the van were in the ignition and we took them and had them duplicated in a couple of hours, made sure they worked and put them back in the van.

It would be too big a job for me to sell the platinum; I just didn't have the contacts. This was big, big time, and so we went to see Billy Hill in Barnes where he was living. He said he'd handle the sale for us and arranged that the morning before the robbery he'd fly to Paris so he'd be out of the way. He was really red hot for these big robberies. What we would do, they would come out in the evening carrying these boxes and put them in the back of their van. There were three or four, and then they'd squeeze in on a bench seat in the front. What we did, very early, was park about three cars in front of them, so that when the van came our motor would pull out to give him parking space.

When they came back another car would pull out so they got the space again, but this time the rear of our van would be back on to theirs. They wouldn't think nothing of it. What we would do when they got in the front to go back to the factory would be one motor would pull up and block them in. We'd open the doors just like the Jockey's Fields. Not a blow to be struck.

We nearly come a tumble. We didn't do it by a sheer miracle; it was a ready eye. Lucky for us Patsy Fleming, who was on the run at the time after he escaped with Alfie Hinds, had seen coppers having a conference on the pavement. He went round again and they were still there and so the job was off. There was no point in hanging around hoping. It was away as fast as we could without drawing attention to ourselves. It come out later who shopped us. Someone who knew something told the coppers because one of us, not me or Patsy, was having it off with his wife and this was a revenge. We never went back, but it could have been a terrific touch. We were talking about really serious money.

Another disappointment came a bit earlier when Jack Spot set up a robbery for us at a factory in Manchester. Spotty liked to be called that because he said he was always on the spot, and there's no doubt a lot of people – Jewish guys that is – liked to have him around them. He provided them with protection, but they didn't half have to pay for it. I remember Nigger Smith – he was as white as me, and I don't know how he got that name – came from Southend telling me in the late 1940s he driven Spot and Machin and the Wood brothers up there and he was told to park outside this factory. Half an hour later, Spot comes out with his arms all round the owner's shoulders. You know the sort of thing: 'Any trouble and you call *me*, Hymie,' and it's big dough all round. Well, not for Nigger; he only got £25, which I suppose wasn't bad in those days. Poor old Nigger; he was a mate of Wally Challis and he got three when Wally got a five in 1952 or thereabouts. Wally was the one killed a man driving Dodger Mullins back from Dartmoor. Wally and Nigger Smith had a crooked motor with a bell under the bonnet. The police didn't have a flashing light in those days and if they'd done a blag and were trying to get away they rang the bell, but they did it once too often. After he come out from that, Nigger ran the Cabinet Club for Aggie Hill.

In the days when Spot and Hilly were still friendly Spot marked my card, and Bill said all right, over the factory, so me and Patsy Lyons took a train up North. It wasn't worth the effort. The tragedy was that day there was a big picture taken in the Cabinet, about thirty people all posed like a rugby team, and Patsy and I missed being on it. Anyone who was anyone was on it – except us.

Billy Hill had all sorts of people under his belt. One of the most surprising was Leopold Harris, the fire-raiser and fraudsman. He'd been done in the Twenties or Thirties, but he was still working as an assessor in the Fifties. He must have been getting on for 80, and still as crooked as he had been in 1933; even better, in fact.

One of the Soho figures of the day owned a French restaurant in Wardour Street. It was very big in its day. Princess Margaret used to go there a lot, but now it's an Italian. He also owned a night-club not far away, and eventually Joe Wilkins (Bert's nephew) and I burned it down.

I'd met the owner when I went in the night-club for a drink sometimes and eventually, since he was having a bit of trouble with punters, he asked if me and Albert would like to mind it for him. Albert dropped out after a few weeks and Joe Wilkins came in.

I don't know why, but the club never did well; it was a nice little place with a band and a cabaret, and he had a licence to drink to 3 a.m. but it never took off. We realised that the only way you were going to make a profit was on the insurance, so we put it to the owner but at first he wasn't really all for it. He said give it two or three months before you do it. In his heart he was hoping it would pick up, and we wouldn't want to do it. After a couple of months we turned up with a can of petrol. At 3.30 everyone had to go. This night we got them out a bit earlier and produced the can of petrol. The owner's nerve went, but we talked him round and sprayed it all over the joint. There was a burglar alarm on the premises, so we came out and put the alarm on. He walked round to his flat which was above the restaurant, but Joe and I hung around. No flames, no smoke, nothing happened. We phoned the owner and out he come and turned the alarm off. We splashed brandy, scotch all over the joint, locked up, and home he went. Half an hour later we had to get him out again. Same thing. I realised now the mistake. No air was getting in, so I smashed the window at the back and that set it up nicely. Inside a couple of minutes the flames were all over the place. The fire brigade from Shaftesbury Avenue just round the corner was called out. They win the day for you. Smashing doors in, spraying everything with water. That's when Leopold Harris came in the next day; he was the assessor for the insurance. We done a few jobs with him before, and had him straight. It had all been set up by me.

I'd met Harris through Hilly, who put me in touch with him and said to go and see him before I did anything. I wanted to know how I could guarantee it would be him and I said, 'How do I know it'll be you?' He said, 'Don't worry. It'll be all right.' He said, 'I will be the one', and I never asked him how. But there he was and he was like magic. In fact he congratulated me on the fine job I'd done. He didn't know how many goes it had taken. It was so simple I couldn't believe it.[8]

Shortly after that I went on the run over Harry Rogers, the bingo club owner, when he wouldn't pay me for the torching I did for him down in Sussex. Months went by. Every so often I got in touch with the owner and he says the money hasn't come through. Then finally he says he's got the cheque and he'll give me my share. So I go to the French bank in Long Acre where he banked. You could get readies easily, and I split it with Joe. To give him his credit he paid up, unlike so many people who if you was on the run thought it was a licence not to pay you. It came to a nice few quid and he paid Harris himself. Then he turned the club into the Hideaway, and Hew McCowan really did it up and made it a really posh place. The Twins fancied owning the club and got nicked in 1964 when they tried to

---

[8]In what was then the longest trial at the Old Bailey – 33 days – Leopold Harris received fourteen years for arson in 1933. He had been a well respected fire assessor until 1932 when it was discovered he had been financing a large number of agents who were set up in businesses with stock of a highly combustible nature. Fraser's story that Harris was still operating in the 1960s is not as fantastic as it may seem. Whilst in prison at Maidstone, Harris was sufficiently well thought of to still be advising insurance companies from his cell which had been turned into an office. Before he was sent to prison he suffered from pernicious anaemia, but in jail he was fed raw liver and regained his health. He was released in 1940.

get McCowan to hand it over to them. They got chucked and the same night took over the club, calling it the El Morocco. In 1966 the owner got twenty-eight days for hitting a parking warden. He was excellent, I liked him.

Billy was into crooked cards as well. He had the 21 Club with Harry Meadows, one of the family who ran things like Churchills in Bond Street – where you got a dinner and a floor-show, but the real thing was the punters could make private deals with the hostesses. Billy's put them on their way and they made the most of it. The 21 was in Hertford Street off Berkeley Square. I think years later the son of one of the Greek shipping tycoons had a room over the top. It was a straightforward gambling club and Bill had these playing cards made where there were certain markings and the only way you could see them was to have special contact lenses or glasses. You could then see the mark and knew it was an ace or whatever. He was getting a good living out of it. He'd play and sometimes I'd help out if they were stuck, because although I'm useless at gambling even I could work out how to do it. I used to do this some evenings when I was on the run, more as a favour than anything else.

A man I did like working with in the early days was Alf Gerard. He was a really big, ugly man, but he was good to have on your side. I was in great demand in the sense of pavement work then; not everyone was willing to do it. Rewards were good but failures could be drastic – topped, ten years, five if you were lucky. You wouldn't go out with the intention of doing untold violence, but with people having a go you had to be prepared for an army to come on you. Remember it was broad daylight. It wasn't like 2 or 3 in the morning when there was hardly anyone about. I was a real live wire.

Generally you worked with your own team of up to about twelve or fifteen. Of course, you didn't work all fifteen in one go, but you were a little group. Alf wasn't one of them, but from time to time he'd stick up a job to us or make what you could call a guest appearance.

Jerry Callaghan was really a better mate of Alf Gerard than me and also he was best man at Dodger Davies' wedding – or the other way round. The Callaghans were a big family from South London. I think their father was a sergeant in the Army, and I first knew Jerry from before the War. The family came from Waterloo in Bayliss Road opposite the Old Vic; then it used to be called Oakley Street. I think our mob had a fight with his school; that's how I first met him. I knew him and his brothers Henry and Mickey. Henry was a very bright man; he went to college if I'm not mistaken. Another brother died in the ring at Manor Place Baths in the early 1950s.

Jerry was a great friend of Billy Ambrose who owned the Pen Club and got shot in it.[9] Billy had been a top class boxer, but the Board of Control suspended his licence when he got fined £50 for receiving – and that was the end of him as a straight man. Ambrose got five years over the Pen robbery. They nicked nearly three thousand of them at Conway Stewart in Stepney.

William Gregory said he had been on the raid and that Ambrose wasn't on it, and he got nicked as he left the court. Then Billy escaped from Hammersmith hospital and he stayed out for nearly a year, until the time when along with Jerry Callaghan he got five years in Manchester for robbery. Jerry'd done a five previously for malicious wounding. There was a whole lot of them arrested in May 1953 over a load of stuff in Leeds which turned up down here. Henry Botton, the man who shopped me over the shooting at Mr Smith's, was one of them and a couple from the Oliffe family was another.

Jerry's brother, Mickey Callaghan, was with the Harris

[9]The Pen Club in Smithfield was reputed to have been purchased with the proceeds of a robbery at the Waterman Pen Company, hence its name. It was run by Fay Sadler, girl-friend of (amongst others) Tommy Smithson, shot by Ellul and Spampinato. Ostensibly the fight in the club on 7 February 1960 involved the non-payment of a small amount of damage to a car owned by a girl-friend of one of the Nash brothers. Billy Ambrose and Selwyn Cooney, a friend of Billy Hill, were shot. Cooney died. Jimmy Nash and two others were acquitted of Cooney's murder. More probably the fight was part of a power struggle for the West End trade.

family when they had a fight with the Carter brothers in the Sunset Club. He could have a really good fight. Henry Botton was either a boxing promoter or manager.

Jerry and Alf Gerard had a garage where there were crooked cars. The law knew about it and were waiting when they came back one day. They steamed into the coppers and got away and went off to Australia. That's in a way how it come on top for Biggsy. No fault of theirs. Somehow the law tumbled they were in Australia, a letter or something got intercepted and with the inquiries Biggsy got uncovered when they were really going after Jerry and Alf. They got caught and deported back here, and I think Jerry got a six or seven and Alfie had a five. Jerry is in a wheelchair now, lives down Gloucester way. Alf's been dead these years. He was a good cook and had a bit of a restaurant once called The Blue Plaice over near Waterloo. He was hiding out from something down at a flat the Callaghans had in Brighton when he died there. I think he had cirrhosis but others say he choked on a lobster, which is more appropriate, him being a cook. His son, Nicky, was another hard man too. He got shot as he left his daughter's birthday party.

Whatever I say about them, there's no doubt the Carters were big on and off in my day in the Elephant. They got their reputation when they did 'Hoppy' Smith. Hoppy was a hard man, into protection, and 'Tom Thumb' Brindle's first wife was Hoppy's sister. Hoppy had a club foot and a built-up boot, which is how he got his name, but it didn't slow him down much. The original fight was in the Flowers of the Forest in the Blackfriars Road, when Hoppy pulled out a cut-throat razor and Johnny Carter got cut when he put his forearm up to protect his face. The return was when Hoppy come out of a pub bottom of London Road. He saw the brothers were waiting for him and, quick as a flash, he picked up a little girl who was standing outside the pub. Of course, they couldn't touch him with her in his arms, but it didn't do him any good long term. They put a V in his forehead, and after that they were people to be looked up to. Tony Reuter, who the newspapers called 'The King of the Teddy Boys', married a Carter sister, and the Roffs were cousins. Danny Roff was shot a bit back as a revenge for the death of Charlie Wilson in Spain. It was all over a drugs quarrel and the mistaken belief that Charlie had grassed up a man called Roy Adkins who also got shot in Amsterdam. He got shot down in a club in New Cross and then when that didn't work and just left him a bit paralysed, someone finished him when he was in the driveway of his home in Kent.

I did Micky Roff in Wandsworth. After I done Carter I was transferred to Leeds, and in that period Micky had come in and he was telling everyone, 'If I'd been here it wouldn't have happened. I'd have done Fraser'; and when I come to Wandsworth I was told this. Naturally, I couldn't let it go. In 1954 at Wandsworth when you'd done nine months you was allowed to go to a lecture or concert in the chapel, say once every Pancake Day. I'd done well over nine months and so I was eligible. I had a tool made and going along A2 to get to the chapel I done him sweet. By the time the screws arrived after they heard his scream, I'd got rid of the tool and was sitting peacefully in the chapel. There was nothing they could do.

After the lecture I was locked up in my cell quite normally, but about 9 o'clock all of a sudden my spyhole went up. This was incredibly late by prison standards. You didn't have radios or wrist-watches, but you got to know what time it was particularly because you could see a clock as you left the chapel. A voice goes, 'You took a liberty with me, Frank, you really hurt me.' And it was Roff. They must have specially unlocked him. I knew his voice, but I knew there'd be prison officers either side of him outside the door; that's the only way they could nick me for him. I said, 'I don't know who you are. Get away, you daft idiot. You're a prison officer pretending to be a prisoner.' He kept repeating it, but I ignored the rest. About 7 a.m the next day I was marched down the punishment cells on report for attacking him. Lawton was the governor, and I was put on bread and water.

I never saw him again after that. By now it had gone round

he was a prison grass, and then Eddie Gibbs did him with a hammer at Parkhurst. Not only was he a prison grass, Micky Roff was one on the outside too. He rushed into Carter Street police station somewhere at the end of the 1950s and gave the numbers of a car, saying men in it had shot at him. This was nothing to do with me. It was a dead straight car and they arrested Johnny Nash, one of the brothers from Islington, and took him into Carter Street. He said, 'What are you talking about?' but in the charge room when John was surrounded by police Micky Roff went up and punched him in the face, saying, 'That's for shooting me.' Subtle way of giving evidence. Johnny couldn't hit him back. If he'd spent four days in the witness box, he couldn't have given evidence more wickedly than with that one punch. Charlie Richardson was also charged, but he was acquitted. Poor Johnny got two years for that piece of wickedness.

Then in 1970 Roffie goes demanding money off a guy who had a garage in South London. The man slaughtered Roffie with a chopper and Roffie nicked him. Thank God he was found not guilty. He's long dead now – natural causes, unfortunately.

Four

I don't think there are any real Mr Bigs any more. Billy Hill was the last independent, so to speak, and before him Bert Marsh – he was as big as anyone. He spoke both perfect English and Italian. He lived in Amwell Street near the Square. It's the ones you don't hear about who are the really successful thieves.

Once the Italians lost their power during the Second World War to the Whites and were interned, Bert Marsh got a bit isolated and he was pleased enough when Billy and Spot cleared them out in 1947. He did Billy a very good turn over the Jack Spot–Albert Dimes fight in Frith Street. It's common ground that Spot was on the way out when it happened. He and Billy'd run Soho between them for six or seven years, but Spot was on the down and he was getting very jealous of Billy. That's why he picked on Albert Dimes for the fight.

Everyone knows they cut each other to bits, and it got stopped when a Jewish lady hit Spot over the head with a pair of weighing scales. They both went to hospital and got discharged. Then they were both charged.

Me and Eva's husband, Jimmy Brindle, and Tony Nappi were up at Albert's house at 22 River Street in Clerkenwell where he lived at that time, to see how he was getting on, and we went downstairs, opened the street door and there were the police come to arrest Albert. I wouldn't let them in, and Jimmy and Tony stood straight behind me. They were trying to push in, but then Albert heard what was going on and said it was all right, let them in. I asked what he wanted me to do, and he said I was to see Bert Marsh and then see Bill.

Jimmy had a motor and I went straight to see Marsh. At the time he had an illegal bookmaker's pitch in Frith and Old Compton with his partner, a man called Buster. I told him on me own and Bert just said, 'Leave it to me.' That's when the police conveniently found the knife just off Soho Square, the very knife Spot had used. Bert had picked it up just after the fight. It was very important in Albert's favour. I went with Bert when he put it in the Square, and then went with Hilly. There was then an anonymous phone call and the knife was found. It was a moody, of course. Then Billy started to go to work.

Just like the comedian Max Miller used to say, 'I liked it in Brighton.' I first settled there in 1955 straight after the Spot—Dimes fight. Funnily enough, just before that Jack had sent word with Georgie Wood to ask if me and Billy Blythe would like to open a club with him, but I said no because I was with Albert and Hilly at the time.

Then after the fight Billy sent me to Brighton to look after Sammy Bellson, who'd been paying money to Spot but who now could see which way the wind was blowing. Billy meant to make sure he stayed with us. Brighton was an open town in those days and Sammy Bellson was the nearest thing to the unofficial mayor. He was born in the East End, done a carpet in 1941 or 1942 and then in 1945 he went to Brighton. It was the best thing he ever done. It was an open town even then. All he did was organise it even better.

By the time I arrived in 1955 it was unbelievable. I remember I once said to him, 'Let's do a bank down here.' I didn't mean the counter, but going in and doing the strong-room, and he just said, 'No, Frank. If you clear the bank out and the deposit boxes you'll get 60–70 grand, a great deal of money, but Scotland Yard know how sweet they have it here and they want to put the block on it because they're not getting anything themselves. Once that bank was done, there'd be such a scream that Scotland Yard would be sent in to clean it up and that could put a stop to a lot of things, whereas now you have five gambling clubs.'

The biggest club was on the front right next to the Grand Hotel in the basement. It was just like that film *The Sting*, except they weren't working a scam. They didn't have to. Anyone could walk in and out. There was cards, dice and bookmaking in the afternoon. All the runners were up on the board. There was roulette in the evening along with the dogs. You could play from sixpence to six grand so to speak. The stakes were what you wanted. Bellson owned all five clubs, but the people who ran them might have a stake.

Then there were the night-clubs. The main one was in West Street where Sammy had the Burlesque. It was over the top of his offices and it was open all night. The others would close some time in the evening, then everyone would go on to the Burlesque. The police would just walk in for their cut. If you fancied doing a jewellery shop, going in with the keys, then the police didn't answer the burglar alarm too quickly provided, of course, they were getting their corner.

Cherry Titmuss and me – in 1955, after we cut the wages bags off some men's wrists – we had to give the law in London £500 to get out of it. We said we'd been in Brighton, and to make it look good they had to send word to the town to check it out. The Brighton law confirmed back that they'd checked up and so really they alibied us. We went to give the Brighton law £500, same as in London, and Sam said, 'Don't spoil them. Just give them a tenner each.' We was feeling generous, so they got a score apiece.

Sam wasn't greedy. If someone wanted to open a club they could do so, and he wouldn't take a cut, but if you wanted a favour and you'd go to Sam then he might charge you. Mostly he'd do it for nothing. He'd pay off the coppers for you and charge a bit for his trouble. You could drink all night, legally, without knocking on doors and getting let in. London faces almost lived there.

Then it all fell apart. Sammy had the Chief Constable in his pocket. He was a man called Ridge who'd worked his way up through the force. I think he'd been gassed during the First World War. There was a man called Bennett who ran the Astor, which was known as the Bucket of Blood because of all the claret spilled during the fights, and he agreed to pay Ridge £20 a week to be able to stay open all hours.

If you've got a copper straightened, then things go along sweetly all round until he gets greedy – and that's what happened. There's the usual things: a drink here, a Christmas turkey there with a tenner in along with the giblets, a weekly pension and money for any special favour.

Things would probably have gone on all right except there was one copper, Heath, who was an evil man. He would threaten and lean on people. That's how they come unstuck. Perhaps Sam slipped up. He could have put a stop to this, but most probably the woman Heath was particularly on to didn't know of Sam or they could have gone to him for help. Anyway Sammy and Ridge – along with Tony Lyons, who owned Sherry's, the pub on the corner of West Street and the front, and who had even more clout than Sam I think – were nicked. The copper Heath and another called Hammersley also got done for conspiracy in October 1957, a year or so after I started my bird for the Spot case. Their dealings went all the way back to 1948.

And then people came out of the woodwork to say how the police been blackmailing them. Sam, Heath and Hammersley got time, but Ridge and Lyons got chucked. Years later, Ridge sued the council for his pension and he won.[1]

Sam went and did for himself when he wrote that story in the newspapers – 'I was the Governor of Brighton but we didn't need bullets, we did it with bribes,' things like that. That was the end of him. He must have needed a bit of quick dough. All his things had been closed down. If he'd kept his box of tricks shut, he could probably have gone back and still had the respect of the law, but by writing that story it was all over for him. Once Sam opened his mouth like that, things tightened up.

I saw Sammy in Pentonville when he was doing his three. He came back to London afterwards and I hear he's still alive. On the other hand, Tony Lyons carried on until he died. He lived in a block of flats going towards Rottingdean. He was very intelligent, shrewd.

But of course this was a couple of years after the Spot trouble and what followed. After Albert and Spot were acquitted, Spot just wouldn't leave it alone and he sent that Joey Cannon from Paddington after both Billy and Albert, and so Billy ordered me and Ginger Dennis to cut him. We really did him when he was coming back to his flat one night. He knew it was going to happen because he kept going into Paddington police station asking for protection, but he didn't know from which direction it was coming.

That's when he went and grassed us up. He should never have done that; he'd cut enough people himself in his time that he should have been able to take it himself. Not only that, but he put innocent people in the nick. Bobby Warren and Battles Rossi was nowhere near the place. I think that was why later Billy decided to have him framed. Now you might not think that was kosher, and I suppose it wasn't Billy's finest

---

[1]It took him until 1963 to manage it. On 14 March the House of Lords overturned the decision of the Brighton Watch Committee because Ridge had not been informed what charges he was to face; nor had he been invited to attend the disciplinary proceedings. Half his pension was paid by the Home Office.

hour, but in a way he did it to get back at Spot for what he'd done to us.

After the slashing I got away to Ireland, and I only came back when I heard Ray Rosa and Dickie 'Dido' Frett had been nicked. You're always favourite when you're away. If I'd managed to stay in Ireland and got captured twelve months later, then I'd most probably have walked out of it. But what happened was, it was arranged that Patsy Lyons would drive Ray and Dido to Manchester, where Bobby McDermott would put them up before we all went to Ireland. Me and Bill was in the other car and somehow we were separated. We went on to Manchester and explained to Bobby they'd be up there shortly. I got the boat and I stayed in a house just outside Dublin. When they asked me at the trial what I was doing there, I said I was looking to see if I could make a living smuggling watches. While I was in Ireland I heard they'd been nicked, and I couldn't get back quick enough. Two things. One, it was because of Dido and Ray. I owed it to them, and I thought that much as Bill and Albert were good I needed to be there superintending things. So far as Dido and Ray was concerned, they were nicked not just for the Spot thing – although they got out of that – but also for cutting Johnny Carter which was my quarrel.[2] They were my friends. They were my responsibility, and I had to do something.

You'd heard of phones being tapped, but like an idiot you didn't really believe it. In those days you didn't think you were that important; spies maybe, but a tuppen'y-ha' penny cutting case? Never! I couldn't have dreamed I'd be nicked, but I was. I was nicked at the airport by Nipper Read, who later went on and nicked the Twins. I was livid, I couldn't believe it.

I got taken to Paddington Green police station for questioning about both cases, and there I got a bit of help. I'd been banged up and I spoke to a uniformed copper who came round the

[2]The Brindle family and Fraser had a violent and long-running feud with the Carter brothers, also from South London. For a full account, see *Mad Frank*, pp. 96, 110 *et seq*.

cells checking we hadn't topped ourselves. I sussed that this copper was sympathetic and I took a gamble. He said, 'You all right?' I said, 'No.' In them days the coppers never stressed did you want a solicitor. Officially they may have been meant to, but it was really up to you to ask for one. Then even if you did, you was at their mercy: 'He wasn't in'; 'they couldn't get hold of him'; 'he won't come out'. All that fanny but, to be fair, solicitors back then wouldn't do things like they do today. I said to the copper, 'Do you know Dave Barry?' He had barrows in the Church Street market off the Edgware Road. In fact, Ray Rosa later married Dave's sister. He said, 'Yes', and so I asked him to get Dave to phone my solicitor to get him up right away. I knew I took a gamble. One, the copper might not do it. Two, he might tell the Superintendent and D.I. Cornish, whose grandfather was one of the famous ones of his time, who was on the case. Then I would be in trouble. Asking for a solicitor – the actions of a guilty man!

To his credit the copper done it – got hold of Barry, and Dave phoned up the brief and he came down. The guy Dave rang was a solicitor's clerk. It was too late for him to do anything about the Spot case, but he did the trick with the Carter case. They asked him to let me go on the ID with Mrs Carter. It was the girl he was living with. I said I knew her, and the brief said that there was no point. What I meant was the real Mrs Carter: his mother, not his bird. The brief stuck it out, saying that IDs weren't meant for people you knew, and so they never put me on it. As Carter's girl had never seen me, she never picked me out at the magistrates' court. She picked out Dickie Dido and Ray Rosa. The police must have told her where they'd be lined up. I got seven for the Spot thing though, so did Bobby Warren. Billy Blythe had a five; Bert Rossi and Ginger Dennis got four each.

They split us up like they did earlier with the race gangs. Bill went to Liverpool, Bert was sent to Winchester, Ginger to Lincoln, Bobby Warren to the Scrubs, and I went to Bristol. Billy died during the sentence in February 1957. He had a duodenal ulcer and he was sitting in his cell when it burst. He'd reported sick two or three days running and they'd given him some mixture; you always got the standard thing whatever was wrong with you. By the time they got him out of the cell, it was too late.

I don't know if Billy Hill's heart wasn't in it any longer, and he tried to go off to Australia with Gypsy Riley. She was a really beautiful woman. He'd always fancied women and Aggie had let him have his way with the hoisters and the toms, knowing it could only last a few weeks, but Gyp was in a different class altogether. Billy had his own numberplate GPB which stood for Gyp, the Poodle, and Bill.

Aggie kept on the Modernaires Club in Greek Court at the Charing Cross Road end of Old Compton Street. If you look today you can still see the door which led down to the basement. It had once belonged to Jack Spot, and she'd bought it off him. Of course, she still had the Cabinet Club upstairs in Gerrard Street. Tommy Steele's father, Darbo Hicks, had the cloakroom concession in the Modernaires. At the end of the War he used to have barrows, and if we had a party he would bring the booze round on them from the pub to the flat where we were. He could sing a bit too, and we'd have a whip for him.

I don't think a straight person ever went into clubs like the Modernaires or the Log Cabin. If they did, I never saw them. The only exception would be on a Monday when the markets were closed. Then the traders would come in for a drink, but they all knew what the score was. They wouldn't have done bird themselves, but they would know people who had.

Gyp got done in March 1957 over a fight in the Miramar Club in Paddington a couple of months earlier. The club was in part of a hotel. Everyone used it for a time, it was very popular. Gypsy was over on Hilly's behalf to show Spot that he didn't run Paddington any more.

A guy called Arthur Ranns had got his eye done there, but

the magistrate wouldn't have anything of it. After a week's lay down, when he heard the case he said the evidence was confused and although she'd been in the fracas that wasn't enough to send her for trial there. Marrinan defended her and he must have done a good job. It was one of the last cases he did before he got struck off.

They'd have let Gyp into Australia, but they'd never let Billy near the place. In fact he never landed. Some copper, 'King of the Detectives' in Sydney he was called, came out on a launch to the boat and marked his card for him. It's funny really, because that copper was just about as crooked as Billy himself. I think maybe he just did it for the sea voyage and the chance to give his book a bit of a gee.

Albert more or less kept his head down after that. He had the point-to-points now and they gave him a good living. What he did was collect their voluntary contributions, really the price the bookies paid for a pitch, but then he went and quarrelled with the National Hunt Committee. He'd always had an interest in horses, and even before then he'd had a jockey or two straightened. I was introduced to one of them who won one of the big handicaps early in the season shortly after the War. I think as the years went on he got slung off. I met him through Albert, and in turn he introduced other hookey jockeys to us. I didn't meet Albert's best man at it – his most crooked jockey – until 1951 or even later.

At first I couldn't work out how they could go crooked, and then it was explained how it was so easy. They could introduce you to the stable boys and you could give them the doping gear. That's where people like Joe Lowry and Charlie Mitchell were so brilliant, the way they had it sewn up. Johnny Barham got nicked in 1965; he got a four. I went into a bit of horse doping, but I never held the needle or shoved the stuff in its feed. I went as a minder to see the stable boys done their job. It's all very well being told it has happened and your money is well spent, but being told and it actually happening are two different matters. So I went to make sure everything was sound. This would be the night before they went to the races.

Although a lot of people did, I never did the dogs. They were just that bit more difficult. They could make quite a bit of noise, and dogs had for many years had that sniff around them. Bill Blythe was great one night; he'd got a lot of bottle. He jumped over the barrier at Harringay when it was all going wrong and frightened the dogs into turning round so the race had to be halted. Then he just jumped back into the crowd and was away.

Whereas with the Sport of Kings it wasn't considered that nobbling would or could be done, you could come a tumble with the dogs so easily. If they started going slow it wouldn't be hard to sus what had happened, but a jockey could hook up a horse out in the country in them days when there were no cameras and no slow-motion replays and no one would be any the wiser. It was the same with the dope as it is today. There'll always be doping. It just seems the authorities take longer to sus out what's happened.

It was funny how Albert always seemed to want to protect his reputation when all it did was bring him more into the limelight. Just after I went down for Spot, he had a run-in with a Tory M.P. who'd called him names and went off to the Commons to have it out with him. Of course the man didn't see him, but it was in all the papers. Then, after he got named in one of Charles De Silva's rackets, he paid a top brief to get up in court and say it was nothing to do with him. The other thing he decided to do was to sue Cassandra of the *Mirror* about something he'd written at the trial. Reggie Seaton, who was prosecuting, said we were rascals, and Cassandra said that Hilly and Dimes were 'disgusting creatures' and he called me the 'murderous Fraser'. So he got his solicitors to write a letter to the *Mirror*.

What happened instead was that, of course, the *Mirror* backed Cassandra and they printed the letters over the front pages for a couple of days under headlines, and it made Albert look a bit foolish. I don't know why he did it; he couldn't win. He'd had a run-in with that William Hickey column in the *Express* and all. After Ginger Dennis came out from the Spot slashing he was with Alfie in a café bar in Frith Street, and William Hickey mentioned he'd seen Albert with girls. They were nothing to do with him – he was a happily married man – and so Albert sued. I think he got nominal damages.

Over the years a lot of us have done it, but even if we've won on paper we don't get no damages because we haven't any reputation to get damages for. Darby Sabini was one of the first and he ended up bankrupt over it, not that it did him much harm.[3] The law doesn't like criminals suing straight people. And if straight people get hurt by us, the law always sees to it we pay. Jack Spot was one. He was having trouble with Duncan Webb, who was in Bill's pocket and was geeing him up. Jack broke his arm and Webb sued and picked up over £700. Then he made Spot bankrupt over the damages. Bill could have helped out if he'd wanted, but he wouldn't.

The only one of us who done any real good in a libel court was Alfie Hinds when he sued Herbert Sparks, the copper. Sparks had put him away for the Maples robbery in Tottenham Court Road in 1953, and then after he retired he had gone and written about how Hinds had done it in the *People*. Alfie was out by now and sued for libel, saying it had been a fit-up, and he won. He had things going for him. He hadn't got anything like the form say I had. He was out, which made

---

[3]In 1926 Darby Sabini brought an action against D.C. Thomson & Co. over an article in a sporting newspaper *Topical Times* on 12 April 1924, written by a former racecourse man Ted McLean and naming him as a leading villain on the turf. The newspaper pleaded justification and Sabini failed to appear at the trial. He was made bankrupt in the sum of £737, the costs of the action. When he appeared at his bankruptcy hearing, he said that he was employed by the Bookmakers and Backers Racecourse Protection Association which, he said, was a legitimate limited liability company. His duty was to sell the lists of runners to bookmakers at 5/- a time and he received some £8 a week commission. *Counsel for the Creditors*: The only bookmakers who buy these cards are those who are compelled to do so because they are afraid of you and your followers. *Sabini*: No.

a great difference, and the police were still suffering from the Challenor scandal. Also, from all accounts Sparks was a terrible witness and Alfie, who had an IQ far in excess of his, was a good one.[4]

It was that crooked barrister Marrinan who egged me on to sue the *Sunday Empire News*. He'd defended Bobby Warren in the Spot trial, and he tried to help me out when I was having a bit of trouble in the witness box by finding out how many telephones there were in a certain room and giving me a signal. Now he wrote to me saying he'd represent me. It was all over Spot again.

Spot had been acquitted when Billy Hill tried to have him fitted up, and the paper said the police had taken a statement from me in support of him. At the time I was meant to have made the statement, in fact I was down the punishment cells after I did a grass in 1957.[5] I was in the strong cell and I'd got five months for the screw and two for the grass, so I lost seven months in all.

The police had never been near me, and I couldn't let it go. Ginger Dennis, who was at Lincoln with me, he smuggled out a paper where I had to sign on the writ. There's no way prison authorities would have given permission if they'd known. Once the writ was issued, then it was all above board and the prison authorities had to go along with it. It was the same brief who'd helped me at Paddington Green over the Carter ID, and he subpoenaed the prison officers with a book when I was at Lincoln showing I really was in the strong cell and there were no visits. It broke the screws' hearts, but they couldn't

---

[4]In 1964 Harold Challenor was found unfit to plead to a charge of conspiracy to pervert the course of justice. He soon recovered and became a solicitors' clerk. His three junior colleagues from the police received a total of eleven years. Amongst the victims of Challenor's campaign to rid the West End of criminals and dissidents, which involved planting evidence, was James Fraser, Frank Fraser's nephew. Hinds was awarded £1,300, but despite this the Court of Appeal refused to quash his conviction. Shortly after, the law was changed to prevent such actions as Hinds'.
[5]The grass in question this time was Harry Cowans, who was beaten by Fraser and 'Mad' Frank Mitchell. The story of his treachery which led to the attack can be found in *Mad Frank*, p.147.

help but tell the truth. The judge himself called it an erroneous mistake on the part of the newspaper. But who cared? I had no character.

The paper had said they'd print an apology and I refused. I think they offered about £25 as well. It would have been a small piece and tucked away. I don't suppose I'd ever have seen it, because at that time you weren't allowed newspapers. Also it was good fun because I could have visits in connection with my action, which was handy. It ran for about two years and came up in April 1959. This was at the High Court. I gave evidence and I was awarded a penny and my costs, so it was worth it in one way.

What came out in the end, so far as Albert was concerned, was just how close he was to Angelo Bruno of the Philadelphia mafia. He really looked after things this end for them when they were bringing in organised gambling junkets before the authorities shut them down. The damage was done by then. The money had been made.

It was Bert Marsh who introduced me to Angelo, when he was over seeing Albert, and I went with Albert to Rome where I was introduced to Lucky Luciano by a man, Dick something, who was one of the few Jews in the Mafia. As I've said before, we had him checked out by Harry Levene when he was over in New York because it was thought he might have been slipped in to us, but it turned out he was kosher. Billy could always get Harry to do a bit of work for him.

Levene took over the boxing from Jack Solomons. They hated each other. Until Levene came along, Solomons had had it all his own way. He told me and Eddie that Levene had been the manager of a big club at the back of Regent Street – I think he said it was the Bagatelle – and the Solomons family had a place in the street market in Ridley Road, Hackney. This was before the War. They supplied fish to the hotels and clubs. But for what they were charging the Bagatelle was eating only a small fraction; they were being charged for non-existent fish, both of them in it together. When it came on top and the accountants got called in, Levene had questions to answer. He wrote a statement and Solomons was nicked, but he got out of it. They never liked each other after that, though.

I'd known Solomons for years through Billy Hill. Spot and Hilly really had him, didn't they? Not fixing fights, although Spot did that a bit, but free ringside seats, that sort of thing. Solomons was just like one of us originally; came from the back streets so to speak and before the War, when Sidney Hulls was the main promoter in this country, Solomons got on the band-wagon with him and rode him out. They put on Woodcock *v.* Harvey at Tottenham Football Ground. In them days that was really unusual. Solomons lived in Brighton and knew Bud Flanagan, who had opened the Albany Club in Brighton before the War. It's still there today, gone through many hands since he had it of course. Later Solomons went into partnership with Bud Flanagan in the betting shops. Me, Eddie Richardson, Jack Solomons, Flanagan – we all went to Cardiff together for a benefit for Lyn James, the Welsh boxer who died in the ring there. About the end of 1964 or beginning of 1965 – something like that. I think Eddie and I put up £25 each.

I liked Solomons and I got on with him, but he strangled the boxers. Levene did look after them better; that's how he stole Solomons' thunder. I've got to say that every year Solomons was very good, though. He would take over the Manor Place Baths and give a charity tournament for needy children and pensioners. I'd do a lot to help; I'd go round to see people, getting them to make donations or take out advertisements in the programme. Vic Rosati was one of them I'd pop in to see; he had the King's Arms in the Walworth Road. Funnily, his brother was the headmaster at the Christian Martyrs Catholic School at the back of the Old Kent Road and he taught my boys. Vic had been one of Darby Sabini's men at Brighton. All the Elephant Mob used his pub. He stayed in it for years until he had to move when they knocked it down for flats. He went into another one at the back of the Elephant.

Levene knew Bert Marsh and Bert Wilkins and he had their money behind him at the start, but he paid them back. There was always an advertisement for Bert Wilkins' club, the Nightingale, in Berkeley Square. Levene was sensible; he paid the boxers more than Solomons and so the managers went with him. But it was through his connection with Bert Marsh that we could use Levene.

I passed the hospital where Albert was dying when I was brought down to London in 1972 to give evidence for Roy Grantham, who turned out to be a grass. Of course I didn't go to Albert's funeral, and I was surprised when a number of others who'd been close stayed away. Stanley Baker remained true though; he attended.

There's always been people who'll put up a job for a cut. History shows that Jew who was nicked for the Pearl robbery all those years ago was a putter-up.[6] The Train robbery was another – stuck up, I believe, by Brixton Jock, that friend of Billy Hill.

In a lesser way that's what we did with the people up north like Abe Tobias, but I think today it's more or less stopped. It's a question of trust. I think people don't stand for things just being put up with no involvement. They either find their own work, or if anyone sticks something up they have to be on it with the team; they have to be part. It could be dangerous; someone who stuck some work up wasn't on it, and it could be traced back, could you rely on them to keep their mouth shut? Take the Brinks-Mat robbery; the guard, Tony Black, he was the organiser's brother-in-law Black, he opened up. He was living with one of the sisters. Of course there's plenty of

---

[6]Fraser is referring to Joseph 'Cammie' Grizzard, perhaps the greatest receiver of stolen jewellery and 'putter-up' of his era. In 1913 he organised the theft of a string of pearls sent from Paris to London. He was sentenced to seven years' penal servitude and on his release took part in a swindle to obtain diamonds. This time he received twelve months, and was allowed to return home before his death on 11 September 1923.

examples of the man who's put something up, gone on the job and then sidled off at the last minute or even been arrested and released.'[7]

I think now you're only safe with your own family but then, when you think about that brother-in-law in the Brinks-Mat, I suppose not always even then.

[7]The Brinks-Mat robbery took place on 26 November 1983 when raiders at the Heathrow Trading Estate stole millions of pounds of gold bullion. The insider on the job, the guard Tony Black, was the brother-in-law of 'Colonel' Brian Robinson. On 17 February 1984 Black pleaded guilty and was sentenced to six years imprisonment and then gave evidence for the prosecution against Robinson, Micky McAvoy and Tony White. Robinson and McAvoy each received twenty-five years imprisonment and White was acquitted. The money was laundered through a series of off-shore companies and a considerable amount was smelted down. A police officer was stabbed to death when he was carrying out undercover surveillance at the home of Kenneth Noye, who was acquitted of his murder but later received fourteen years for receiving. In the late 1980s and early 1990s, a series of trials resulted in the convictions of a number of people for handling the proceeds. A further set of actions in the civil courts resulted in the retrieval of the money, which had been multiplied by a series of highly successful property speculations and investments, some organised by solicitor Michael Relton who received a twelve-year sentence.

Five

When I was working it was a proper working relationship all round. Everybody's equal, but out of that equal there would be one or two who would voice an opinion a bit more firmly.

You wouldn't choose to do a place near your home, not if you could avoid it. It would depend on how skint you were. The Eldorado ice-cream job was near home, and where the Oxo building robbery took place – I was literally born round there, but we still done it. If you've a choice you don't, but that was such a nice thing you couldn't very well pass it by.

We found our own work outside big firms. We'd go our separate ways looking around, and then we'd have a serious look on a Friday. The next week we'd all look, and one would go in when the cashiers and clerks went in from the firms just to change down a £5 note, something like that. You could openly see what money they were getting from the bank. Then the report would be 'Yes'. Say there's £2–3,000. You wouldn't look again unless it was in a very busy area when you'd have to pay attention to the traffic. The following week or the week after you'd do it. You'd do them on the pavement outside the bank or the firm, whichever was the best for the car and all round.

Sometimes outside the bank or the firm wasn't too good. The men who collected the money often walked, and preferably you'd do them in a side street. If they went by car, then in the side street we'd put a couple of crooked cars so when they arrived they had to park away down the street out of sight from the main road. You'd spread the motors out so it would be impossible to park in between. These would be cars we'd nicked; they'd be well rung and would be driven away afterwards because the police would have no idea they'd been involved. No one had any idea of taking numbers. Cars could be parked all day long, very few people had garages. In the course of a day, I've gone back with my pal and just got in and drove the car away. It seems incredible.

The notes weren't necessarily new at all, and we never had to have them changed – not once. You could safely say in a good year you'd do twelve or possibly fourteen, and you'd reckon to get around three grand between us on each. There'd always be four: two on the pavement, one in the car, and the other who would collect the car or pretend to chase you. Officially he was a dead straight man with a straight motor. There was a bloke we had from Borstal; he was a foreman carpenter. He never did any other single day and never looked back. He'd have a drink, a couple at the most, and then he'd be gone until the next bit of business. Wound up a very rich man, God bless him; a man who really made a success of crime in every sense. To his credit he deserved to. He never wasted his money, kept a very low profile – never went out drinking, and disciplined himself extremely well.

When you got away in a car, about three turnings away there'd be a van you'd have parked for you. You'd get out, all go in and the driver of the crooked car would get out and make his own way. That car would be abandoned. The van you got picked up in was a ringer, so if the numbers were took it wouldn't make any difference. There would be quite a lot of coins, because with everyone paid in cash a man's wages might be £6 which would be in notes and 18/6d which would be in silver and copper. We'd have two suitcases for the stuff, and we'd go to someone's house. In my case I'd have to fly straight home because I was always being put on IDs. I never got picked out, but my brother did once after we'd changed jackets so it was a bit of an iffy parade. It was getting in the newspapers with them calling us 'The Friday Gang', in the dailies along with the three evenings, the *Star, News* and *Standard*, and the police were just coming round on a regular basis. Newspapers like to put a name to things. When I was a kid in the 1930s there was a gang they called 'The Evening Dress Gang' because they used to steal men's dinner jackets and ladies' gowns, but they never amounted to much.

Several of the jobs we did was with Albert Baffey, who was a top driver in his day. He was with me over the Oxo and the United Dairies and the Royal Northern Hospital money in the Holloway Road. Jack Rosa should have been on it but he'd had a row with someone, given them a belting and got two years, so he was unavailable so to speak.

Every Friday the cashiers would go and get the money from a bank near the Seven Sisters Road; then they'd walk back with it. We had our usual newspaper van and took the money as sweet as you wish you could get. That very same night I was nicked for it at about 9 o'clock. Albert lived then in Burma Road, Stoke Newington. He'd bought the house and he was looking after a guy on the run – Wally someone, I forget his second name. He'd given over the top floor to him, but he'd said, 'You're foolish stopping with me. If they ever do nick me and you're here, you'll be nicked as well.' Albert got nicked that evening as well, and so did Wally. They didn't put Wally on an ID. I think they knew the SP and that he wasn't working. Me and Albert went on a double parade and neither was picked out.

A couple of weeks later Jack Rosa got taken out of Pentonville for some check-up at the Royal Northern and got chatting with the staff there. 'Only last week we were robbed of all our money,' they said. He said he nearly replied, 'And I should have been on it,' but thank God he didn't.

'The Friday Gang' had to end, and it did when I got bird for punching a barrister in Bolsom's in Mayfair. When I came out they were tightening up a bit and it was getting very dangerous. 1 couldn't keep having that luck. I'd done every day of the six months and then was out four days and got nicked trying to get Jack Rosa's defence money out of a hotel off the Strand. I got chucked on that one, but I was out only another four months when I was done for a warehouse at Bedford. Charlie Gibbs was with me then, one of the top thieves before the War, and during and after too. His sister, Carrie, was Alfie Hinds' first wife. Teddy Gibbs was on it and all. I was the only one, I'm happy to say, who got nicked. Best only one than more. Later Charlie got ten years PD and got cancer very early into his ten. He was one of the first prisoners to be allowed out a week or so before he died so it could be at home.

Crime as you get known is like a network; people know you, you know them and if there's something to be done up North sometimes they'd rather have a London outfit who's in and out rather than do it themselves. Friendships are made in prison, or approved school, and then you get introduced to people who have been in prison. In turn they introduce you, have a drink, a bit like a convention of lawyers where they have outlets all over the country. The big men? In Manchester you had Bobby McDermott of course, a great receiver. In Glasgow there was Mendel, and Cronin till he got poisoned in the 1940s. In Leeds there was 'Blondie' Higgins because of his fair hair. In Sunderland there were two brothers who did a five for manslaughter; one had the cat; a good family.

In Blackpool there was Abe Tobias. It wasn't as good as Brighton but it wasn't too far behind. There were spielers there, and of course Jack London the old fighter; his family minded a few clubs and that. Albert Dimes was on the run up there during the War after he had deserted. They had good clubs in Blackpool. It was rest and recreation, and if you had a load of tom to knock out they'd be queueing up to buy it off you in Blackpool. The police had been sweetened. In them days no one even believed anything like that. They were more crooked than even today's I suppose, for the simple reason who would ever believe a policeman was crooked back then? That's how they fitted people up and got them out as well. They had a licence in every sense of the word.

There were no motorways until 1959, and then the M1 that only went from London to Birmingham. And remember petrol rationing was in force quite some time after the War. So you were better going by train and then nicking your motors up on the spot. You'd pick the team down here, you'd have a look at it – one or two of you. You'd expect them to have a stow in someone's house, and to say where you could nick motors and where they could be rung very quickly, or there'd be no scream for so many hours and that would be the extent of the help you'd get from them. Then you'd go up a week before to have a look, because if it was a pavement job it would be something which would go either every day or once a week and most things then were pavement. Then you'd come back, put the others in the picture and maybe go up once more for a final look, then a week later you'd go up the night before, work the next day, and it would be up to you whether you wished to stay or come back. Jack Rosa once flew down from Blackpool; me and Patsy Lyons went back by train. Then after the job you'd go back and share. Depending on how much was involved, they'd get the same share, but say over £2,000 they would get slightly more than we did. It was all cash. You didn't need a slaughter.

You'd do a job up North maybe four times a year depending on whether it was possible and, of course, people from the North would come down here. Motorways have made life a lot easier.

There was also some exchange in robberies between the French and the English, although I didn't personally work abroad. Of course, shoplifters worked all over and so did creepers.[1] If a French team was coming over to work they'd notify someone like French Lou – who by the time he died had a lovely off-licence in Soho – or Albert's elder brother, 'Italian Jock' Dimeo, who was also well known. Just as when I had to go abroad, people in Paris were notified to give me a bit of help.

Italian Jock died before Albert. He'd got him out of the Mancini[2] trouble. In 1942 Italian Jock and 'Scarface' Jock Russo were in Bobby's Club, which was in Rupert Court off Rupert Street, and they cut Dodger Mullins and Archie, Billy Hill's brother. Bill had already been nicked with Teddy Hughes and Jock Wyatt over the post office. So when later Russo came to Dartmoor, Hilly done him there. He'd got three years and was in at the time Archie got cut. It could take several years to repay a striping, but repaid it usually was.

Albert was a relation of Russo, and he got up the fake attack so Jack Spot could be done. People say, how could Billy Hill do something like faking a case so that Spot could get convicted? Wasn't it all against the rules? Well, Battles Rossi and Bobby Warren were innocent of the attack on Spot, and so the rule book got torn up. I was there and said, 'It's on you, Jack,' so he had time to do whatever he wished. He could have fought back if he'd not been a coward; no one was masked up. Of the five of us, two were innocent.

That's why the rule book was slung out the window when they got it up for Spot. It was something I wouldn't have wanted to have done, but I could see they were trying to get Bobby and Battles out and if that could help – well, who would worry about him? There was always the possibility that someone straight who identified a person on a bank raid could have genuinely thought the man was on the robbery, but in Spot and his wife's case they were definitely innocent.

[1] Originally specifically pickpocketing a woman's skirt, 'at the creep' came to mean small-time thieving of offices or flats, particularly when they were occupied. Even later it meant stealing from unoccupied buildings, and this is the sense used by Fraser.
[2] See *Mad Frank*, p. 119.

It's common enough to stick someone's name up to help you get out of trouble; but you have to ask permission first, or they've got to be dead so it doesn't matter to them. Even then you should talk to the family, see if they mind. If you did it without asking, you could expect a smack.

When Harvey Holford did his old woman in at the Blue Gardenia night-club down in Hove, one of his problems was that he'd got an illegal firearm and it wasn't for the first time either. I was very friendly with him and I went to see him in Brixton. Now he'd got to have some fanny about what he was doing with the gun in the first place, let alone shoot her. It was during the time there were these gaming tables where you could play Legalite, which was meant to get round the gaming laws about roulette. What he wanted to say was that he was mixed up with Billy Hill and Albert Dimes, and he was in a bit of trouble with them, so it was for his protection. At that time Billy was a household name. He even crops up in that film with Peter Sellers and Terry-Thomas, *Carleton Browne of the FO*, when some prince or other isn't wearing a dinner jacket when he goes to a night-club. They want to throw him out, but someone says the man's a prince and the head waiter says, 'I don't care if he's Billy Hill. All right, let him in, but don't take a cheque.' That shows you how you had to dress in them days if you went out at night.

Anyway, I went to Bill and he said of course if it would help him. Albert went off alarming about it; he'd become respectable and had a betting-shop licence. Of course it came out in court, but it did Harvey some good because he got a manslaughter and four years. I think at the end of the trial Albert got a brief to stand up and say it was rubbish and he'd never threatened him. Albert also was very friendly with the TV man Bernard Braden, and he had it mentioned on his television programme. Hilly didn't mind at all. It was water off his back by then.

Joe Wilkins, who was the nephew of Bert, did it to me when I was in prison. I'd been very friendly with him over the years and we'd done a lot of work together, but he never asked permission. He got into trouble in 1987 when he was caught sunbathing on a boat *The Danny Boy* which had a million and a half of puff tucked away. He tried to row himself out, saying I was one of the biggest dealers on the Costa del Sol and he was afraid of me, but since I was in the nick I couldn't see how that could be. If he'd sent a message asking permission, I'd have said by all means, but I was surprised to read about it in the papers. I saw towards the end of last year that he was still on the run. His name came up the other day when a copper said he had been approached by Wilkins about getting drugs down from Scotland.

Another time I had my name stuck up was when some geezer escaped on a horse from Dartmoor. Of course, when he was picked up the papers said things like Dick Turpin. He put out the story that he'd escaped because he was afraid of me and didn't want to go back to the Moor. I never knew who he was, never seen him to my knowledge and he got transferred, so I suppose good luck to him.

Sometimes it works but more often it doesn't. When the police shot poor Kenny Baker dead in a snatch on a Securicor van in Reigate in 1990, Mehmet Arif and his brother Dennis were along with him. Dennis ran it that he'd lost over £100,000 gambling and he was into Kenny Baker for £60,000, and as a result he'd been made to go along on the blag because he'd be shot if he didn't. The trouble was the pros could show he'd been at a big wedding at the Savoy along with Kenny only a few weeks earlier. Kenny's family didn't mind, though they were quick and right to point out he'd never have forced anyone to go out with him. Kenny shouldn't really have been working like that; he was well in his fifties by then.

If you go away, you hope your mates are going to look after your wife or your girl-friend. Once upon a time before the War you could reckon they would, but now that's more or less history. Then those who didn't go down helped out the one who did, but anyone with a realistic sense of intelligence would only expect that to happen if them that got away did fairly well while the man was doing his porridge. Then they would be expected to play the game – very much so if they were doing well. If they wasn't doing well, then you wouldn't expect it. You must be realistic.

People have said they've grassed because when they've been away the rest of the team hasn't looked after the wife or girl-friend. But that's no excuse to grass. Even if they were doing well and haven't looked after them, then it wouldn't justify turning them in. In no way whatsoever. Even if they had looked after the girl, the grass would have come up with another excuse for grassing. It doesn't put them in a good light if they should have been putting money in, but the fact that they haven't doesn't justify grassing.

You wouldn't go to see a wife or girl-friend on your own; that might embarrass her, or give someone the wrong idea. You should go with your own wife or girl-friend or your sister. Or you could go with another man, but not on your own.

Usually it was regarded as bad manners if the girl started going out with someone, but of course if there was a top man involved there was exceptions. It was the same as being a soldier and going to war. They should remain faithful. Of course it didn't always happen. Members of the man's family would be given the unpleasant task of going round to see the woman and give her a warning. It could be anything: 'Drop it out or else.' Mostly they would be completely cut off rather than anything physical happen. She wouldn't be invited to parties, she'd be completely isolated and would have to move away. They would be allowed girls' nights out at the pub; they'd be allowed to dance; they could socialise to a large extent, and you must remember amongst the top thieves most of the women were very intelligent and could enjoy themselves without getting too much involved. They treasured the respect they and their children had, and this kept them on the straight and narrow. It means that they would be treated with the utmost respect and liking wherever they went.

The realistic, sensible guys would blot them out and that

would be the end of them. Send a message that it was
finished. Them that wasn't sensible would hang on in, causing
theirselves a lot of grief. But some couldn't cope. One of the
best men I was in the nick with was Nicky Kiley. He had
film-star good looks, very handsome, very smart. Him and
his brother, they hung around Soho. Neddie, the brother, was
a nice man.

Nicky got ten years for a security van in 1953, and the
American girl he was living with at the time came on the
visit and told him she was leaving and going to America
with a guy. She must have sent him a 'Dear John' already
and he knew what was coming. He smashed the window in
the visiting room – and it wasn't fragile glass either. Then he
did her with a bottle he'd somehow smuggled down. To do
that, he had to lean through to reach her. You can imagine the
scenes in the visiting rooms – screams, blood, smashed glass.
He'd been very good to her and he was very bitter. It would
have been something like, 'This'll be our last visit.' He knew,
and that's why he went tooled up. Lawton, the governor with
whom I had all the trouble and whose son was the judge at the
Torture trial, never nicked him outside and he was weighed
off by the visiting magistrates. He lost about twelve months'
remission and got bread and water. Today it would have been
headlines; then there was nothing in the papers. Last I heard,
Nicky had got Alzheimer's and was in a hospital. I don't
know what happened to Neddie; I don't think he ever did
any time.

That sort of thing happened many times, but Nick's was
highlighted. Girls have been attacked on visits over the years;
it wasn't uncommon. It was something no one could legislate
for, because at the time it wouldn't enter the man's head, but
when she give him the news it could spark it, particularly since
there's no glass between the pair of them.

Now the world has got more used to women going off, but
years ago it was a dreadful thing. Women were treated more
like chattels in all walks of society, but now it's more of a free

market to use a common term. Women are stronger in speaking up for themselves, more independent.

On the whole the men were fairly good; they had a loyalty to the women they were with, and they stuck to it pretty well. That part is still very much the same. Most men, before they reach that stage they've sowed their wild oats and enjoyed themselves and are content to be with that same one. They've more or less got it out of their system.

Before the War, the places to go were clubs and they were very hard to get into. There was the Embassy in Bond Street where Ambrose's orchestra played, and in the top hotels. I did go to a couple as a young boy but mostly people kept to pubs, afternoon drinking clubs, spielers and parties. There'd be certain houses where you could always have a party or pubs where you could drink upstairs. If you had it in the bar, it was like a morgue. Then there were the spielers.

During and just after the War, all day, every day, you'd be drinking somewhere if you wasn't working. You'd meet in a pub at 12 and drink till 3 p.m. Then you'd get a taxi and go up West to drinkers like Aggies or the Cabinet. You'd stay there till 6 o'clock and then go to the pubs till half-past ten. Then you'd have a couple of drinks in the Eleven o' Clock House which the Sabinis had in Clerkenwell. *Then* you would get a couple of crates of booze and go to a party. I know it sounds daft but you'd do it day in, day out. On the other hand, you could do it for £30 a day. There were toms in the clubs, but you didn't need them; they were for the punters. Really it was the hoisters who were the good fun girls.

Then later came the clubs like the Astor and Churchills. The Bag O'Nails had always been there of course, just by West End Central police station. The Nash brothers had an interest in the Bagatelle, which was just off Regent Street. Then there was Tolaini's Latin Quarter – they were a family who originally had a café in Stoke Newington – and Al Burnett's Stork Room. You could get straight through there into the Society in Jermyn Street. Then later on there was Danny La Rue's. He only opened the club when Bruce Bracey wouldn't give him and the others a rise when they were working at Winstons. And of course there were drinkers all over Soho like the Nut-House, where Spot did Harry White once and for all when he and Hilly were taking over Soho. Before the War Tommy Ling, who was at school with me – his father had a drinker in Cecil Court off the Charing Cross Road. We'd go there even though I was only thirteen. I loved it. Tommy had great kudos from it. In them days, having a club up West was a big thing.

I was never a gambler. Really I was bored to tears with it. That's where Albert and Hilly really liked me, that I didn't do my money. Joe Lowry was a fantastic gambler. Albert himself was too. But, no matter how straight the game was, there was always the whisper that it wasn't. The trouble with thieves is that many of them are great gamblers, and they think they're better card players than they are. The people who played were nearly all crooked themselves, so no way was it easy to cook up a crooked game for them. Those games were for the mug businessmen who went to the clubs. As I said earlier, Billy Hill was ace with the cards; they were specially made and marked, and you had special glasses and you couldn't lose. It was magnificent. These were for the businessmen and this carried on even when gambling and the clubs was legal. You had rich punters coming to them from all over the world in the early 1960s, and the games were rigged specially for them just as they'd always been.

There's always been a fascination as between show business and gangsters. People in show business do things the way they want to do them, different from the normal man and woman in the street. Gangsters like show-business people, and the other way around. Of course, a lot of them come from the same walks of life as we do and so they've known us all their lives. Second, in show business, as Stan Baker used to tell us, the villain or the bad boy in the film nearly always steals the film. Look at Humphrey Bogart, Edward G. and Jimmy Cagney – and so it's gone on right to the modern day: Gary Oldman, Marlon

Brando, Robert De Niro, Al Pacino. The public likes villains, they've nearly always got the meatier part.

Show-business people hang around observing gangsters, so if they get a role they have an idea how they talk, how they act, their way of life. I believe that all dedicated actors and actresses are always studying life and the people in that life when they're off-duty. Waitress, bank manager, cab driver, politician – something they must automatically observe. Same as if a good thief was going to pose as a policeman, he would remember how policemen talk and their habits when he plays that role.

When Alf Fraser was doing five years and I was working with Eddie and Charlie Richardson, I got a message from Jimmy Robson, who was himself doing twenty-one years in Parkhurst. Actually he got twenty-four years – fourteen preventive detention and ten years imprisonment consecutive for gelignite and a tie-up in Bristol. He'd appealed and got it reduced to twenty-one years imprisonment. I went to visit him and he told me he was a Red Band in the gym. 'Frank, the first time in history an outside football team can come in and play the prisoners. Get a team together, it'll be a great opportunity.'

We made ourselves busy. Lonsdales, the sports equipment company, had just opened in Beak Street and they were very good. They sent a letter addressed to the sports officer saying they'd sponsor a team, and he sent a letter back saying that would be all right and we could bring 16 or 17. I think he was a bit worried about bad publicity, but he came through. We had to get there at a certain time. I came over from Brighton and the others came down by car. We met at the ferry and then got taxis the other side. We weren't obliged to sign in. It was before Blake escaped, and Category A didn't exist.

Away we went. A number of the team had done a bit of bird, and so when we got to the gates we let all the straight ones go in first and us others came in a minute or so after them. We went in the prison bathroom – changed into our kit, us who were playing. When we got on the pitch there was deathly quiet, people recognised us. We all did our best to make out we didn't know each other, but my old pal Jimmy Essex, who'd been acquitted of murder twice and was doing eight, he was playing, so was Jimmy Robson. We was shaking hands all round the touch-line and the prison officers were scratching their heads. We were giving tobacco and cigarettes to the crowd. The ball was continually kicked out of play to give us a chance to talk. After the game we all went in the bathroom to change. It was wonderful, absolutely magnificent.

We'd been put down as Lonsdale's team, but in fact it was really the one that Burt McCarthy, the boxing promoter, had put together as the Soho Rangers to play for charity. The accolade of all happened. As we're going out of the gate, the Chief Officer and Governor said would we go into the officers' mess. They'd laid a meal on for us and the Governor gave a talk thanking us. One of us thanked him. 'Will you come back?' How we kept a straight face I don't know. The Chief Officer looked at me as we were going in the mess. He knew he knew me, but he couldn't place me. The penny dropped but it was too late. I made a fuss of him, and that was good when the speeches come out. I'd chinned him when he was a prison officer; I think it was at Wandsworth.

By the following Sunday it had leaked and in the *News of the World* there was the headline: SOHO RANGERS HAVE THEIR AWAY MATCH AT PARKHURST. Tommy Gibbons, who was the publican of the Thomas A'Becket down the Old Kent Road, and a former top heavyweight himself, was very good. He wrote saying what harm has it done? He was smashing. It helped to keep everyone happy. First and only time it ever happened. Lovely history. Four years later some of the officers were still there when I was back. In a way it may have led to the riot – I'd made fools of them and they weren't at all pleased.

Stan Baker was upset because he wasn't invited to the match. I don't think his film contract allowed him to play, but he was the sort of manager. The only reason we didn't was because it could have been seriously bad publicity for him. Terry Spinks, the boxer, was one of the team; he just thought he'd be doing a bit of good for people. The Rangers ran about two years. We used to get good crowds and Alfie Hinds – the prison escaper who'd been done for the Maples burglary and won damages for libel from the copper who nicked him – played for us once. The papers called it his first away game. It was for a children's hospital down at Foots Cray. The Arsenal man Frank McLintock came along, but he didn't play in case he got injured. Then me and Eddie and Leslie was all nicked over Mr Smith's and it all faded. Bill Stayton disappeared. Tommy Wisbey's brother, Georgie, who was a straight man, and Albert Dimes played. Tommy McCarthy, who had the Log Cabin Club in Wardour Street, was also in the team. I think he was related to Burt and Les but I'm not sure how. His partner in the club was George Walker, the boxer Billy's twin brother, who'd been Billy Hill's man years earlier and went on to be a big city figure. I see he got acquitted on a big fraud the other day. Good luck to him.

I knew Stanley Baker through Albert Dimes long before I knew Charlie and Eddie Richardson. After *Zulu*, Baker gave my youngest son a shield and spear; he still has it. Stan's father-in-law was a fruiterer in Spitalfields and Billy Blythe minded it for him. When Albert was nicked over the fight with Spot in Frith Street, Billy asked if Stan would make a contribution to Albert's defence, and it was through that link that he met Stan when he went round to thank him afterwards.

But I knew Stan's father-in-law even before I knew Stan. In turn Stan met Charlie and Eddie through Albert Dimes. Albert was a gambler not a drinker, and Stan liked a drink, so I would go out with Stan. Then when I was with Eddie and Bill Hill and Albert, Stan would come with us to the Rib Room at the Carlton Tower in Chelsea.

Stan wasn't a crook; he just liked being with crooks. But he was clever enough not to give anyone the chance to have one over him. One night I asked if he would like to go to the Astor and he'd said to me, 'Let's go to Churchills. I understand one of the girls fancies me.' Churchills was considered a high-class rip-off. It was strictly for out-of-town businessmen, punters like that, but I said all right. One of the girls there did fancy him. We collected her and went over to the Astor where we had our photo took, but he was clever – at the moment the flash went off he moved away so it looked as though she was with someone else and not him. He wasn't putting himself in anyone's hands.

The media weren't on to people like they are today. Unless it was flushed on their plate, they didn't go snooping around for it. That's why someone like Stan got credited for organising us into that soccer team, the Soho Rangers. Everyone said what a good fellow he was for doing it, even though it was really Burt McCarthy.

Stan pitched in when Johnny Sullivan got nicked for the Biggs escape. Johnny was brilliant. He and another man sort of blocked the screws when Biggs went for the wall. That was a funny old escape. It came off in July 1965 and was highly planned of course but Andy Anderson (who was later with me in the Parkhurst riot and got chucked) and another man climbed the wall along with Biggs and the other three they were meant to be rescuing. At the top the men couldn't just push Andy and his mate back into the yard, but they didn't know what to do; they certainly didn't want them along with them, and so they gave them a couple of quid and some boiler suits and sent them on their way. Andy knew about Eddie and me at Atlantic Machines, and he made his way over to us. Stan was there at the time and he put in for Andy, so it was natural he'd give a few quid for Johnny.

Johnny got nicked of course but the judge, Carl Aarvold, who was dead keen on tennis, gave him a sort of gee saying it was wrong but nevertheless was something like the public school spirit. We had a whip which got Johnny and the other man £430. The money was sent in by Eva. Like I said, Aarvold had give him a gee when he sentenced him and that's what

Eva put in the letter to Johnny congratulating him on what he done. The letter was opened by the screws and given to the Governor of Wandsworth, who got in touch with Scotland Yard. Nearly £500 was quite a lot of money; you could buy a part vacant freehold house in Tottenham or Brixton for that. Tommy Butler, who ended up in charge of the Train investigation, come and took the money and then raided Eva, saying it was Train money and what had she to say about that? Eva said it wasn't. Her husband was a bookmaker, she told him, and they'd had a legitimate whip-round and she sent it legitimately by registered letter. Butler was beat and he knew it. He had to give her the money back.

This was November 1965, so we paid the money over to a solicitor to hold for them. Four months later Butler nicked me for the murder at Mr Smith's. I was the only one. I got chucked, of course, but he had his knife into me. He was always convinced I was in the Train robbery.

I knew Richard Burton and Elizabeth Taylor through Stanley Baker, and for a time back in the 1970s there was talk Burton would play me in a film. It was in the newspapers, but nothing came of it.

Tommy McCarthy's Log Cabin downstairs in Wardour Street was a brilliant club, and he was a brilliant host as well. He never had afters and he closed about 11. No band, lovely little club. There was great music of the day on records, but there was no gambling. Where he was good was, he always paid a round himself if he knew you. He wouldn't ask, he'd just send it over with one of the girls. On a Friday we would start off there and then go round to Charlie Chester's, where Eddie Richardson and me were on a pension, and then on to the Stork or the Astor or the Society. Al Burnett ran the Stork. He had the Astor off Berkeley Square in 1945 and like an idiot he let it go; it was something he always regretted. Bertie Green owned it after that; he had it for years.

I can't fault Al. He introduced us to everyone; cut the bill when there was a party for me after I came out from the Spot slashing. He had the write-ups about him in America when he did some sort of soft-shoe act, and he had them all framed about the place. He could sing, dance. He was great, he'd always sing 'Any time you're Lambeth way' when I come in. He was a character. When we all got nicked about the machines – when the police said Eddie and me had leaned on the club owners to get the machines in their places – he never said a wrong word about us. There again, not one club owner come and give evidence against us.

You could go straight through the kitchen of the Pigalle into the Society. It must have seemed like the cellars in New York and Detroit during Prohibition for them. Straight people went to these places for nights out. Some knew who you were, and they loved it and tried to get in your company so they had something to talk about. All the stars loved being seen with the Twins and so on. It's nothing new. Think how the people used to go up to Harlem in the 1930s after a night out for an extra spot of slumming. I think they like just that little bit of thought that it's going to be dangerous, or they'll see something their neighbours haven't seen and so they can talk about it.

Six

In a way it paid to get the cat, or the birch for that matter. With the birch, like the cat, a stroke was reputed to take two months off your sentence. Fifteen strokes equalled thirty months. This was an unofficial tariff. That's why Billy Hill and Jock Wyatt asked for the cat when they done a post office van in July or August 1942. The trouble was Teddy Hughes was with them and, when they were taken down for the doctor to examine them, he wasn't fit enough so none of them got it. They got four and he got three, then he got that twelve for the airport. Teddy was very ill in hospital by the time he got the eighteen months in Wandsworth, and he died in the early 1960s.

Up until March 1948, when you had the cat for an offence in prison you lost remission, got bread and water, everything. Then Chuter Ede, the Home Secretary, was urged to do away with the cat by the do-gooders. Certainly not the prison officers. The Prison Officers' Association was powerful and they weren't having it, so the Home Secretary did the next best thing. He said if you had the cat or the birch in these circumstances, you got no other punishment. So everyone was lining up to get it! Of course the screws didn't like that one bit, and as the years went by they made sure you were charged with two offences: gross personal violence on the first and assaulting a second officer who was pulling you off, so you got the cat for the first and then loss of remission for the other. But for two or more years, it was wonderful.

The authorities thought the cat was worse, and I never knew them to stop no matter how bad a man's back was. If you screamed out they'd love it. But the screws knew the birch was worse. Your shoulders are a bit manly but your bottom is tender, and there was the humiliation of your bare bum being seen by everyone. I got the birch when I did the screw 'Holy Joe' in Rochester for looking at me in the bath. It wasn't a matter of getting the birch first and, if that didn't stop you, getting the cat on another occasion. You could get either. For example, Timmy Noonan who was with me in the Parkhurst riot had the birch twice and Frank Mitchell – who escaped from Dartmoor and the Twins got acquitted of killing – he had the cat for doing a screw in Pentonville in about 1958 and then later when he was at Hull, he done another screw down the punishment block and got the birch.

When I first had it, it was a tremendous leg-up status-wise in a way, to get the birch or the cat. The War had just started and most men were abroad, in an Army prison or on the run. If anyone got the birch or the cat along with the bread and water that went with it, you gained a reputation. You looked as though you were something special to the others. If you did a screw, you had more chance of winning the pools than not being brutally beaten up afterwards. There were no visits, no media interest. The beating-up rather than the birch or the cat, and the sheer injustice – that was what stopped many people when they badly wanted to do a screw. It was a real beating.

When I first went into prison, literally every second of every day a prisoner lived in fear of the authorities. You couldn't talk in the workshops, and your cell bed had to be up against the wall until 8 in the evening. If it was down or your blanket was on the floor, you were put on report. Then you didn't know for sure you were on report until the next morning when the screws would burst into your cell and take you down the punishment block. Today you get a form 1127 which tells you what it's all about.

A bed was a heavy bed-board with short legs, maybe two

inches, so you slept just that bit off the floor. That and your mattress had to be up against the wall and all blankets had to be folded neatly. In some nicks I mean *really* neatly or it was on report, and that meant a certain bread and water punishment and loss of remission. The Governor did have the right to give you a caution, but you have more chance of winning the lottery now than you had of getting one of those.

It depended on the prison whether you had a chair or a stool in your cell. Tables were a lump of wood stuck in the wall, and there was a wash-stand. There was no running water in the cell and no hot water except in the bath house. You got a bath once a week if you were lucky; it was up to the screws. At least, except in the wartime, you got your own water.

You were at risk twenty-four hours a days from the screws. After you finished on the machines or the mailbags, or in some nicks making brushes, you did a cell task – and that was sewing more mailbags or possibly making more brushes. You had to do so many a day, and if you didn't complete your cell task then it was report again. Mailbags was eight to the inch. You had to do it after breakfast, lunch and tea, but some prisoners tried to not do it after tea. In them days cells had gas light and it was murder on the eyes, not to say soul-destroying. Even if a man sewed his mailbags, a wicked officer might put him on report for not doing eight to the inch. That would be par for the course, and was how I got put on report at Feltham. The screw said I wasn't doing it properly, but I was. Whatever I did, I did properly. If I wasn't going to do it right, I wouldn't do it at all. It was funny how screws changed. You could see the new ones come in and they'd be all bright and in their own way quite kind, but within a few months the system and the other screws would get to them and they'd be just as bad as all the others.

I only ever worked in a brush shop two days. It was when I came out of Feltham and was sent to Wandsworth, the same time that that chaplain caught me with bread and cheese. After I'd done my punishment, it was out of the cell and into the shop to work.

It was Canadian Johnny nicked my brush in Wandsworth, the second day I was in the shop after I'd finished my punishment, and I did him for it. He was a deserter from the Canadian Army, and was doing three years' penal servitude for a hold-up.

In the shop you had to do at least one brush a day, and if you didn't you'd be on report for not doing your task. You had a sort of glove to protect your hand, and you had to pull the bristles through. My position was directly under the prison officer sitting in a raised chair. He'd only got to look down and there was me. You couldn't talk because you were well away from the next person but, come what may, every day someone would be on report for talking.

When you'd done your brush at your table the bristles were always uneven, so they would be collected by Canadian Johnny. He would take them across to a machine where they'd be trimmed and then bring the brush back. At the end of the day Van Been – I think the screw was called – would come round with another prisoner to inspect the brushes and to mark down that you'd done one or two.

When Johnny never returned my brush, I put my hand up to the screw for permission to speak, and since it was about work Van Been said I could. I went over to Johnny and asked, 'Where's my brush?' He said, 'You don't give me a brush.' I then realised what was going on. If he didn't give it back, Johnny could then sell it to another prisoner for a couple of roll-ups which if you smoked would be like a godsend. You only got 11d a week if you were really very good, really dextrous, at making brushes. The average was more like 5d or 6d. I didn't smoke, but I would buy tobacco – you couldn't buy nothing else – and I would sell it off for food. A cleaner or someone in the kitchen could get a loaf of bread for you. The prisoner Johnny would sell the brush to, wouldn't know it was mine. He'd just think it was a bit of luck that Johnny'd got a brush over so he didn't have to work so hard to keep up his quota.

I asked again, and blatantly he said the same thing. You

must remember that I was 19 and had just come off bread and water, and he must have thought I was a right mug. I was skinny as anything. If he'd been a Londoner, he'd have known about me and that I had a reputation.

Then more than now, if anyone was a rebel in prison they got a reputation. They were someone to be respected, admired, looked up to, call it what you like. It's no exaggeration. You were putting your life on the block, and you'd be lucky to survive. How many men do you think were killed in prison? There were many – even if they held an inquest, and they didn't always do so. Guys were found hanging in their cell when everyone knew, no way, no way. Even though I was young, I had a track record, and the fact that Johnny didn't know that was what made him pay.

By the side of his machine he had a load of handles which went into the yard brushes we were making. I picked one up and I really done him. He'd done something which was outrageous. It was deliberate. If it had been a mistake you could have ironed it out, but it wasn't.

The alarm bells went and prison officers come and I was dragged out. Now I was brought up in front of the Visiting Magistrate, and I got another fifteen days No. 1 and twenty-eight No. 2 and loss of remission of another sixty days. What with the trouble in Feltham, that was all my five months' remission gone.[1]

I had told the magistrates what had happened, and later Canadian Johnny wrote a petition saying that he'd provoked me and that he'd struck me first. That wasn't true, but he'd learned who I was and now he went 100 per cent in my favour. Canadian Johnny came completely round the other way. He couldn't do enough.

When you got over twenty-one days No. 2, the next seven days you did on ordinary diet. So in fact you only did twenty-one out of the 28 days. If you had forty-two, you

---

[1]No. 1 and No.2 were forms of severely restricted diet to which men on punishment were subject.

got a break of seven days after the twenty-one and then went back and did the rest. When I'd done twenty-five or six, the Visiting Magistrates called me up and said in the light of his petition my punishment would be terminated. I didn't get any remission back, I noticed. Then two days later there was the incident when another Canadian guy was getting topped and I was in trouble again for breaking up my cell and – they said – having my light on so the enemy bombers could see in the blackout. I never understood that. The light switch was on the outside: all they had to do was switch it off!

I never saw Johnny again in the prison system that time, but I heard he'd got more bird and was at Parkhurst with some pals of mine and had a bit more penal servitude.

Then in early January 1949 a man got shot dead in a bank raid in Bristol. What the police did was, they patiently went through everyone who'd had a conviction for a firearm offence and had them arrested and put on an ID parade. Canadian Johnny had a conviction for guns, so it was his turn now to be arrested and put on the ID for the Bristol bank killing. So sometime in 1949 the police raided his flat and found he was putting up a guy who'd escaped from Dorchester prison. They also found a gun in the flat. The pair of them had failed in a robbery on some railway embankment; there'd been a stoppo and they'd got away. The Flying Squad said the raid was nothing to do with the escape and when they found a gun it was a bonus. So they put them on IDs for the robbery as well.[2]

I was in Brixton on remand over a torch I was meant to have stolen. I hadn't for once, but I still got put away although the first time the jury disagreed. Patsy Lyons got twelve months

[2]About 3 p.m. on 7 January 1949, a gunman shot cashier George Black in Lloyds Bank, Knowle, Bristol. A greyhound trainer tried to stop him but the man said he was collecting a debt, hit him and ran off. There were a number of suggestions that the man was an Army deserter, an Irishman, a Londoner, that he had been with a woman in a stolen car two hours before the raid, that he had gone back to London from Temple Meads station, but inquiries petered out. No one was ever charged. In this context a stoppo is a chase by the police. It can also mean a rest from work, a breather.

for it and all. We'd been put on some IDs for smash-and-grabs we'd done, but we hadn't been picked out.

It seems silly nowadays to think you could be remanded in custody on suspicion of stealing a torch, but I was in the hospital under observation because I'd just come out of Cane Hill. Johnny sent a message to me asking if I would go on the ID parade with him and give him some help. So I said of course I would. That was allowed in prison; you could go round and pick the men to stand on the parade with you.

At that time the police looked on prison officers as scum, below their dignity, and treated them like that. The screws knew this and they hated the law, so on a prison ID you had a chance. The police would do what they could to avoid an ID in Brixton, and the screws would let the cons do more or less what they liked.

Every time a witness came up to the parade I pretended to be holding a tommy gun, spraying people with bullets and saying, 'I'm the man who killed him. Pick me out.' They had lots of witnesses including a priest or chaplain who was in the bank at the time, but no one got picked out. Everyone was fooling about and even one or two of the witnesses were laughing. 'Don't you dare pick anyone out except me,' I was saying. I didn't get punishment. After all, I was in the hospital for observation.[3]

Canadian Johnny did a bit more time for the gun, and in 1953 he was out and then nicked again for shooting at a police officer, which wasn't sensible. He was found dead in a police station cell. I'm convinced he did that murder in the bank.

Bent identification parades outside prison were common. Any I didn't get picked out on was on my own merits, but Hilly had done some wonderful things on them. For him, the copper in charge would put someone else entirely – not the

---

[3]Identification parades continued in prison until the late 1960s and, as Fraser indicates, they were often a farce, with the men, chosen with care from the ranks of the inmates, cat-calling and hooting in an endeavour to intimidate or distract witnesses. After continued representations by the police, the practice of holding parades in prison was abandoned.

suspect – on the parade, so it wasn't surprising he didn't get picked out.

But it happened more often that the police fixed the parade in their own favour. It was a lucky touch if it was the other way around. It was common if you didn't have a really strong brief there, and even then he couldn't always protect you. When you went on a parade you knew your chances were not good. That's why everyone asked to have theirs in Brixton prison.

Apart from coppers, Bill also had a couple of doctors on the books. If I'd got away after the shooting at Mr Smith's there'd have been no problem in having me patched up. There was always a couple of sporting medical students who'd have been prepared to try their hands.

On the other hand, we didn't have much faith in lawyers. Even Billy didn't feel comfortable with them. Marrinan was the only one I was really comfortable with, thinking that he would fight like a tiger. There were others alleged to be good, but you didn't trust them to make a defence for you. That's where G. L. Hardy and Joe Yahuda had good reputations. You knew they would fight, but you couldn't expect them to do anything crooked for you.[4]

The finest bit of news I heard in 1946 was when the Governor of Liverpool said that for the time being cell tasks were being stopped because they couldn't get the material. In fact it never came back. That was the best bit of news for many a year.

Going back though to that time in Wandsworth after the brush incident, I went back down the punishment block and then on to H1 where I got into more trouble over the topping of the Canadian, Gauthier. Then I got sent to the Scrubs, where they was going to give me electrical shock treatment.

---

[4]Looking through newspaper cuttings and law reports, G.L. Hardy appears to have had the great professional criminal practice of the 1930s and 1940s. For example he appeared for most of the defendants in the Lewes racecourse affray, and not under the Poor Persons' Defence Act which was the rough equivalent of legal aid. Yahuda's brother was acquitted of fraud in the 1980s. The evidence against him had been that of a supergrass, but anecdotal evidence from former members of his staff indicates that he was sometimes less than careful.

Churchill had authorised when he was Home Secretary. Other than that it was like a Sunday meal. Sunday was known as 'Floating Fat Day'. You had a tin for your meals and a second tin slotted in on top which had a potato, almost always in its jacket. Underneath there was a thin soup with a bit of meat, but it was always fat. At Christmas you'd sometimes find a bit of lean meat.

By 1957 we were getting regular films for long-term prisoners. In Dartmoor in the 1950s there was a film club with a film every Sunday. It was there a guy got stabbed to death in 1960 or 1961. He was doing 12 years for a sex offence.[5] I was in the prison at the time but because I was on a special stage – you had to have done at least four years of your sentence to be on it – one perk was you got to watch television on a Sunday and sometimes they showed football matches. They weren't live of course, but it was still football and that was wonderful – much better than the films in the C. of E. chapel where if you was at the back you couldn't see anything.

Even so, the films was pretty tame. No sex or violence, of course; so we never got shown anything like that film with Margaret Lockwood as a highwayman, *The Wicked Lady*. I read somewhere recently how a judge had criticised a Borstal for showing *The Colditz Story* about the Second World War escape, after which a couple of people had done just that. He had the Governor called before him, who explained that it was meant to be showing the boys the value of teamwork. But I never got shown anything so instructive.

You've got to stand by each other in prison, but there were

---

[5]Harold Dennis Thirkettle was stabbed to death during a showing of *The Blue Lamp* in the prison chapel at Dartmoor on 14 June 1961. A man with a number of convictions, he had been serving 12 years imposed in June 1959 at York Assizes for the manslaughter of the woman with whom he had been living. When she had said she was leaving him for another man, he had attacked her with an axe. Matthew Nwachukwa was charged with Thirkettle's manslaughter. Nwachukwa, who was regarded as an informant, had himself been stabbed during the film and – pulling the knife from his back – stabbed the two men nearest him. Neither had been involved in the attack. He was acquitted.

some surprising people who didn't. For example, I'd known Alf Gerard for years. I only did one crime with him – a wages snatch on Southwark Bridge. He was reliable. Prison-wise I wouldn't have been too keen from what I heard, although I never experienced this myself because nothing cropped up when I was in prison with him. In 1972 when there were a series of sit-downs over conditions, Alf Gerard was at Albany prison and he didn't come out. You have to stand up with your fellow prisoners. I think Alf was doing nine years; it was after he and Jerry Callaghan had done the coppers and had been brought back from Australia.

Everyone has to come out for a sit-down. Men of the calibre of Alfie and Charlie Kray, they never took part and it gave other prisoners the excuse not to take part either. It caused dissension and weakened what the prisoners were fighting for – better conditions. It led to a fight between Stan Thompson – who escaped with the Jimmy Moody that was shot – and Alfie, when Stan accused him of being a scab. Charlie Kray was simply ridiculed by his fellow prisoners. Home Secretary Maudling had made an order that mere sitting-out would not be put on report. All we were doing was sitting out in the sunshine; those sitting would shout 'Scab'. The Prison Officers' Association had a meeting because the officers were furious, but then the Poulson affair broke out and Maudling resigned. The next Home Secretary listened to the prison officers and made sitting-out and refusing to go back in the cells an offence.

Timmy Noonan later pulled out Brian Mottram's pacemaker because he knew he'd gone out thieving with Duval, who'd given evidence against us in the Torture trial. Mottram should have realised you can't do things like that. He'd got out of the Torture trial because he had a dicky heart and went into palpitations in the cells before the hearing every morning. It was said he played with himself before he was due up the steps in a morning and this brought on his tremors but, of course, I never seen him do it. The doctors said it would kill him if he ever went on the trial and so he got chucked. But he managed to survive trial a few years later when he was done for fraud with Jack Duval, I notice. He got eight years and his wife kept trying to get the sentence cut because he wouldn't live through it, but in fact he didn't die until years afterwards.

A lot of people fouled their cells both during riots and at other times. They did it to stop the screws attacking them or they'd fling themselves at the screws and smother them in it, but I never did. I was too neat. During the time I acted mad to get to Cane Hill I did it on the floor, but I never smeared my cell. I was too tidy. Talking about excrement, I did get a bit of my own back on the screws. I tipped a bucket of mess over Parr, the Governor, and when I was put on report I told the Visiting Committee that he'd said, 'You've ruined me, Fraser, for the rest of my career I'll be known as "Shitpot Parr".' Of course he never said that. His claim to fame was that he put down the Hull riot in October 1976.

After that when I was done for assault on the screw 'Pissy' Bamford, I said at the Visiting Committee in my defence that the reason I'd tipped a pot of piss over him was because he'd told me he had a fetish and that he liked urine being poured over him. He was a man I'd done seriously because he'd given Doreen one when she tried to stop me getting a beating. I said how he'd apologised, saying he deserved getting a broken jaw, and now could I do him a favour as he had this kink. I said of course. 'I like urine being poured over me. Could you pour some?' I said, 'Get someone else.' Then he looked round to make sure no one could hear and said, 'Normally my wife does it but as I've had a row with her, she won't and so would you?' I said, 'I should think so! You'd only put me on report for assault.' He said he'd give his word he wouldn't; then he looked round again and said, 'Between me and you, Fraser, I'm known in the prison service as "Pissy" Bamford.' I said to the magistrates that I felt so sorry for him that I went and done it. Then he went against his word and he put me on report. The girl taking it down and one of the magistrates were putting their hands over their mouths trying not to laugh. The only one who wasn't laughing was Bamford. Of course it was all lies, and he never asked any such thing. By now I was really enjoying myself. There was nothing for me to lose. I was down the punishment block already; they'd piled on everything they could, and I'd lost all my remission so I just got another dose of punishment. It may seem spiteful, but it was one way I could have just a bit of a victory.

Seven

In his book, *Autobiography of a Thief*, the Train robber Bruce Reynolds said that when he first went into the nick in 1951 the big men there were me, Kiley, Stanton and Steel. I can't remember Steel at the present, but I think the Stanton must have been Siddy who did a bank over at Richmond in the 1950s, broke in with the keys, took a load of gear and then went back in again. He was with a Welshman who cut his hand on the glass and left part of his finger; they got his prints from it. I was with Siddy in Dartmoor; he come from Fulham way. He can't mean Alan Stanton, I'm sure, but he was the one who got a screw shot and I was involved.

The Alan Stanton I knew got nicked with Lennie Osborne over a bank in Birmingham; then they were brought down to London for a GBH on the police and I think they got slung on that. This was well before Osborne became a grass. Whilst in Wandsworth at the end of 1973 they were allowed appeal visits on the ten years they were doing; as both were Category A men, they would be in boxes with glass between them and the visitor, and a prison officer sitting one on either side of the glass supervising the visit. You could only talk about the case or the appeal. A prison officer put them on report for not talking just about their case. It was just before Christmas and they got bread and water, and when Alan come up from the punishment cells he said, 'We're going to have the screw shot outside. Is it a good idea?'

I said, 'Terrific, splendid.' By the time they could arrange it all two months later in February 1974, I was down the punishment block again. A prison officer was shot at Wandsworth just outside the gate, early in the morning. Just one at random. I was one of them blamed, I'm happy to say, but since I was down the block I couldn't have done it. The man down the block with me – Jake Prescott, one of the Angry Brigade[1] – got blamed as well, so I got moved along with Jake to Gartree.

Although we got the blame no one got nicked for it at all until years later through Lennie Osborne, who had been a good man in his time. That was his step-father's name: he was Johnny Osborne. Back in the late 1950s, probably 1959, someone give Len the tool to do a grass and a makeshift key – anyone a bit good could make them – so he could get in the man's cell. He got three and a half years on top for that. Unfortunately, it was the wrong cell and he slashed the wrong man. Funnily enough there was another Lennie Osborne lived in Wandsworth at the time, and when it was announced he was getting married he started to get hate mail because of the slashing. He had to make a statement that he wasn't *that* Lennie Osborne, that in fact he only had one leg after being run over by a bus at the age of eleven, and he'd nothing to do with crime at all.

When the two-legged Lennie finished that five and a half years he come round to Windmill Street to give me a message from Alfie Fraser, and I gave him a few quid. He was only out a month I think, and he got nicked for the robbery at the Bricklayer's Arms at the beginning of the Old Kent Road when the money arrived for the Christmas Club payout. He was the only one who got nicked, but he kept his mouth shut. You couldn't praise him highly enough then – that would be Christmas 1964.

[1]The Angry Brigade was a group of anarchists who in 1971 carried out a series of bombings particularly in the London area, including one on the Barnet home of Mr Robert Carr, then the Minister for Employment. On conviction, members received heavy sentences. The attacks led to the founding of the Anti-Terrorist Branch (C13).

He finished that ten years and then came out and got that other ten years at Birmingham. He was still good then. When he come out from that was when he shot a security guard. He must have thought they were going to throw away the keys, but that's no excuse. I know he'd done a five and a ten and than another ten off the spin, but I've known others who'd done equally as much if not more and they never grassed.

I don't think Lennie would have done it if his step-father had still been alive. He was a terrific man – him and his brother Teddy both. They came from the Elephant, into a bit of everything but 100 per cent stand-up guys. I was with Johnny Osborne when Billy Hill had a crooked screw at Wandsworth. I was doing two years after a smash-and-grab went wrong when the getaway car wouldn't start. At the time I was working in the laundry and I was on C4. I should have been C3 but there wasn't any room and I went back into me cell. Then doors were left open – nothing in the cell to nick. I thought my pillow was disturbed and I went to straighten it. Behind there were two ounces of tobacco. I thought it was a wicked screw getting it up for us. Johnny Osborne was the cleaner and I rushed along and told him what I'd found. He said he'd hide it and keep his eye on it. Then a screw comes on the landing and I'm locked up, but my cell weren't searched so I knew it couldn't be a fit-up. Since I never smoked, later I told Johnny to share it out and take some for himself.

In those days you had to wait eight weeks before you got your first visit, then every four after that. You only had a letter a fortnight, and I couldn't exactly write out, 'Who's sending me tobacco?' A week later I come in from work – by then I'd been moved from C4 to C3 – and Johnny told me there's another two ounces. 'A screw come up, went to your old cell, looked in and see your card wasn't there and asked what happened to Fraser? I told him you'd been moved, and I watched him and he went into your cell.' This went on every week. Then when I got my visit I told Eva and asked her to check up. I thought it might be her brother-in-law Tom

Thumb Brindle, or even her husband. She made inquiries and Mikey Harris – the one Billy Hill cut twice, but who was in between cuts so to speak and friendly with Billy just then – told her. She came back and told me that Billy'd got a screw straight. I said, 'Tell them I don't want the liberty.' I didn't smoke, and it was a liberty if I kept on accepting it. She said, 'Well, it's already paid for three or four months.' The screw never spoke to me or me to him. Then Billy himself come in when he got three years and I thanked him. I said, don't do it any more.

Billy himself got nicked because a screw called Croucher, who was a right dog, found the two ounces. There was no way he could have had it legally. You had to do three months before you earned, and by the time you got paid it was fifteen weeks at the earliest and then it would be fourpence, sixpence. Elevenpence was the most, and you had to have a plum job for that. If you were in the laundry and could get on to speciality work in Wandsworth – which was ironing prison officers' white summer jackets, or on a modern machine in the mailbag, or working with a civvy electrician or plumber – you could get the eleven pence. If fifty out of 800 were getting 11d that would be a lot. Billy got three days No. 1 diet, loss of remission and bread and water for the tobacco.

The good news was that Chirpy Downes – I think he was Terry the boxer's uncle – he and Lennie Smith, they done Croucher and a principal officer, 'Jazzer' Smith, in the chapel after the service and both got the cat over it in 1948. Gave him a terrific belting after the service. I don't know if Bill paid them.

What people did was, they had joeys sent in. A joey was a threepenny-bit, and a whole lot would either be slung in over the wall to a Red Band who wasn't likely to be searched or given to a bent screw. The screw could bring in either tobacco or threepenny-bits. That would be safer for him. If he was searched and found with too many on him, he could always say he was saving them up for his little boy. To buy tobacco and cigarette papers, you had to go to the canteen and a screw would come in with a suitcase with them in it. He wouldn't know how much you'd earned; but if you hadn't been in prison long enough to have earnings but you had some joeys, you got hold of a guy who'd been in a while and had a decent job, and you got him to buy an ounce for you. You didn't even go to the canteen for the first three months. In fact, you never got unlocked for recreation.

In 1945 I saw the first screw sent to prison from Wandsworth. He'd been crooked for years, even at the Moor, and like an idiot he had allowed it to become too well known that he was doing business right, left and centre. He was one of the screws who took me to Wormwood Scrubs where I was meant to have electric shock treatment. I knew he was crooked, and he knew I knew. I said, 'Ever get round the Elephant?' and then a wry smile come over him because he knew I was having a bit of a dig. He was doing too much with too many, but no one had lollied him.[2] Even the mugs were beginning to know he was doing it. Then while he went on holiday registered letters kept on coming to his house. The post office was very efficient then, and the postman would go to a neighbour's house to get it signed for. Just his luck that particular neighbour handed them in to the authorities. They opened the envelopes and there were these slips, 'This is a quid for X,' and so on. I think he got three or six months and did it at Bedford.

At Christmas a crooked screw would always fetch in a bottle of scotch, and you'd go round to give your pals a drink. I remember in 1943 Billy Howard had one sent in, but I wouldn't have one. I'd never drunk scotch and I didn't want to start. Christmas and Boxing Day you were sweet. It would be very, very rare for a turnover or spin. Other days every so often mobs of screws would search, because a whisper had been round that you were a tobacco baron.

The screws like Croucher would come in your cell in the

[2]Here to lolly is to inform and comes from lolly-pop = cop. In Australian criminal slang, a lolly is a confidence trickster's victim.

first three months and sniff. Then if there had been tobacco that guy'd be turned over. A mate wasn't allowed to give you one; you could smoke when you'd been paid and not before. Croucher was a dog. Later he went to Ford and him and a Principal Officer died in a car crash. When I heard the news it made me think there was someone up there.

Any prisoner who got out without losing a day's remission would think he was dead lucky. It was just so easy to get into trouble. First, a prisoner couldn't smoke for three months; second, he couldn't talk in the shops; third, he couldn't have anyone else's library books. When the screws swooped on a landing for a search, they'd look at your library card and it would show what books you'd got marked out to you. They'd check, and if you had someone else's book then both of you got nicked – automatic bread and water. Strangely, you never got one or two days; you always got the three days and anything up to fourteen days' loss of remission.

Going back to the shooting of the screw outside Wandsworth in 1974 (see p. 110), when Lennie Osborne and Stanton had finished their sentences and now Osborne was nicked for shooting a security guard, in the course of his confession he mentioned the shooting of the screw and named Alan Stanton and how it was done and planned.

The actual shooting had been done by an Italian kid, Tony Baldassare, who later barricaded himself in a flat in Streatham and shot himself in a siege.[3] He collected lighters. He must have had hundreds of them and when his body was found he had one in the shape of a coffin with 'Anthony Philip Baldassare born 21 August 1939 London SW' on one side, and on the other side 'Died—' engraved on it. People said he was as well hung as John Bindon

[3]Baldassare killed himself in Gleneldon Road, Streatham on 25 January 1985. He had been on the run since failing to surrender at the Old Bailey the previous summer when he had been accused of a £200,000 video theft. He was suspected of carrying out over a dozen robberies and he had shot a police dog, Yerba, after a foiled bank raid at Petts Wood, Kent in August 1984. Before he died he set fire to a considerable amount of money so the police would not get it.

was. I don't know myself, but if he was it must have been something.

Tony's sister was living with Osborne, and when Lennie named the people who'd done it he said the kid's sister had helped arrange it. Can you believe the wickedness of saying that? She immediately denied it and so did Alan, but another one of them, like an idiot, put his hands up. The other ones who said 'on your bike' – they never even got nicked. The screws couldn't remember what the people looked like, so it was confessions or nothing.

Alan Stanton died four or five years back. He was let out of Maidstone and sent to an outside hospital with a couple of weeks to go. He'd got cancer and the screws sat by the bed until just a couple of days before he died. Then he was doing fourteen years for a load of charlie.[4] He was a terrific fellow.

What you had to do in prison was stick together, since any sign of dispute between you was exploited by the screws. Even small things like the time when Frank O'Connell – who was done for manslaughter when Joey Martin shot the milkman in a raid in Wood Green in the middle 1960s – was in Leicester with us. Someone had brought some money in to him and it had been found in his cell, so he was on bread and water. We were having a film and Frank wasn't going to be allowed to see it, so Tommy Wisbey and me said we didn't want to see the film as we were going on exercise, which we were entitled to. We said we weren't going to watch a film while a man was locked up, and the others agreed with us. We went on arguing with the screws and eventually they said Frank could come out; but if the Governor came round, then he'd have to go back in his cell. What we were really doing is showing the others what they could have done for us when we were on bread and water but they hadn't done it. Tom had a straightener with one of them over it.

Sometimes, of course, you could be wrong about things, I

---

[4]Cocaine.

admit. In 1953 or 1954 when I was in Wandsworth you were allowed to buy a jar of Brylcreem in the canteen. Lawton was the Governor at the time. I used to treat myself, and one day the jar was missing and I was told the cleaners did it. I got a bar of iron and on the exercise did the pair over the head. They'd already denied it, but like idiots they were flash. Their tone implied, 'So what if we did – what are you going to do about it?' I'm sorry to admit now that they didn't have it; it was a guy from the library who'd taken it. A party used to come round with books on a trolley. You'd get the four books from a guy eight cells away and they'd be swapped. He was completely bald, so I never suspected him, and by then he'd been moved. I wasn't nicked but an innocent man was. He was quite famous. 'Give me the bar when you've done it,' he said. I did, but when he dumped it by mistake he let a screw see it and they assumed he'd done the cleaners. But he was staunch, he never said nothing about me.

When I was on hunger strike, if they gave me bread and water I'd sling it back. That was pride. I didn't want to give them satisfaction. But it was foolish of course, because it just gave them more satisfaction when I chucked it back because they knew I'd have to go on and wouldn't accept it in the evening. Nine or fifteen bread and water meant that if it was nine days you'd do three on and three off so in fact you got proper food (if you can call it that) on days four to six, and then back on bread and water. I'd eat the ordinary diet, so out of the nine I'd do six on hunger strike.

How I survived Leicester after I'd done the Governor there, I don't know. I did about fifteen days. This was a proper strike by me. Daft, call it what you like, but I never cheated. If I cleaned me cell up it was spotless; if I smashed something I did it properly. If I went on hunger strike I did that properly as well. I was force-fed during the War and just after. You're strapped down and they forced your jaws open so a lump of wood with a hole in it went into your mouth and the feeding tube went right through. How I've got teeth left I don't know.

Eddie Richardson, Jimmy Fraser and me at the Chalk Lane Hotel, Epsom in October 1985

Talking to one of my coach tours as we stopped at the Repton Boxing Club

Waxwell Place in Camberwell before the war.
It looks peaceful but the coppers didn't go down even in pairs

Battles Rossi is in the glasses, Tommy Wisbey is on his left shoulder, boxing
manager Ambrose Mendy is kneeling down and the boy who got convicted of
Mrs Gold's murder when Battles got acquitted, is grinning behind my left
shoulder when we went on a visit to prison

Arthur Thompson

Billy Hill

Train robber and good friend Roy James

The only two good conduct certificates I ever earned. The first they gave out like lavatory paper at my school and the second came after I spoke at a lunch

This was the day of Tommy's release from his Train Robbery sentence and he's with Renée, Marilyn and baby Jonathan

Terry Venables (third from right) and my nephew Jimmy (second from right) at Terry's Sportsman club

Marilyn and James Pavanelli (man who swindled her) in Rome

Derek Lewis when we attended a lecture he gave at Wesley's Chapel in the City Road

Barbara Windsor, me and Marilyn at Barbara's 60th birthday party

'An old TV star takes pity on a vagrant and gives him a scarf and a Gannex mac' said Ted Rogers

When we left Barbara's birthday party the photographers wanted me to propose to Marilyn, so I did

The cafe was hard work but good fun but we couldn't make a go of it

In the dressing room before the successful show at the Jermyn Street Theatre

Left to right: my two sons Frank Junior, David Fraser and Jimmy Fraser (nephew)

On holiday in Cancun

Me and Danny the dog after he found my chain

I think the rules and ethics then were more strict. Also, prisons weren't so full up and they had more time to devote to you.

Just now and again you could get a half-way or even decent screw. A First Officer at Strangeways, he was always decent to me. I'd met him when he was a strong-arm screw at Leeds and when they were putting me in a straitjacket they would always put a few punches in to go along with it, but he was decent. He wouldn't bash me about like the others. He always pulled his punches, made it look as though he was going along with the others, but he never did. But he couldn't of course tell them to stop; he'd have just looked silly.

When I was being sent round the prisons, changing every two months, I bumped into him regularly every time I came back to Strangeways. Sometimes he would even let me phone Eva. He'd open me cell up: 'I'm just taking the Cockney fucker to my office to check something out.' Then he'd take me in, shut the door, phone Eva and let me talk to her. In the two months I'd be there, he'd always let me have a couple of phone calls. He never took a penny, nor asked for one. I said he could have a drink but he wouldn't. He kept his eyes on the screws as well so that I didn't get into too much trouble.

At Strangeways he managed to get me up into the wing and into a cell on A2 with great big windows. It seemed to have windows all the way round, and while he was there I always had that same cell when I went back. That was where me and Stan Carnall saw a flying saucer one night. Stan was in the wing opposite and he mentioned it to me. We didn't tell anyone because they'd have thought we were really mad, except it was on the local radio the next day. It was floating dead still and then it went straight up, apparently.

Even when I was at Winchester in 1984 and I'd heard that the next day I was going to Strangeways, the screw helped out. Someone had marked my card unofficially that I was on the move and luckily Eva came to visit me the day previous. Usually they just came in the cell in a morning and said I was off. This time I knew, and Eva said she'd get in touch with him. I told her he'd retired, but I knew he came from Leeds and Eva managed to trace him. She phoned him and he was terrific. He got in touch with the Chief at Strangeways and the next day I had the same cell on A2. He used to talk to me sometimes, and once he said he'd been offered the chance to go on the course as a governor but he thought he'd retire. I said he should take it, but he'd had enough.

Maybe I shouldn't write this, but back in the really bad days there is no doubt those regimes did frighten people into not going to prison. If they went, they did their best not to go back again. Even now when conditions are much easier there's still the freedom lost. You can never replace that.

If prison did one good thing, it was introduce me to books. I started reading P. G. Wodehouse and I went on to Somerset Maugham, Sinclair Lewis, Theodore Dreiser, and Margaret Mitchell's *Gone with the Wind*.

I think we did some good with the Parkhurst riot in 1969. Most of us got convicted, but the jury threw out the ridiculous stuff like incitement to murder and we did show the public what the conditions were like in prison at that time. No one had taken much notice before, but when the judge said the marks on our back showed we'd been beaten then some people did sit up. Genuinely, we never knew if we would come out alive. Also there were a few resignations afterwards. That big Scottish man, their hero in the riot – after we're all knocked unconscious and were coming round and there the prison officers are standing up and pushing us back with the riot sticks, I said 'Let's have a fair fight.' But all the big Scotsman said was, 'You're fucking mad,' and he turned round and walked out. Someone slung a billiard ball and knocked him out and I got charged for it. He resigned a few months later. A big blond one quit and became a cab-driver up in Hull. Another went to Canada. It did make a difference – not much maybe, but a difference.

I did a bit of good in a way later. In a small way I set the trend going so that now solicitors and counsel can defend you in front of the Visiting Magistrates. You could get more time before the Visiting Magistrates with no representation and really no rules than you could in front of a stipendiary who'd have made sure you had a brief. In June 1975 I was in all that trouble in Bristol – I'd lost about 700 days remission – and there was a whip with Billy Hill and the others to put up the money for an application to the High Court so I could be represented when I went on a punishment hearing. I had Stephen Sedley, who's a judge now. He lost first time round and then appealed, but he came up in front of Lord Denning who was the Master of the Rolls and we got knocked back by him, which was par for the course at the time. What I can say is, we went as far as we could. The legal papers made a noise about it and a couple of years later the rules were changed.[5]

What you didn't do inside or outside prison was grass people, but that bit of code seems to have gone out the window. Now it seems you can and no one minds that much either. Look at that Don Barrett; he was a supergrass twice over. He wasn't the first, but he must be the most villainous of them all. Nowadays there are so many grasses, and half of them don't tell the truth. That's the tragedy; it makes it worse still.

If someone has been a grass outside, then there's no way you know what prison they're in; it would be just rumour. They'd be tucked away in an open prison or even given a new identity and told to get lost. That's what happened to the electrician in the Bank of America case – given a new life – and when they finally arrested the man who they thought was the mastermind of the whole thing, Frank Maltby, they didn't dare bring him out of hiding and so they had to let Frank go.

When I was at Norwich prison in about 1979, the third of the big supergrasses was nicked at Norwich airport. The grass was Charlie Lowe and apparently Barrett really steamed into him. I was locked up at the time and Barrett was still finishing his original big sentence. Around the time when he steamed into

[5]*Fraser* v *Mudge and ors* [1975] 3 All ER 78.

Lowe, I was going backwards and forwards to Norwich. About 1983, when I was back there and Barrett had officially turned supergrass, the screws told me that the beating of Charlie Lowe was deliberately planned. It was just to show me and others like me that Barrett had steamed into a grass and so he could be trusted. It had impressed me; I'd thought, 'Well done.'

It seems even then he was grassing in the prison, but there again you can never tell if the screws were just jumping on the band-wagon. I took that into consideration in my own mind. When Barrett was in with me in Hull, he was officially all right. He was doing eighteen years for good robberies and everyone spoke well of him. He had been put away through Bertie Smalls originally. When the committal proceedings was going on and Diane Smalls was giving evidence, she was getting a hard time from the defendants and she just shouted back, 'What about Barrett?'

Barrett officially turned grass in 1981 and he got fourteen years halved to seven, which meant he was out in a bit over three years. Ronnie Darke[6], who'd done eighteen years for a security van, knew Don Barrett well and I think he was on that same robbery. His credentials at that stage were good but, after Barrett turned supergrass the first time, Ronnie Darke still introduced him to a guy called David Croke who was kidnapping supermarket managers and telling them he was strapping gelignite round them to make them open the safe.

Darke made the introduction, never telling Croke who Barrett really was. He should have shot him, let alone given him an introduction. Instead he puts the guy up to Barrett and Barrett puts him away. I was in the nick with him. Ronnie's not been heard of in years. Barrett's out now, and I wouldn't be a bit surprised if he's still putting people away.

What's funny is how you can get really decent men who in the end will go crooked. Ginger Randalls – there was a stink about his name. He was very game in his day, but when I was

[6]He should not be confused with the Johnny Darke killed by John Bindon in a fight.

in Birmingham after doing the Governor of Exeter I remember reading a paper and there was a big article in the *People* that he was a grass, although he denied it. I'd thought Ginger Randalls was dead game until I read that. The reporter Tom Bryant wrote about him, Frankie Hulbert and Hugh MacLean, and later MacLean did a series about how he'd shopped people. And that sort of stuck to Ginger. That would be very early 1960. Frankie Hulbert, who we used to call Frankie Alberts, he slung himself off a roof. He was in Wandsworth with me in 1944. It happened at Ponroy Street, New Cross, where he lived and he was being given a spin. He was a pal of Dodger Mullins.

When Joe Wilkins and me looked like having the Starlight Club in Stratford Place off Oxford Street, and we were minding it for a few days to see how it went, Randalls come down and I wouldn't let him in; I told him he was a wrong 'un. At Parkhurst in 1969, a day or so before the riot, his son was just finishing five years and I give him Eva's phone number to alert her what was going to happen and say we needed all the help press-wise, and he did it. I told him I regarded his father as a grass, but the kid still done it for us. Not a case of like father, like son.

There was a whole clique of them. Red-Faced Tommy Plumley was one. He was a friend of Frankie Alberts. Tommy was a grass, but people subtly put up with it. He was a very likeable man really. You could use him to get into the coppers, get a bit of bail, shut down a bit of evidence. He always had good jars[7] and his other line was to have coppers straightened; he was the first you would go to. He had a very good line in diamonds; you had to be a real expert to know the stuff he had was fakes. He could sell you stuff and, if you never had to pawn it or wanted to sell it on or insure it, your wife could wear it for the rest of her life and no one would be the wiser. Then Tommy shopped a few people about the time of

---

[7]Jars are diamond rings. The derivation comes from jargoon, a stone resembling a diamond, and was once standard English. The verb to jargon means to show a person a genuine diamond and then sell him a paste one.

the Kray trial and he got three years. The police heard him in a café opposite the London Sessions building when he was trying to set up an alibi. Three of them got nicked, and during the trial Tommy changed his plea and pulled the others down with him. I expect some pressure was put on him by someone: 'If you don't do this, Tommy, then we'll let everyone know you're a grass.' Something like that. He did his time in the hospital at Wormwood Scrubs. I think either he had diabetes or that was part of his reward. He was in there when I had a lump in my stomach and I went for an operation in 1960. He ended up with a petrol station in Hoxton. No one really saw him after that and yet he was everywhere before.

Harry White, old Alf White's son, had it off with the wife of the man who ran The Albion near Ludgate Circus for years. Both Harry and the man were straighteners, and the pub itself was a meeting place if you wanted anything done. It was there that the famous fight between two coppers took place. A D.I. was trying to get the other – who was the officer in the case – to get a man out of a robbery, and he was offering £10,000 which was big money. The other was trying to tape-record the conversation, and they had a roll around on the floor.[8]

Another of that clique was Buller Ward. If someone stuck something up to him, he'd stick it up to someone else. He'd pass info on, sell a bit of gear, get a cut here and there. Personality-wise he was a likeable fellow, but he was a grass when he was nicked with Leslie Payne long afterwards at Winchester. Then it all come out officially. Reggie Kray cut Buller Ward and he never took any reprisals. He was a good man in his day, but he was part of the Red-Faced Tommy syndrome. Buller could have a good row so Tommy would always associate himself with people like that, hand on the back of their shirts.

Looking back at the late 1970s–early 1980s, the era of the

---

[8]Following the incident in 1970, Detective Superintendent John Keane received three years' imprisonment. On his release, he became a clerk with a firm of solicitors.

supergrasses, it never really concerned me because I was in the nick anyway, but there was a whole collection of them and they all acted like each other. Roger Denhardt was about the cleverest of them but him, Leroy Davies, Osborne all come in Wandsworth around 1973–4 before they went hookey. They were all brash, the 'kill'em and eat'em' type. They were geeing themselves up, but underneath they knew their true character. You couldn't call them modest. Everyone has to be brash when it comes to it, but not when there's no need for it.

Roger Denhardt was the best of them, brains and workwise that is. When I first met him he looked like an all-American college boy – big, tall and very handsome. When he was a kid back in the 1960s he was the original British 'Bonnie and Clyde'; he and a girl-friend and a couple of others robbed banks and post offices. The police was very afraid he'd shoot it out with them if he was caught, but one day he just walked into the nick and gave himself up.[9]

He'd got thirteen years for robbing a security van in Hemel Hempstead after Leroy Davies grassed him, and when he was on another trial for conspiracy to pervert the course of justice he just went hookey. In about 1979 he was at Chelmsford and a fellow prisoner cut him, and he shopped the guy then. That should have been enough. People then should have dropped him out, but with them internal things it wasn't headlines.

There's no doubt he had a lot of charm and what his great

[9]He told the police, 'During the past three years I have wrestled with a strong desire to confess my crimes and to a great extent put right the damage I have inflicted on my fellow citizens . . . It is really the only honourable course a man such as myself has left to take. I have caused a major schism within my family. This act of informing is the most positive proof I can give that I have concluded my criminal career for ever.'

His subsequent evidence cleared up 329 crimes involving £3 million of stolen property. Twenty-nine people were jailed. As a thank-you for his co-operation in what came to be called Operation Carter,' he received an eight-year sentence concurrent with his thirteen-year term and was released from prison in 1981, having obtained full remission.

In 1986 Graham Sayer, who had twenty-two years' service behind him, was convicted of robbery at a post office in Mansfield. He had used his mother's car as the getaway vehicle and had spent so much time near the store that his number had been taken. Dennhardt was by now safely in Spain.

feat was – after he came out, what he did manage to do was turn a copper called Sayer, the detective sergeant who'd been assigned to be his minder. They did a post office up in Mansfield together and the geezer got nine years.

The other thing you don't do is nick people. You take and give your lumps and bumps and you don't go to the law. Lennie Garrett and his brothers were all good boxers before the War; then Lennie turned professional, and he was one who did let the side down. Ted Broadribb, who was secretary to the Boxing Board later on, was his manager, and when Lennie was nicked pre-War Ted spoke up and he got out of it, but then he got Borstal so that was the end of him as a professional. Later he escaped from Lambeth Magistrates' Court. There was a flat roof with iron bars and his brother Jimmy Garrett climbed up, sawed through the bars and next morning when Lennie arrived and was allowed to go to the lavatory he was through a fanlight and away. This was about 1941.

The Garretts came from the Elephant, and Lennie was in Portland with me. In 1943 I did some villainy with him in Flint Street at the back of the Old Kent Road, next to what was then the police station. We'd been out at the jump-up and we pulled up in the van we'd nicked: me and Jimmy Stevens and Lennie, who was getting on the phone to the guy who was going to buy the snout. Jimmy and me were still in the van with the crooked gear and we didn't realise the scream was up. You think you've got half an hour or so from one side of London before they come looking for you the other side of the water, but this time they must have come out quicker than we thought. Me and Jim got away and made ourselves busy with a good story about how Lennie was in the phone-box by chance. They never got their cigarettes back and the proceeds helped to pay for his defence at County of London Sessions. I was nicked myself for something different by the time he got a not guilty.

In early 1942, to make matters better still, Jimmy Garrett was now on remand at Feltham. A guy had sawn through the bars of his cell and he got caught in the grounds and sent down the chokey, so his cell was empty. Outside your official cell there was a big board with your name, but if no one was in the cell then the board was reversed and so the screws didn't bother to go in. Jimmy was orderly on the landing, so he'd be the first prisoner to be unlocked in a morning. He just went along to this man's cell and turned the board round showing a blank. The screws didn't even bother to look through the spyhole. The bars hadn't been repaired, and he was through them and clean out over the wall.

People still thought they'd never get caught. If you kept out, you was out. You always thought you could stay out for the year or so. If you escaped on remand then there was the chance you could get your case together, see a few witnesses, put a bit of dough about, but otherwise inside a month you was up at the Sessions.

Once he'd stopped boxing, Lennie Garrett cut quite a few people and he also got cut. This was where he went wrong. Jimmy Robson did him after Spindles Jackson had chinned him in a fight in the pub, The County Terrace, in the New Kent Road. This would be the end of 1944. The revenge came in early 1945 when Lennie and a whole pack went to Jimmy Robson's flat in Brixton Hill. They smashed their way in even though Jim and his wife Toni had put a wardrobe up against the door. They gave Toni a slap and they cut Jim to ribbons.

When he come out in 1952 from doing some bird, Lennie and Danny Swain had a straight fight outside a pub in Camberwell. Swain couldn't half punch; he hit Garrett so hard he fell down and broke his ankle. With that, Henry Botton went and did Garrett with a starting-handle. Garrett nicked Swainey and he went to the Old Bailey and got found not guilty. Garrett should never have nicked him; coming from a good family like his, he knew the rules. About three or five years ago, I read in the *South London Press* that someone cut him to pieces in his own home in Camberwell. He'd answered the door and he got cut. No one got nicked this time so far as I could see, but of course he was an old man by then.

Eight

I have to be fair. I was never really a good escaper myself. I was never in the general prison population long enough to get invited on one, and the only time I was – when Alfie Hinds had an idea to break out of Pentonville – I got moved before it went off. Mind, I did try a bit when I went to the Feltham Borstal, but that was kid's stuff. A rush at the wall one Sunday morning and it was all over in five minutes. No planning, no nothing.

Before then the approved school had been very strict. They had the cane across your arse literally for nothing. That was St Benedicts in Reading, which used to belong to the guy who owned Huntley & Palmer. He gave it up to help keep boys straight for good motives. But it didn't. I escaped on the day I was sent there and I got away completely. I just ran off and jumped on the back of a lorry. Then I changed lorries and I got to London. I wasn't out long. I didn't go home, of course. My sister Peggy was married by then and she put me up. Her husband was well into communism, and he must have seen this as some sort of a challenge to fascism. Even if he didn't, he let me stay when it could have meant bird for him if I'd been found there. This would be 1940.

Then I was caught on a smash-and-grab at Bravingtons in King's Cross when Patsy Fleming got away and I was sent to Arndale. By now I'd escaped from the remand home a few times, and I'd been put in prison and was taken straight to

Arndale. I escaped again from there, this time with Jimmy Essex and Jackie Barratt, one of the family from Clerkenwell. Jimmy Essex eventually got done for murder twice and got a manslaughter on both cases.[1] The first one he was with 'Dido' Frett and Danny Swain, but I'm pleased to say both of them got away.

Anyway, at Arndale we just unscrewed a window and were off, but we were caught the same day and they took us straight back. The screws from the approved school would go out with the police to look for you. We got the birch when we got back.

A bit later I escaped yet again, once more with Jimmy Essex, and this time we got back to London. That was really the last time I had a successful escape. I stayed with my sister Peggy again and we were out nearly three weeks. Then Essex and me and another guy were doing a tobacconist's shop in the Kennington Road when we got surrounded by coppers. I managed to get on the roof and jump over, but when I jumped down it was right into the arms of that crooked copper Ken Drury's father, who was on the beat over our way.

Quite wrongly, I got the blame for the time a gun was found on the train going to Dartmoor, and it was nothing whatsoever to do with me. It was all down to Nobby Saunders. He'd been done at a court-martial in France after the invasion and it got made up to fourteen years. Then he escaped and went on a jeweller's with Tommy Jenkins, Harry Boy's brother, and shot at a policeman. Tommy got eight and Nobby got life.

In 1957 he'd done about three or four years, and the idea was for him to escape when he came up on the train from Dartmoor. He'd saved his visits for a year so that he could have them at a local prison of his choice. The gun was organised by some very well-known brothers from South London, and it really was a work of art. Firstly, the gun had to be got into the prison, so

---

[1] The first was over a fight at the Elephant coffee stall in London Road and Essex received three years. The second charge resulted from a fight in Armley prison and this time he received ten years.

it had to be taken down overnight and hidden either in the quarry or on the farm where people worked outside. Those people were trusties and would hardly be searched when they came back into the prison; just a pat down, window-dressing really. They would pick it up and get it inside the prison. Don't forget this was before the Mountbatten inquiry, after which all the security came into force.

When you left Dartmoor on escort or discharge, you went down to the punishment block on the afternoon of the day before so you did not come in contact with anyone. You took your sheets and towel down with you in a pillow case. You'd be searched, but if you had a decent job and were trusted it was really only a pat and the screws didn't bother with your linen – which is where the gun would have been. The next day you would be searched before you left, but as you'd been in solitary it was only another pat. You'd have the gun under your cobblers. So now the gun had got out of the prison again and on to the train. Once you were on it, although everyone would be handcuffed to someone else it was a fairly relaxed atmosphere. It was an open special carriage and the screws were going on holiday in a way. The screws went up to London on escort and then had a booze-up with their mates at the 'Ville. You could be sat next to who you wanted, and this is where they done a magnificent feat. Someone going up for their visits passed the gun to Nobby.

Next he asked to go to the toilet to do a sit-down, and that's literally when Nobby's arsehole went. Going in for a sit-down meant his cuffs would come off for those few minutes. What he should have done is come out with the gun, said 'Stand back', pulled the emergency handle and taken his chances. He might have had to shoot someone and there might have been a hero, but I doubt it. I don't think the screws would have been too game. I don't think he'd have had to shoot anyone, and he could have jumped off. But, there again, killing a screw was a topping offence. That's when his nerve went; he hid the gun behind the cistern, did his business and come out. Why didn't he do it straight away when the gun was slipped to him? Well, that would have sort of compromised all the others. Now, if he'd come out of the toilet with the gun they could have jumped off with him if they'd wanted, but if he'd done it before he'd gone in then the screws would have known the gun must have come from one of the men on the train.

When the cleaners cleaned the train next morning, they found it and there were the headlines: GUN ON DARTMOOR TRAIN. I was mentioned and it was suggested the gun had been left as an escape for me. I was going down to the Moor that day handcuffed to Billy Ambrose. On that train it was the custom that friends could bring all the food and smokes that could be eaten on the journey. That's when Billy, Albert and Eva had brought us food, but because of the gun the screws wouldn't let them give it to us. Bill had been on the journey himself and knew what to do. As long as it was smoked and eaten by the time the train arrived, it was all right. The P.O. in charge – he was the one I got the cat over at Shrewsbury. He'd nicked me for being saucy and I did him. This time he bottled out same as Nobby'd done twenty-four hours earlier: backed off. I kicked up, yelling and screaming. I was going, 'It's because of you and me in the past. 1945.' Then the P.O. came up to the carriage window and allowed just me to have the food, but Billy and Albert had really done it in style and there was more than enough for all of us.

In 1960 when I went back to Dartmoor, Nobby Saunders was now a Red Band doing well. Then he got the hostel at Leicester. He met a girl there and to his credit was never heard of again. It might have turned out for the best, but he was weak when it come to it. At least eight people were involved in putting themselves at risk for him.

The authorities at the prison weren't having too good a time when I arrived. The next day they lost a bloke called Albert Fowler, who got off the Moor in poor weather making really good time. It was reckoned he covered five miles in six hours, which was fast going in the fog. He got nicknamed 'Foxy' by the newspapers because the local hunt sent the hounds after him, but they couldn't get a scent. It wasn't the first time he'd gone either. In the past he'd slipped a prison escort, escaped from juvenile detention three times, and this was his third escape from prison. He stole a boat and ran aground and then got caught driving a car up in Northumbria about two months later. He went down for an additional eight.

Saturday you only did a half-day's work, and then that ended in June 1961 when Georgie Madson tied up the screws in the mailbag shop at Wandsworth and ten of them escaped.[2] He was doing a preventive detention of 10–14 years for robbery; good thief, safeblower, everything. He was known as the Major-General, and this time he was doing eight for some safes in a laundry in North London. It was a really good escape; about ten of them got away and some of them stayed out a long time, but they got reeled in one by one and there was some heavy bird on offer. I knew George very well, he was a good man – came from Enfield way. I heard a bit ago he'd died.

It was shortly after his escape that the order came out for no more work on a Saturday morning. The Prison Officers' Association used it as an excuse to say they couldn't guarantee security. George did us all a great favour with that tie-up and escape. People should always be grateful to him.

Georgie was a good escaper as well as being a good thief. In April 1943 he was in Wandsworth serving two years. He'd been up a ladder with a couple of others in the laundry, repairing and whitewashing the roof. A prison officer come in the main entrance and delivered a message to the officer in charge. It was a nice spring day and the officer went straight out again. There were doors and gates, but because of the weather the doors were left

[2] The plot was organised with a former prisoner, Ronald Jeal, who had been released three weeks earlier and who provided the cars. The escape was on 24 June, and the warders were overpowered and a bench placed against the wall. When questioned by the police, Jeal said, 'If conditions were better in the nick the fellows would do their bird without moaning.'

open. He went through the gates, slammed them but didn't lock them.

They were watching from up the ladder expecting him to come back and lock it, but he never did and so they came down into the laundry. It was a great big place where the screws couldn't see everything and Georgie and the others tried the gate. It opened so they went back for their ladder, up the wall and as they were getting up, old Charlie Atwell, the prison officer in charge of the gardens, chased them but they got away. In them days there was a sort of gentleman's agreement that if you escaped from prison and you kept free for the remainder of your sentence, then it got wiped out.

So after the two years was up – when he'd done his time, so to speak – George came back with his solicitor and demanded his clothes and they had to give them to him. He was a great escaper, was George. Neville Craig, the brother of Christopher who was with Derek Bentley when the copper got shot, escaped with him either that time or on another occasion.

George escaped again in September 1960, this time from Exeter. He and two others got out in their lunch hour, using a builder's scaffolding which had been left in the yard, and over the 20-foot wall they went. Then they nicked a car. They were out a bit, but it was one of those escapes which can't last.

Eddie Gibbs died in the summer of last year. In 1949 he'd got the cat for doing a P.O. at Wandsworth. I'd known the man when he was a screw at Lincoln and he was a dog. Eddie was right to do him. How he got the cat was, he had some keys made and sawed through the bars of his cells. About 5 p.m. the orderly officer would double-lock the doors, winter and summer, and that would be that. But when Eddie got out he had the cell door keys as well as those for the double lock. He also had the keys to where the ladders were kept in a hut with a tuppenny-ha'penny padlock on it near the prison cemetery.

There were no patrols, no dogs in those days. Security in prison grounds wasn't tight at all. He started to open up some of his mates, including Jerry Callaghan, from their cells. In the course of doing it he come a tumble. Some screw must have clocked him and gave the alarm. He got back out into the grounds and threw the keys away, but he had to be captured. In the confusion everyone else got back in their cells. While he was doing his punishment, that's when he got eighteen of the cat. Like I've said, in those days, if you got the cat it was the end of your punishment.

Then Eddie was at Dartmoor doing five years when Billy McGuire, who was about 19 or 20, got fourteen years for shooting at a copper. He must have got that sentence in 1950. What he wanted to do was a screw. He knew he'd go down the punishment block for it, and Eddie did a deal with him that when he'd done enough with the screw he would let Eddie drag him off. Same as the Berts, and same as Jack Rosa and Billy Hill. Billy McGuire got the cat and Eddie got about a year off his sentence. That would be about 1952 or 1953.

Eddie was a bit of everything. Later on he got a ten, and by now Billy McGuire was still doing his fourteen years when they sent Eddie to the Moor. They shipped him out because of bad feeling between him and McGuire, but it was all put up. Eddie became a Red Band at Exeter. In October 1959, when me and Jimmy Andrews did the Governor and the Chief Officer after Jack 'The Hat' McVitie had been slaughtered by the screws, Eddie was terrific; he was the one who smuggled the notes out – threw them over the wall, and a guy who'd been released that day picked them up and posted them on to Billy Hill. It was headlines in the *Daily Mail*. By then (since February 1958) prisoners were allowed to have newspapers. Billy got Captain Hewitson M.P. down to see me and later to ask questions in Parliament about my beating and, although I was in punishment and didn't get the papers, news was smuggled down to me.[3]

Billy McGuire eventually got parole and went out in about 1961. Then he got another two years. He was in the 'part worn' stores in Wandsworth when I came in; he helped to give you

[3]See *Mad Frank*, pp. 83–5, 160 *et seq.*

your clean gear. That would be about 1973, and then he just disappeared. I heard he was another who died of cancer, three or four years ago.

Some people just can't settle and do their bird, even soft bird. Kenneth Neal was one of them. He was never anything special, just a fraudsman working for Charlie, and he wanted to come home and see his family. I think he'd been a publican once. He kept screaming that he wanted a bit of help. He was in Ford, and you can't have it much softer than that. To be in Ford then was a big, big plus. It was very easy-street, far removed from a closed prison. Johnny Barnham and I went to see Alfie Fraser who was in Parkhurst, and when we got back off the island we went straight to Ford to see Joe Lowry who was doing time for dog-doping. By the time we got there it was too late for a visit and the screws wouldn't let us in. It gave me the opportunity to look round, so when it came to getting Neal away it was no problem. There used to be a chain-link fence which stretched part of the way around – the rest was open and he walked out. An open prison was what it said: an open prison. He didn't really need any help except having a car waiting. It was just like walking out of your own front door. Then he went and became a dog. He got a bit more bird and went and hanged himself. It was the same with one of the fraudsmen in the Kray trial, a man called Michael Kenrick. He was serving a five-year stretch and thought he was going to get more on top, and so he did himself. In fact the pros never offered evidence against the others in his case, so if he'd had more bottle he'd be alive today.

'Rubber Bones' Webb, he was another good escaper. He got off the Moor. I never knew what his first name was. It was in November 1951 and I met him when he was on the run. He dug a tunnel in his cell and went along the tunnel into the grounds. There were no patrols then, no screws, no dogs, no floodlighting. Once you were in the grounds you'd meet no one, and it was over the wall with a rope and hook. He come to the West End, and it was there he was picked up.

He wasn't a good thief, I'm not knocking him there, but he was a good escaper. You can't knock that.

The best riot at Wandsworth involved Jimmy Andrews and Tommy Harris, an Irish kid whose brother Martin escaped with Jack 'The Hat' from Lincoln prison in about 1960. There was also Johnny Cotton, who was then doing four years and three months, and he was waiting to go to Dartmoor instead of a local prison. At least you'd get some association there. When you'd done eighteen months in Dartmoor or Parkhurst, lag stations, you went on second stage and had a grey suit with a ring around to show you had done that. Another six months and you went into a blue jacket, and when you'd done four years you got a ring round your blue jacket to show you were special stage. Then you had meals in association at dinner, and every evening with a wireless. You couldn't make tea, but you could at least mix. If you were put on report, in addition to your bread and water you would lose so much stage, which meant you went back to the first stage for a month. Later in 1955 Johnny did a jeweller's and got a ten, along with Johnny Cohen who got double.

They all had a pact that if any of them got nicked for talking in the shop, they would have a riot in the mailbag shop. The screws nicked Johnny Cotton and before he went in front of the Governor he had a bit of a confrontation – great big man he was, 6 foot 2 or something – and as soon as they heard he'd been punished the others in the shop kept to the pact. Cotton had been badly knocked about when he went to see Lawton, and this made them more determined. I didn't know this at the time because I was in the strong cell in E1.

There was a little cobblers' thing in the mailbag shop; there was a bench where two or three prisoners would be repairing shoes. Jimmy Andrews and the others went and took the hammers and steamed into the screws. It was one of the best ever. A fellow called Tommy Flack from the East End and a couple of Scots, Benny Stewart and Willie O'Dare, were on it as well. For about ten minutes they had complete control of the shop before the reinforcements arrived. A hundred or so could have escaped; the screws ran for their lives and Alfie Hinds was shouting, 'Open up.' Alf had the foresight to plan an escape, but he didn't have the bottle to do it on the spot. There was a ladder and they had the screws' keys. There was no security fence at Wandsworth, but they were so excited they never dreamed about going over and none of the other prisoners had the brains to jump on the band-wagon.

That was the only thing I can say about Lawton. No one ever got took outside for sentencing if he could help it. What he did with these men was, after they steamed into the screws they had barricaded themselves in a screw's office in the mailbag shop, and Lawton brought in steam hoses. The windows were smashed and the hoses turned on. The screws had been really done with the hammers, but they got their own back. Wandsworth then was so violent. Lawton had given the screws *carte blanche* to do what they liked.

Franny Daniels was at Chelmsford before the War with Bill, and he took part in the strike they had in the summer of 1938. The strike was over conditions, which were really rough. It was when Lawton was C.O. there. Lawton'd been upped from plain screw to Principal Officer at Brixton and then to Chief Officer at Chelmsford.

The Governor at that time, as governors go he wasn't bad – he was with me at Liverpool years later. What he done was against all the odds really. He sided with the prisoners and suspended Lawton: it was unheard of. Lawton appealed, and a Commissioner was sent down by the Home Office and interviewed every prisoner – about two hundred of them. Quite a lot of the prisoners went crooked and Lawton was reinstated. The Governor was sent to Gloucester or Dorchester which had about only eighty prisoners; it was a right come-down for him. Then after that Lawton was promoted to First Chief Officer at Pentonville. The 'Ville was bombed and closed and he was sent to Wakefield as a Deputy Governor and then to Oxford as Governor, which was when his career took off.[4]

You couldn't ever win on a strike or a riot outright, but what you possibly could do was change conditions a bit further down the line. I think the Parkhurst riot changed the system. Miller, the Governor, was weak but he was a brilliant PR man. When the Visiting Magistrates come round, he really looked the business, but he was weak. The Deputy Governor was also weak – not villainous, but weak. I bumped into him later when he was Governor of Exeter and he was quite OK. In that sense the riot was worth it because it did get a bit of publicity. It should have got more, but it did show up what conditions were like.

[4]The long-running and often violent feud between Lawton and Fraser, culminating with Fraser's verbal attack on his son, then Mr Justice Lawton, at Victoria Station and the subsequent Torture trial, is described throughout *Mad Frank*.

Nine

Some people are with you all through your life. Ruby Sparks was one of those, and he did me right all the way through. It was Ruby stuck up the London Airport car park to us when I was working with Eddie and Charlie in the early 1960s. He was the one who introduced us to the guy who gave us the details.

I'd always kept up with Ruby. When I come out of Broadmoor I went into The Favourite, a great big pub he owned just by what was the old Alexandra Park racecourse, and he gave me £25. It don't sound a lot now, but then it was £500 or maybe £600 in today's money. I got on very well with Ruby. He'd more or less packed it in by then, but late in life he got nicked for a sort of scam. I think he got six months for a fraud. It was down at Brighton, I believe.

He was a good entertainer; he had a very good voice, and of an evening he'd sing. His girl-friend, the 'Bobbed Haired Bandit', had just faded out of the scene as she was getting older. She got six months from Dodson at the Old Bailey for harbouring Ruby after he got off the Moor, but the judge called her back and reduced it and after that we never really heard of her. There's a story that she's still living, but I don't know if it's true. Ruby's escape had been brilliant. Of course he could never get to the keys the screws had on them, but he managed to get close enough to remember what they looked like and then when he got back to his cell he'd work on a blank. He got his money together by running a crooked dice game in the prison, so when he got over the wall he had five or six quid which in those days could get you quite a long way. Ruby was getting quite a bit of publicity, and people were suggesting he should be prepared to do a bit of GBH if need be when he went on a robbery, but that wasn't his game. Me, I wouldn't have minded at all, but Ruby was just a thief. Later he married a very decent girl called Ann who kept him out of real crime for the rest of his life, although he could always point you in the right direction if you were a friend.

You'd have phone numbers to call. Although in them days people like us didn't always have phones, we all seemed to, but, although I got caught over the phone when I was in Dublin, generally there was none of this tapping going on. Least, not that we knew. Very occasionally you'd meet people for a drink and discuss a bit of business. Ruby told us about the car parking and introduced us to one of the car-park attendants who told us that those about him in the swindle were giving him peanuts and he deserved more. Funnily, a bit earlier when me and Eddie Richardson flew back from Manchester where we'd been for a couple of days, we got our car and when the man on the gate gave us a ticket we couldn't believe it. We went off alarming. Much more than we should have paid; we knew then it was a fiddle. Then we all burst out laughing because they were rascals like ourselves. We paid our money and left. We knew it was a fiddle, but we thought it was just a couple of them working together. Every week Ruby was getting something, and he introduced us to a man who put us right in the picture. At this stage Ruby and the man were thinking that sooner or later it might leak out, because they were on a grand scale and they were afraid the Krays might make themselves busy. They knew with us they'd be completely safe, and there would be no liberties – it would be perfectly worthwhile slinging that bit of money out.

The man said we should take over, and if we did then everyone would get a fair share. So me and another kidnapped two of the men who he told us about. We just picked them up near the airport when they came off work. We took them to

Atlantic Machines, which was off the Tottenham Court Road, and had a chat. It was very successful. There were two rooms downstairs in the cellar which were a bit like cells. We shoved them in and said, 'Which would you like to die in?' They couldn't tell us quick enough, and after a couple of hours we just drove them home. All you need to do in a snatch like that is come up to the people and shove them in the back of a car. It's the speed which does it; that and determination, showing that you mean business.

We then went to see the geezer who owned the car park. It wasn't an NCP in them days. He was quite happy, only too pleased because he knew that, in its own way, it would all be straight and above-board and now no one could muscle in. What we were getting depended on the take, but on average it was a couple of grand a week and we shared it out. Ruby got his corner every week, and he was happy. In fact, they were right about the Twins wanting in. One of their complaints against Charlie and Eddie was that they wouldn't let them into the car-park touch.

There was a bit of trouble the first week or so and then I took 'Dummy' down. I never knew his real name, but he was uglier than the Hunchback of Notre Dame. I thought I was seeing things when I first saw his face in the Log Cabin. When I was introduced to him, right away I could see the potential. He didn't have to say anything, and in fact he never spoke much at all. You just used to have him stand there. At the car park they couldn't hand over the takings quick enough. He was always used for the occasions like I just said. I don't think he was too bright, but that was how he made his living.

Patsy Lyons was another I kept in touch with for a long time. He was the man who I did Palmers Court with all those years ago at the end of the War, and who got caught because we were greedy. It was stupid. We'd decided to do another jeweller's that afternoon because we had only got about £2,000 each for what we'd stolen. Like fools, we used the same car. I can't think how we did it: just couldn't believe we could be caught. The number plate had been taken and we got nicked coming out of the Rotherhithe tunnel. A policeman coming from Tower Bridge had received the number of the car which had been used. When we arrived out of Rotherhithe, as we got to Old Street there was a chase, traffic blocked us in and we had to make a run for it. Two of us got away. That was a lesson to always leave yourself a way out. I got away, but I didn't do so good with the tunnel the next time, coming back from a raid on Benfleet Town Hall where we'd got a load of clothing coupons.

We picked the shops we did because we had a man on the tweedle[1] who, if he liked the stuff that was in them when he went in about his own bit of business, he would mark our cards. Then one of us – it was usually Patsy because he looked so smart and distinguished – would go in and have a look round. That day, I was the one doing the blag and Patsy was the driver.

Johnny Macdonald was the other man who got nicked that day we tried to do two jobs. I saw him recently and we were having a laugh. When he was on trial for that blag, they had a witness who had a shop opposite. 'What drew your attention to the robbery?' asked the counsel for the prosecution. 'Well, I thought a buzz-bomb had landed,' he replied and everyone started laughing. What it had been was me with a cosh smashing all the windows of the shops in the courtway to create a diversion and stop people having a go. Johnny lives over Blackheath way now. The other who got away was married to his sister, Marie, and had been a prisoner of war and got back to safety, so escaping was his line. Johnny Macdonald himself was a great escaper. He got out of Sherwood Borstal with Harry Boy Jenkins, and then in the 1950s he got out of Brixton.

It was Harry Boy who got topped for the de Antiquis killing though some said he was grassed up. I did quite a lot of work with him; he was one of the gamest fellows you could ever wish to meet in our world. Kathie – the mother of my three eldest

---

[1]Tweedle is a false ring or sometimes watch used to deceive jewellers or pawnbrokers. A jeweller is shown a ring which is then switched for the tweedle. 'On the tweedle' is the confidence trick of substituting the rings. The phrase dates from Victorian times.

boys Frank, David and Patrick – her brother married Harry Boy's sister. Kathie's brother Albie was a very nice man, much nicer than his sister.

When someone was topped it was sad, of course, that's common sense; but it was part of the job, and was the main hazard. Otherwise, don't do it. When someone got topped, I never thought it was time I turned it in. In a few cases people did but not outstandingly so, although it was a deterrent to them who wouldn't have been in that type of robberies anyway. I think even if hanging hadn't existed, they wouldn't have gone in for that type of crime.

When you went on a smash-and-grab or outside a bank, getting the money there was always that possibility that someone could get killed – not willingly, but it could happen.

No one went out with the intention of killing anyone – you did your best to avoid it – but if it happened it happened. But on bank robberies and smash-and-grabs guns weren't carried. Anyone who turned up with a shooter would be slung out immediately by a real professional because the public were encouraged to have a go. There was even a radio programme, *Have a Go*, with a song 'Have a Go, Joe, Come on and Have a Go'.[2] It wasn't specifically at people stopping robberies, of course, but it was the spirit of the time. Straight men were just back from the War, and they thought nothing if a gun was produced. They wouldn't dream that anyone was going to use it, and even if they did they'd still go for them. Not like today, when they're repeatedly told not to do anything. It was a different culture. You had the First World War heroes and the same after the Second World War. All wanted to be heroes.

---

[2]*Have a Go* was an enormously popular radio programme starring Wilfred Pickles. Violet Carson who later appeared in *Coronation Street* played the piano and Mabel, Pickles' wife was 'at the table' with the questions. There was another catchphrase 'Give him the money, Barney' when the contestants answered four simple general knowledge questions, for which the top prize was £1. The Barney was Barney Colehan, later head of Light Entertainment at the BBC. The origin of the phrase was probably from between the wars when it was used as an encouragement to a very shy man: 'Have a go, Joe, your mother'll never know.'

If you carried a gun, you could be forced to use it whether you liked it or not. In Harry Boy's case, it was one of the others who had the gun and I don't think he even knew that the man had it or, if he did, it was only at the last moment. They went to do a jeweller's in Charlotte Street in Soho, and they had a young boy with them who didn't do what he was told. Instead of waiting, he just rushed in, and someone pressed the alarm. Then as they were getting out there was a lorry blocking their way and two men tried to stop them. One of them, Alex de Antiquis, who was on a motor bike, got shot.

It was September 1947 when 'Harry Boy' was topped along with Chrissie Geraghty, who came from over West London and who he'd met in Sherwood Borstal. I was away at the time, but I came out about a month later and the first week I went round to his mother to pay my respects. She'd written to Lawton, who was the Governor at Pentonville, to ask for his clothes, and she showed me the letter he'd written back to say that Harry Boy'd been hanged in them but she could have his belt, braces and shoelaces which had been taken from him if she wanted. She never did.

Patsy Lyons and Johnny Lewis, who was another great escaper, got out from Wandsworth in 1945 when there was a lot of repairs going on because of buzz-bombs, and they slipped off C Wing's exercise one Sunday afternoon, rushed round to reception and on to a roof where there was a ladder lying about. Their cards had been marked by Jesse Piggott, who had a job in the yard. Patsy Lewis got caught right outside the prison by P.O.s coming on duty. He and Johnny just walked straight into them, but Johnny got away.

Both Ruby Sparks and Patsy was on the same wing as me when that Canadian Emile Gauthier was topped in the September of 1943. He'd bren-gunned a woman to death in Brighton because she wouldn't go out with him, and another couple of people got hit as well. The jury couldn't agree first time round at Lewes and there was a re-trial at the Bailey. This time he was convicted, but the jury recommended mercy. The

Home Secretary wasn't having any of it, and he was executed in Wandsworth. The night before he died there was an air raid, and it must have got to him because he steamed into the warders who was with him, which didn't do him no good at all. When I heard what was going on, that was when I smashed up my cell in support. When they finished with him they smashed my barricade down and did me. Then they threw me in H1 where there was two strong cells. He was in the condemned cell for sixty days, which was then the longest anyone had ever been in.

The people I know who've been in the condemned cell, it didn't appear to have affected them. The classic case was a fellow who was sentenced to death and the other two got out on appeal. Leslie Martin was his name, and he was known as Curley. This was before the War when, if you had a good point of law, no matter how guilty you was then you won. But after the War they brought in the proviso so the court could say well, that bit of your trial was wrong but there was still enough evidence without it.[3]

They'd tied the woman up, and the handkerchief they'd gagged her with had Martin's laundry mark on it. Like a fool he'd used it without thinking. He'd say, 'Don't forget, Frank, make sure your handkerchief don't have your laundry mark on it.' It was a *cause célèbre* case because two of them walked out. Very few people, particularly women, got tied up then. Not because they might die, but if they were caught it would be a long sentence and the police would be likely to nick anyone who happened to be around, irrespective of whether they had anything to do with it or not, so we didn't wish it on the others.

---

[3]Leslie Martin, Albert Ansell and Walter Ross were convicted at the Central Criminal Court on 27 April 1934 of killing Eliza Ray at 47 Handcroft Road, Croydon. It was believed the 75-year-old, who collected rent from a number of properties, kept £3,000 at her home. Her equally elderly lodger went for a regular walk every evening and while he was out she was the victim of a robbery in which she was beaten and asphyxiated. The convictions of Ansell and Ross were quashed by the Court of Appeal on 15 May on the grounds that certain evidence against them had been inadmissible. Martin was later reprieved.

Funnily, Wally Ross, one of the men who had their case chucked by the Court of Appeal, seemed to follow Curley Martin round the prisons. He kept on getting twos and threes and ending up in the same place.

I knew the one who killed Tommy Smithson quite well. Spampinato was his name. It was over Smithson trying to put the arm on some Malts to make them pay for his girl-friend Fay Sadler's defence, and they weren't having it. He was in the condemned cell and, of course, there were two screws working in shifts in with him twenty-four hours a day, even when he's asleep. So one night he decided to have a J. Arthur. Now you had to keep your hands over the top of the sheets so the screws could see you weren't trying to cheat the hangman by doing yourself with a bit of glass or something, and they can see his hand going up and he's making a noise so they call out 'Stop that!' but then they all burst out laughing. He told me that in Dartmoor. Later he turned a wrong 'un. When I was there he'd done about four years and he couldn't speak highly enough of Bernie Silver and Maltese Frank Mifsud, but when he came out he turned them over.[4]

George Silverosa was an Italian I knew out of Clerkenwell. He had done a jeweller in the Hackney Road, was captured, convicted and sentenced to death. He was in the condemned cell at Pentonville in 1942. Because of the War the prison was really closed, but anyone who committed murder north of the Thames – well, they were hanged at Pentonville. He asked to burn his letters personally the day before he was due to die, and as the prison was empty apart from a few working in the bakery they let him go with officers. What he did was pick up an iron bar, did a couple of them and tried to escape. It was a good go, but they never dreamed anyone would do anything like that. To make a request like that when the prison was full they wouldn't

[4]Both were tried in 1974 for the murder of Smithson, who was shot in 1956. Silver was acquitted of conspiracy and Mifsud's conviction was quashed by the Court of Appeal.

have considered it, but with the prison empty they allowed it. I think after that they closed down the bakery. He was hung the next day. I'd been in Borstal with him. In a way I was lucky. The other fellow who went on the job with him had been in the same Borstal. It was just as well I'd never got to know George better, or it might have been me.[5]

I heard from a screw that when Harry Boy Jenkins had been in the condemned cell, the morning he's due to hang the priest comes in. Harry Boy was an R.C. and he tells the priest to push off. 'Why, what's the matter?' asks the man. 'I'm going to see your Governor in a minute,' is what Harry Boy said. I don't think a screw would invent that. He'd be much more keen on showing what a coward Harry Boy had been.

Unfortunately Patsy Lyons went wrong. Basically, Patsy was now friendly with Charlie Mitchell. This would be the early 1970s when Mitchell's name stank. He was a big man with huge shoulders and a good set of teeth who had a bookmaking business down the North End Road in Fulham. He also was a prime horse-doper, fraudsman and thieves' ponce, and was another to change sides.

He had been a long-time friend of the Twins, running long-firm frauds for them[6], and he was so well thought of he went with Charles Kray and some others to Toronto to talk to a Canadian mafioso about washing bonds. That was when they were all arrested and deported. Charlie Kray didn't really trust

---

[5]Sammy Dashwood and George Silverosa battered the 71-year old pawnbroker Leonard Moules to death at his shop when, on early closing day 30 April 1942, he was putting up the shutters. They had been at a loose end and decided almost on the spur of the moment to commit a robbery. Silverosa's palm print was found inside the safe. Each blamed the other. Both were hanged on 12 September 1942 at Pentonville.

[6]A *long-firm fraud* (or LF) is a lucrative, simple and relatively easy swindle to operate. A business, say, in children's clothes is set up and goods are bought on credit and paid for. The operation is expanded to take in household goods, ladies' clothing, sweets and so forth and more credit is obtained. When a substantial line of credit has been established very large orders are placed and the goods are sold off below cost. The proprietors vanish. The more complicated versions involve giving references and cross-references for other companies. Even in the 1950s a properly run LF could produce a profit of between £100,000 and £150,000 with little risk to the operator who would never be seen on the premises, leaving the day-to-day running in the hands of front men.

him and he was right not to, but the Twins wouldn't have it that Mitchell was a wrong 'un. They got suspicious towards the end because when I was with them when they was on remand, they asked me about him. Did I think he would give evidence? I said I didn't think he would, but he shouldn't be trusted. I said this because he had so much money and, if he could, he'd use it to get out of things one way or another. I was only half right.

And so it was proved. During the waiting for the committal he changed sides and told Nipper Read, the copper in charge, that there was a contract out for both him and Leslie Payne, who'd been the Twins' financial wizard and who was also grassing them. The idea had been that Mitchell should put the money up for the hit-man to come over from the States. He saw which side his bread was buttered and so he turned grass. He was just let to walk free. He gave evidence at the committal proceedings, but he went off abroad and didn't turn up at their trial.

The other thing Mitchell had was the great con-man Charles De Silva in his pocket. He was poncing off him, taking about 75 per cent of his earnings. Charles was about the best con-man amongst the top ranks, but for some reason he was dead frightened of Mitchell. For a time the Twins took Charles away from Mitchell and protected him. That may have helped to turn Mitchell, though there was still no excuse for it. De Silva was very handsome, something like Ceylonese; could have been Omar Sharif's brother from his looks. He was an extremely good-hearted man and money seemed to mean nothing to him. Once when he had a chauffeur he made him drive him in a Rolls down the King's Road to a café where he liked the breakfasts. He was very partial to bubble-and-squeak. He visited me in prison when I was doing the Spot seven and sent in a nice few quid.

In conning people there's really two sorts. There's what's called the long con and there's the short con. The long con is what you see in films like *The Sting* where a whole betting shop or broker's office is fitted out so that punters, sometimes only one, can be conned. And everyone in the place – all the girls working the machines, all the betters, the visitors – they're all in it, except the one who's being taken. Of course this takes a lot of time and trouble.

One long con of Charles's which didn't seem to need much equipment was when he said he was setting up a syndicate to buy and then sell arms to the Falangists who were going to overthrow the Franco government in Spain in 1961. Shares in it were £20,000 or £30,000 a time, depending on how much profit you thought you were going to make. That didn't really need anything more than an office and his contacts. But he could work a short con just as well. Because he was dark skinned he could easily be an Arab prince if he felt he needed to be, and the story is that one day he sold a Grimsby fishing fleet sight unseen to a farmer who he met in the first-class breakfast compartment on the Hull to King's Cross train. The man had money from a syndicate to buy in Smithfield market, and by the time the train pulled in the platform Charles had the money.[7]

He was also involved with Billy and Albert and a Mayfair solicitor over a fraud selling chinchilla rabbits. He told the punters there were to be chinchilla farms in Ceylon, and made quite a bit of money while it lasted. The solicitor got chucked and Albert and Billy were only mentioned, but Charles got six years in June 1961. He was very thick with them. Just before he got done they took him to Munich, and they all sent me a postcard.

Two things he did were really high class. He wanted to impress a mug and he got them both invited to No. 10 Downing Street when Harold Macmillan was Prime Minister there. Charles had been on some charity run by Lady Macmillan and he went over to Macmillan, put his hand on his shoulder and whispered something in his ear. Charles used to say the punter

---

[7] The scam may not have been quite as quick as that but in 1961 De Silva, who had arrived in England from Ceylon in 1947, was prosecuted for selling a fishing fleet to a Yorkshire farmer he met in a Kensington hotel. The non-existent trawlers were meant to be coming from Sweden and going to Ceylon. Amongst his other sentences, he served time in Switzerland and was jailed for four years in 1951 in a conspiracy to swindle Selfridge's over nylons.

was really impressed, but all he'd been saying was, 'Thank you for inviting me.' The other thing was that he once found an American who liked schoolgirls and he got a whole load of tarts to dress up, told the Yank they were from a convent and charged him £25,000 for the name and address of the mother superior.

Once the Twins went down Charles lost their protection of course, and he killed himself in a hotel when he was awaiting trial at the Bailey; took an overdose.[8] Some people say that he was killed to prevent him talking to the police, because there's no doubt he could have put a few faces away. It wouldn't be the first time it's happened. He was a devout Catholic, used to go to mass in Mayfair every Sunday when he was out and not working. His real trouble was that, like so many, he was a degenerate gambler. He was in Parkhurst when I took the football team down.

There was another con-man who committed suicide in prison. I can't now remember his name, but he was about as good as Charles. This one was an adopted son and he'd been given a public school education. In 1941 he pulled up round the Elephant in a car which had a coronet on the door and took Jimmy Brindle, Jimmy's mother and a couple of others to Harrods and Selfridge's and spent a fortune with duff kites[9]. They never had gadgets to detect things then. If the guy had plenty of front, it was easy.

When I had this pitch at the point-to-points after the War,

---

[8] The allegation of the circumstances surrounding his death is made, *inter alia*, in Derek Raymond's *The Hidden Files*, pp.111–12.

[9] Duff dates from the turn of the century and means spurious or counterfeit. Slightly earlier, at the duff related specifically to passing false jewellery. It derives from dudder, a term in use in the 1750s and relating to a person who passed ordinary goods as smuggled goods at fairs, getting a higher price for them. John Poulter, in *The Discoveries of John Poulter* (1754), suggests they often obtained double the true price, so the word dudd may itself be a corruption of double.

Kite, meaning paper, comes from tramps' slang of the 1850s. Kites were originally paper stretched on a frame. In this sense of a worthless cheque, it originated in the twentieth century and comes from America where the expression was a business – as opposed to a strictly slang – term. Kite can also mean a letter, a worthless person, a gang leader or a prostitute.

he comes along with his latest girl-friend; she looked like a rich widow. He says, 'Hallo, Frankie,' took us round to his car, betted with us knowing that with the horses he backed he couldn't win. He was just pushing a bit of dough our way. Same lady some months later, he knocked her about and got ten years for GBH and fraud. He must have done it a bit severely and she turned him in. He and Charles De Silva were the last men you'd have thought would commit suicide, but I think maybe they realised their days of being brilliant con-men had come to the end of the line.

Anyway, a few years after the Kray trial, Mitchell and Patsy Lyons were in a car in Fulham. To this day I don't know what Patsy was doing in the car with him, because he'd been such a good man. He shouldn't even have been talking to him, let alone sitting with him. Maybe it was because he'd married a girl from Fulham and had a stall in the market near Mitchell, but that's no excuse.

Johnny Barnham came along and gave Mitchell a coating; they used to be great friends, but not when he turned crooked. When Johnny put his head through the window to stripe Patsy, Mitchell pushed up the window and drove off with him jammed in it, so Johnny was dragged into another car and got his leg broke. Patsy then went and prosecuted Johnny over the striping; he'd needed about fifty stitches. I think Barnham got some bird, eighteen months or so.

I was gutted. I'd known Patsy Lyons so well, and I'd have put my life in his hands. It was a great tragedy, him of all people giving evidence. He never said it was Johnny, but there again he never said it wasn't. In my book that's just as bad. He just faded away, and he died a few years ago.

Johnny and his brothers George and Tommy were from a famous boxing family in Fulham. Tommy did an exhibition film with George Daley which they showed to schools – showing the sheer science of it and so making boxing respectable. Johnny's a black-cab driver now. He got four years for horse-doping in about 1965 when Joe Lowry got five years. That was Mitchell's real game – him and Peter Coulston, a big fat guy who was with us in Wandsworth in 1966–7. They were the kings at that. I even think some newspaper ran a story 'King of the Dopers' about him. Mitchell went off to Spain after that. He got hit over the head with a bottle and killed in a bar there. I'm glad to say the waiter who was charged got slung. Anyway, wherever he's buried there'll be a notice: Don't Walk on the Grass.

Of course, just as you can get good people you can get wrong 'uns. It's the same in any walk of life. One man who was wrong was Georgie Sewell. He used to say he was the Sabinis' right-hand man and liked to be called 'The Cobblestone Kid' because he said he was a really good street-fighter. In that book *Britain's Godfather* he's made out to be top class, but he wasn't. If you believe he was a right-hand man of the Sabinis, you'd believe anything. Georgie Shillingford, who was an uncle of my wife Doreen and a great pal of Harry Boy Sabini, was the last person who'd have had anything to do with Sewell.

There was no doubt that Sewell could fight, but if he lost he nicked you; it was as simple as that. Eddie Raimo, who glassed Billy Hill and who was with Alf White, was one of those prossed by Sewell; he got two years. Back in the late 1920s Sewell also prossed Georgie Shillingford, who was only 19 at the time and got 15 months, and Toddy – I can't remember his other name now – from Hoxton, and that's not the right thing to do. Toddy got a four. Sewell wasn't a reliable man. He was a prosecution witness in the murder trial at the beginning of the War over the killing of a man in Kilburn and let Jimmy O'Connor, the one they called Ginger, down very badly. What had happened was, Ginger had let him have a nicked watch and chain a few weeks before the killing but Sewell, who had something to do with the copper Thorp, said he'd sold it to him after the murder. Ginger got the death sentence, but it was commuted almost on the morning he was to be topped. Ginger came out and asked Sewell to tell the real truth about the ring or watch sold on the robbery; but he wouldn't do it, even though the man's relatives said he'd never owned a watch and chain like the one

Sewell said he bought.[10] Sewell really did let him down. He was offered £10,000 to tell the truth, but he was scared of the police if he went against them.

That murder was a funny thing altogether. I don't think O'Connor was on it. Buller Redhead, from out West London way, got a not guilty alongside him. I was inside with a lot of men who were half or more involved in that. It was an old man, a sort of retired coal merchant called Ambridge, who was found dead on his bed with his head bashed in. Ginger O'Connor got some bird shortly after that, and they nicked him for the murder as he left the prison the following January. Sewell really did stitch Ginger up. Not only was there the thing about the watch and chain, but he said Jimmy had made a complete confession before him and his wife saying he was there and had told his mate to stop bashing the old man, but he'd continued.

For a start, O'Connor swore that Freddy Andrews from Camden Town had done the murder. Not that there was any evidence whatsoever against Freddy. Freddy was doing four or five for cutting an American soldier somewhere in London, and O'Connor started writing petitions when they were both in Dartmoor together asking to see the police so he could blame Freddy. O'Connor was hated in prison for it; he was thought to be a wrong 'un. It is tough if you are innocent and you're doing life, but you just don't go putting people in it. Same as if you're going to be topped. Unfortunately you've got to be topped, you can't just grass people up. I think O'Connor came out around 1952. He did very well for himself; he started to write and had some plays performed, and he married a brief but eventually that broke up and I hear he's not well and is living alone in Paddington.

One man who has done well on the outside is John McVicar. He was a great escaper – better than he was a thief really. Now

---

[10]O'Connor was convicted of the killing of George Alfred Ambridge, a coal merchant found dead at 2 Hampton Road, Kilburn on 12 April 1941. Ambridge had been beaten about the head. O'Connor was sentenced to death before being reprieved. He served just over ten years, being released in 1952. Afterwards he became a journalist and married the barrister Nemone Lethbridge.

he's a writer and a broadcaster. His sister had a baby by Billy Gentry who was with Shirley Pitts, the hoister, for a long time. When McVicar escaped from the coach at Winchester in about 1966 he got nicked with Billy, and I think they both wound up with fifteen years, something like that. Billy was in the shop with me at Leicester when Tommy Wisbey, Bobby Welch and I did the Governor, Steinhausen. Billy was in Leicester security, and he was with us in Durham too.

Later Billy got ten for the mailbag when his girl-friend put him away along with Tommy Wisbey and Jackie Mullins, who was Dodger Mullins' stepson. I never knew that until I was nicked and found out Jackie's real name was Dore. I know it's right because Jimmy Brindle and me were had over a car and Jimmy said he'd borrowed it from Jackie Mullins. The coppers said, 'No, his name's Dore.'

Billy did that ten years and then got another ten, I think, for another security van. I know when I got the bird over the coins in the late eighties he got his bird about that time. He was a very handsome man. After he came out he opened a pub, and then he went out to Spain and fell out there with someone who fractured his skull. Then after that he settled down with a girl: he'd be in his sixties now.

We got into judges on the odd occasion. It was difficult but not impossible. For a start you had to get the case in front of your man, but in them days judges would say, 'I'll deal with that one' and so on. Don't forget there was only a handful of judges and cases and courts compared with what there is today. It was like when Freddy Andrews nicked Billy Hill for cutting him. Bill always said he could get into judges occasionally but I never knew if it was true. Not that Billy ever boasted for the sake of it. On the other hand Billy was a man who cold have a quarrel. There'd been bad blood between Billy and Freddy for a long way back. In fact another man had cut him on Billy's behalf. Billy wasn't going to be fool enough to do it himself; like he was always miles away at the time anything went off. Bill paid Freddy a nice few quid to sweeten him, and there was an understanding that if he was ever in trouble in future Bill would look after him. That's how Freddy Andrews came to get his skull knocked in on a boat to Tangier.

One of Billy's great pals was a man called George Ball who was also a pal of Freddy Andrews. George and Billy had done time together when they were nicked in a smash-and-grab raid in 1940. Billy got three and Georgie a two. Now he and Freddy were both on the run for some metal down in Hampshire; and when the trip came up George said could he bring Freddy along with him, and Billy had to keep his promise.

Because I was in the nick I only heard about it afterwards, but it was a highly publicised thing at the time. Billy organised a boat to go to kidnap some Sultan or other from Madagascar and return him to Tangier. It seemed like a crazy idea, but Billy always maintained he'd been promised £100,000 to do it and he had some money up front. He certainly took along a high-class crew. He had Eddie Chapman, the safe-breaker, with him; George Walker, the brother of Billy the boxer, and the one who later went on to be a big nob in the city before his company went bust; and Franny Daniels was there as well.

On the boat Freddy Andrews must have been slinging his weight about a bit, because one night there was a terrible fight between him and Georgie Ball. George Walker broke it up, but then Georgie Ball took on Freddy with a hammer. Freddy ended up with a fractured skull so, one way or another, Bill got his pound of flesh all round. They never kidnapped the Sultan, of course; they never even got within a thousand miles of Madagascar. All that happened is they got in a fight with the locals and were thrown out of Tangier. Georgie Walker was a nice man. No side to him. I bumped into him two or three years ago at a boxing dinner on the Isle of Dogs. George and I hadn't met for years, but he greeted me straight out. I don't know what's happened to Freddy; I should think he's well dead by now. I don't suppose for a moment George knew anything about the kidnap and, of course, nothing came of it even if it did happen.

Over the years I met Eddie Chapman a lot, sometimes at Bill's flat in Barnes. He was a legend even in those days. He was another very handsome man, very tall, who came from Newcastle, and he'd been a top safe-breaker before the War. He met up with another top breaker whilst he was in Lewes prison and served a sort of apprenticeship with him before branching out on his own. Then he was nicked in Yorkshire over a breaking in Edinburgh and taken back to Scotland. It had all gone wrong. He'd split up from the older man and had a couple of apprentices himself by then. They were going to do the Co-op in Edinburgh and they booked into a hotel for the night. Eddie was trying to open the skylight when it jammed, and he smashed it just as a copper was doing his rounds. All hell broke loose of course. One of them broke his ankle trying to cross a railway track, but Eddie and the other man got back to the hotel. He can't have been thinking straight. He should have just gone off down the back stairs, but instead he went and paid the bill. I think they got as far as Scotch Corner when they were nicked.

Somehow he was given bail and the three of them carried out a sort of crime wave, breaking safes wherever they could until they had enough money to go over to Jersey before they were nicked. Then one of the boys did the most stupid thing he could have: he sent a bottle of perfume to his girl-friend and signed his proper name. The police were on the lookout and saw what the postmark was. It was only a matter of time after that, which was when Eddie was nicked again. He got two years in Jersey just before the War.

He was caught with a man whose father was a judge in Burma or somewhere like that. For a sentence up to that you stayed on the island. If it was over then you were brought to a mainland prison. That's how Eddie was captured by the Germans and this man wasn't. I can't think of his name now but I met him in prison in the 1960s when he was well into a ten for a load of tom – a very nice, very well-educated man.

Then in a way Eddie had another stroke of luck when the Germans invaded the Channel Islands, and he was recruited by them. He was parachuted into England as a spy and he contacted the authorities here and became a double agent. After the war he was allowed off his sentences, and that film *Triple Cross* with Christopher Plummer was made about him. He never did any more bird, but he'd done about four years before the War. He was still working, of course, but he had other talents in the straight world as well and he was doing both. He knew a lot of people who stuck work up to him – jewellers, flats, houses, mostly where there'd be a load of tom or furs – and sometimes he'd pass it on. Then he and his wife bought a health club out near Shenley and did nicely out of that. I used to go there from time to time, but it was a long way out in those days. Five years or so ago he retired to Tenerife, but I just heard he died back here in December 1997; he was 83.

I reckon Hinds and Eddie Chapman were the best safe-breakers in my time. And only a bit behind them was the Scot, Johnny Ramensky. He was another with a brilliant war record. The authorities let him out of prison and sent him to work behind the German lines breaking safes in captured headquarters. He did fourteen in one day and got the Military Medal. Poor Johnny's trouble was that he couldn't stop doing safes. I think after his discharge from the Army, on his way back to Glasgow he stopped off and did one. Of course, there was only half a dozen people in the country who could have done it, and the police didn't have to be Brains of Britain to pull Johnny in. He was also a great escaper. But he started to get more and more bird, and he was 66 when he did his last job which was a large store in Ayr. He was nicked on the roof and died in Perth hospital after he'd collapsed in the prison there. I met him about the one time he and I were out at the same time, when I went up to Scotland for a bit of work and stayed with Arthur Thompson.

I knew 'Scotch' Jack Buggy slightly. We'd been in prison together and outside we had a drink together but he wasn't really my cup of tea; maybe it was just I didn't know him well enough, because he did what he could for his mates. He was a great pal of Roy James, and he got killed over trying to find out where Roy's Train money had gone. This was the thing with those who were actually on the Train robbery and went on the run. They had to leave their money behind with others to look after, and not everyone did it properly. In fact, apart from Tommy Wisbey and maybe a couple of others, I don't know of any single man who got nicked for the Train who didn't get really ripped off by someone or other. But Roy's money was outright stolen. Roy used to say sometimes that the figure in that book *The Train Robbers*, when it said that the man minding it had £74,000 off him, was right.

Though he was born in America, Jack Buggy worked out of Glasgow – that's how he got his name. I met him in prison when he was doing nine years for shooting a guy, Robert Reeder, outside the Pigalle which was a swanky night-club off Piccadilly. He was a game one. He'd tried to go back-stage to invite Shirley Bassey, who was the cabaret that night, to a private party and Reeder, who wasn't minding his own business, had hit him over the head with a plate. They'd both been thrown out and that's when the shooting started. Suddenly in 1967 Jack just disappeared – off the face of the earth if not the sea, because his body was found floating off Seaford bound up with wire. Someone had shot him.

The inquiry turned on a little spieler in Mayfair called the Mount Street Bridge Club where they played kaluki. It was one of Albert Dimes' hang-outs. Of course the coppers couldn't get anyone to talk, but years later they arrested Franny Daniels. One of a team of Australian shoplifters who was doing nine years for blackmail thought he'd like a bit of early remission, and he made a statement. Along with Franny was Abraham Lewis who just worked in the club but, I'm pleased to say, they both got a not guilty. Years earlier the police had also been to see Franny's nephew, Waggy Whitnall, over in Austria somewhere, but nothing had ever come of it. Rumour has it that before Albert Dimes died of cancer he confessed to the priest that he was there in the gambling club when Jack got shot. At least, that's what

Billy Hill told me when he come to see me at Dorchester that last time before he died himself. Albert's relations have said that's a load of rubbish, though.

I don't say for a minute that Franny had anything to do with the Buggy killing, but overall he was a lucky thief. Look how he escaped from the Airport job. He came out of The Cut near us. Earlier, before the War, he nicked a painting and tried to sell it back to the insurance but the company doubled on them and some poor sod, nothing to do with it, who was just in the wrong place at the wrong time, got penal servitude for the job. The man went off his head and was sent to Broadmoor in about 1940, and with remission his five years would have finished in 1943. But you had to do every day of your bird in Broadmoor then; there was no remission. When he finished his time at Broadmoor, they sent him straight to Cane Hill and that's where I met him. Of course, you can't blame Franny for not going and putting his hands up and saying, 'Please, officer, it was me.' It wouldn't have helped this other geezer if he had done.

Archie Hill, Billy's brother, was another lucky thief and a good one. He was good with a razor too. There was a man he done one side of his face and Jackie Burr, who was a good rascal out of Camden Town, done the other so it was like the chinstrap soldiers in the Guards have. This was about the end of the War, and we called the man Colonel Chinstrap after that character on the radio in *ITMA*. Archie wasn't the one who wrote the books about prison; he only did two bits of bird in his life. There was a month earlier on for doing a copper, and then twenty-one months – and that was lucky as well. They were found wheeling a safe across a pavement in Manchester in 1948. He never did another day in his life. On the other hand, he had money behind him and money makes your luck. If you have it, you only go out when you think things are in your favour. If you don't have money, you can't be picky and choosey. Archie died in Portslade during the riot trial.

I remember in 1951 I was skint. Then we all used to meet of a lunchtime in The Primrose, a pub off Spitalfields Market; some days it would be three or four of us, other days it might be as many as ten or twenty. This time I was late, and the only guy who was there was a man who used to do the offices in the City. He asked if I fancied having a try with him and I said sure, since I was skint. Anyway, although it wasn't really my game I went along with him, straight at the creep.

If you get stopped it's, 'Yes'm, can I help?' or 'We're looking for so and so, blank blank.' Now it was six and the City was closing up. All of a sudden we saw a tobacconist's closing on the corner. It had shutters and padlocks; there was no way you could break in unless you had equipment. The fellow with me saw there was a door with offices, so he said we could go through the panelling to the cigarette shop. We smashed our way through without making any noise and we got in and brought out everything we could, and took it to a bomb-site opposite. There were sacks there, and we loaded everything up. Then we phoned up Harry Barham, who was Billy Blythe's brother-in-law. He came round and bought it off us, loaded the car boot, and in less than half an hour we had our money. Harry got it very cheap, but he was entitled to it. We were all happy and I was well pleased. I did get to The Primrose a bit late that day.

When you're skint, there a temptation to take a chance. If I'd had money, I'd have said tomorrow's another day without kicking panels in like that. We'd no gloves, transport, nothing. The man and I had a couple of drinks and went our separate ways, but that's a hard way of making a living. Still, we were lucky.

On the other hand, Alfie Fraser was just unlucky. He was no relation, although when we were in the same nick he used to say he was a cousin so we could meet. He did the Martins Bank in St James's Street in February 1955, when he got over £23,000 from tunnelling. It was a great job, sheer artistry. He and his mate got in through the next-door building which was being done up, and came up against an iron grating they couldn't shift. Then they had a go at another wall and there was a place right up the top where they could pickaxe a hole they could squeeze through. They did that right enough, packed the safe with jelly and ran some wires into the street and blew it up from there.

The police could time it exactly because the caretaker two doors away heard the explosion, looked at his watch and went back to bed when he found it wasn't his own place had gone up. He said that he'd heard hammering for six hours after the explosion – that's how long they were in there – but he never did anything about it. He'd have been on to Scotland Yard before the echo went nowadays.

Alfie was one of the few capable of doing it, so again the police job in finding the villain was quite easy. There would only be about thirty people in the country who could have done it. The copper Ted Greeno made out there was brick dust where they tunnelled through, and there was brick dust in Alfie's shoes, though he had a receipt which showed he'd bought the shoes after the robbery. Alfie always said Greeno took out the car carpet, put dust from the cellar on it and said, 'That's how you got dust on your shoes.' He got 10 years. I believe he was fitted up. It was so easy in them days. Alfie did the tunnel, but that isn't the point.

Percy Horne, Billy Hill's great friend, did Alfie no favours in that trial. He'd been in Wandsworth with me when I had that near miss with the padre and when Billy Benstead got the message in. Percy Horne really let Alfie down rotten. They'd been at Borstal together, and they were very close. Alf gave Percy his money because Percy had just done that Borstal and a six months. He hadn't done any bird since 1942 and his Borstal had been in 1928 or 1929, so to all intents he had no form. Now he was a wealthy scrap merchant – very big, breaking up ships. All of a sudden Percy got a phone message: 'Get rid of the money.' It was in the cellar of his house. Percy had ample time to get it and drive it to a safe house, but his bottle went and he never did. He was too frightened even to drive it away. They searched Percy's place as he was a great friend of Alf's; you didn't have to be the brightest of people to work out who might have the money and, of course, they found it. 'Who does it belong to?' And he went and told them it was Alf's. Percy was found not guilty. He could easily have said it was his own money and that he was just trying to avoid tax; he knew our rules and regulations. So he wasn't very popular for a bit. He'd been well liked, so no one went and hurt him, but no one was going to get lumbered with him again either. Later he redeemed himself when Billy Hill was very ill. The black girl Bill had been living with had taken an overdose and Gypsy wasn't around so much, so Percy went and looked after him.

I worked quite a bit with Alf Fraser. He was intelligent and one of the gamest you could ever meet. What he did at Parkhurst in 1958 was a really good stunt. If you saved your visits when you were in Parkhurst or the Moor, you could go to your home town and have them all there. But you had to save all twelve; you couldn't just save six. Alfie came up from Parkhurst, and the 'Ville – where I was at this particular time – wasn't too bad. You could go in a cell and have a good chat. Jerry Callaghan and Nicky Kiley were also up from Dartmoor on their visits. That's when Alf told us he'd got this crooked screw; this was so we'd know he hadn't gone on the side of the authorities when it all came out. The trick was usually for the screw to lose his keys and a prisoner to find them, but Alf went one better. 'He won't lose his keys, but he'll drop his wallet which has his fortnight annual holiday money. I find it and hand it in.'

It may seem petty in the grander scheme of things, but it meant a lot. Those people who had PD only got a sixth remission, but it was always possible to get reclassified as an ordinary prisoner if you did something outstanding. This was Alf's way to get off PD and so get a third remission, and it worked.

He came out from doing that ten years and wasn't out too long before he was nicked going into some luxury flats in Belgravia with some keys. That dog Harry Rogers, with whom I had all that trouble in Brighton and who was trying to do me for demanding with menaces after I done a bit of arson for him, was going to be a witness for Alf and put up an alibi, but he let him down same as he let me down. Alf had to plead guilty and he got another five.

He died in 1976. His first wife had died while he was away and he'd remarried and was living down on the South Coast. One morning he went down to make a cup of tea and just collapsed.

Another really unlucky man was known as Aussie Joe the Bash. I forget what his real name was. Something like 1928, he did a jewellery snatch in the Haymarket in one of them little shops with fancy windows. It went off well and they was back in the car, but someone hadn't shut the door properly on its catch and when they turned round a corner at speed it flew open and the tom fell out. Ruby Sparks was on the first one with him, and so was Jim Turner – who was with Ruby when he was nicked and got five years' penal servitude followed by a straight five, ten in all, for doing Mappin and Webb, the jeweller's in Regent Street. Jim Turner got away from Wandsworth; he slung a rope over the wall and shinned up it with Ruby behind him. They pulled Ruby down and said who are you, and he had the presence of mind to say he was Jim which gave the man a two-day start. I think he was out about six months.

Thirty years later, Joe did the same shop again. This time he was with Teddy Gibbs, who was the brother of the burglar Charlie Gibbs. Joe did the windows and they were away in the car when a bus pulled over and blocked them. Teddy got nine years' PD; Joe got four because he was about 70 at the time and he hadn't done any bird for years.

About the unluckiest man I ever met was called Noller Knowles. I've no idea what his first name really was; he was just Noller to us all. He came from Notting Hill and I'd been in Borstal with him.

Noller had a girl with whom he split up, and now she was having it off with a Scotsman. There were roadworks up the Earl's Court Road at the end of 1949 or beginning of 1950, and I was driving with him past Earl's Court tube station, which is opposite Exhibition Hall, when he saw this Scotsman. He jumped out, picked up a tool from the roadworks and really done him. The guy nicked him for it, so now Noller was on the run.

He had a gun on him for protection, a revolver so big he couldn't get it properly in his pocket and so he had it with the muzzle pointed up. He was going to sell a bit of tom off the Portobello Road in Latimer Road where the railway bridge goes across the road. Noller was ringing the bell for the fence, and as always he had his hands in his pockets and he touched the trigger. There must have been something faulty with the gun. Anyway, the bullet went up through the mackintosh, took his nose off and went into his brain and killed him. There was a terrific funeral; he was a very popular man.

Paddington in its way was just as big for us as Soho, if not bigger, and the Bayswater Road's a long one – Marble Arch down to Queensway and even beyond – and in the Forties and Fifties every 10–15 yards there were brasses. There'd be two or three in a little group standing talking, and then about fifteen yards along another group. This was literally all day; they got there early in the morning, and they stayed till late at night. They rarely stood on the park side, which I think must have been an understanding with the police. I know there was a Norwegian Seamen's Mission nearby, but the girls' trade must have come from blokes in cars and they done their business in them. I never went with brasses, but guys I was driving along with would say, 'Slow down, I'm going to have that one,' and hop out of the car. It was a miniature Soho, with dives and spielers. In a way it was better than Soho. Where they were lucky, Soho was the known area where the hot light was on, whereas no one knew Bayswater except the punters who used it.

They weren't Messina girls.[11] Those had their apartments

---

[11] The Maltese-born Messina brothers ran vice in London from the 1940s until the 1960s and, after they were imprisoned and deported, still left a legacy behind them in the form of leases of flats and houses. A substantial contribution to their downfall was made by Duncan Webb, the crusading journalist from the *People*.

in Mayfair and Soho in narrow little streets like Shepherd's Market, whereas Bayswater was one long road. The girls there were mostly run by Malts. There were very few black people around in those days. In Notting Hill and Paddington there were the clubs. There was a hotel which had a club in it and still does; mostly renowned for Sunday-afternoon drinking, it is. When the pubs closed people steamed over there. You mostly went to a drinker and then on to a house for a party.

The pikies[12] were the ones who ran Notting Hill and Paddington. As I've said, Percy Horne was big there as well, and the Cannon brothers were very big too. Nobby Cannon is Joe Cannon's brother and so, I think, is Billy. Joe was a dog, and the other brothers dropped him out. He was the one who got recruited by Jack Spot to shoot Hilly and Albert when they were both acquitted after the fight in Frith Street, and he was the one I did in the nick because he was a grass. I tried to put his eye out, and if God had been with me that day I'd have done it.

You tend to think that London has all the best thieves, but it isn't so now. My experience with Liverpool used to be that they were just big dockers who got nicked for fighting and leaning on bookmakers. Stevie Porter was one of the governors in Liverpool in 1945. He got five years for leaning on a bookmaker, demanding with menaces. Steve was just like a strong-arm man; he wasn't a good thief, but in Scotland Road no one would go out of their way to upset him. Five years' penal servitude was a long stretch then.

Another man I knew from Liverpool I met in Broadmoor. Nobby Clarke had a hard life, flogged for mutiny during the War and again he got the cat in Liverpool in 1946 for rolling drunks, robbery with violence. He turned to forging post office books. In them days you could only get a small amount out at a time, but if you had a good team like I was on in London and enough books, then you could make a decent living. The penalties were high. If you got caught, you could expect some decent bird. His

[12]Strictly, pikies are gypsies from the old turnpikes they used. Over the years, a piker has come to mean a cheat.

partner had nicked stuff from him and so Nobby did him. The body wasn't found and then Nobby and his girl-friend went to the nick for passing the books. It was while he was inside they found the man's body[13]. So they did Nobby for murder. He got life and went a bit strange, so they put him in Broadmoor. That was when he went and killed another man, so they shipped him back to the prison system and he died at Parkhurst.

Where good-class thieving is concerned, the people from Liverpool didn't used to have a clue, but since them days they've come on a bundle. This was the general trend as the years went by, and they've improved tremendously. Years ago the top thieves were in London, and they recruited people from Newcastle and Scotland who had been miners and could use explosives. They would bring the explosives down and do the safes for you, but as a general rule that's all they were requested for; that and a bit of GBH. The London thief had never been brought up with explosives. When the War was over there were a few who had served in the Forces and so they had a better knowledge, but there weren't a great many of them.

More recently there have been some good ones from the North. Tommy Comerford was one. When he did that bank in Liverpool in the late 1960s or very early 1970s, it was outstanding. It was a clever inside job, very clever; a brilliant robbery. They got in through a secret passage left over from the First World War, opened up the strong-room and had a right touch in the safety deposit boxes. That was an all-Liverpool side. The next thing, though, he got nine plus for drugs. He was a very likeable guy, both in prison and out.

[13]John Whyte's body was found in a ditch near Nantwich, Cheshire on 16 May 1966. William John Clarke was convicted on a 10–2 majority at Chester Assizes, and his girl-friend Nancy Hughes received three years as an accessory. Clarke had already been in Broadmoor after slashing another prisoner with a broken bottle.

Ten

Like I've said, I was the youngest of five children. Three of us never got into any trouble at all, but I did and the sister next to me, Eva, she was a bit wild like me.

I was away when both my mother and my father died. My mother was a lovely hard-working lady; honest as they come, and gullible with it. When Eva and me nicked some and give it her, pretending we'd found it, she would thank the Lord for having such lucky children. She couldn't have thought we'd have been thieves.

It really hurt my mother and father when first I got nicked and then Eva. On the other hand the War was soon on, so people had other things to think about. Also, being a criminal wasn't so bad during the War in a way because it was a new world society-wise, not as restrained as before when you had to do this or that. The War opened up the floodgates. There was no unemployed and everyone had a job, so there was plenty of money about.

I wouldn't have my mother or father come and see me in prison. I never had a visit off anyone apart from Eva and later my wife, Doreen. Often they used to travel together. Not to the Isle of Wight because Doreen could just come over from Brighton; but if it was, say, Durham, they'd share the journey.

My mother died when I was in Norwich. This was in 1982, when she was about 85. I knew it was likely to happen and

I'd said I wanted to be quietly told on a visit. I said to Eva, don't make application for release. I didn't want to go on a visit handcuffed so the papers and the prison officers couldn't get any joy out of it. She had a big funeral; some of the Train robbers and Charlie Kray were there. Charlie Richardson and Patsy Murray, the nephew of Billy who's in the football photo with me, thought they was doing right sending a telegram saying condolences – they meant well. The screws rushed over to my cell saying, 'Telegram, Fraser. Your mother's dead.' Of course they'd read it and it seemed to me they were gloating. I said, 'You lying bastards, she's still alive,' and I chinned one and got put on report. This was 1982, as I said.

My father had died during the Parkhurst riot trial in June 1970, and they kept it from me until I was sent a bit later to Wakefield when Eva and Doreen told me quietly. I didn't want it in a letter, visits during the trial were very difficult, and they couldn't mouth it across the court. I don't know what I'd have done if they had. That's how I was, in the nick. I couldn't see any joy for fellows being taken in handcuffs to a funeral. When they get out, no matter how many years later, they can do that privately. It's an individual choice, but that's mine.

I first got back in touch with my sons when they were in prison. I'd not seen their mother Kathie in years and, like I said, I never wanted visitors from the family apart from Eva and then later Doreen. I didn't see them when I was out. They were only small when I got done for Spot, and I'd been in and out for the years before that. My first boy Frank was fifty-two in September. David was born in May 1947, then Patrick in January 1951; he'd only have been six. Then one by one they contacted me when they were in the nick themselves.

I messed up one visit with my eldest boy Frank. He was doing five years for some tom behind a false wall in his house when they arrested him over 'Operation Carter'. He's asked to see me and I'm at either Gloucester or Dorchester, I forget which, and he's in Long Lartin, which wasn't far and gave me a ride out. At that time I was on the travels: two months in a nick, and then on. The screws in some of the nicks could tolerate it. 'He's only going to be here two months and we'll leave him alone; give him a visit and that'll keep him quiet.' So I was taken out for the day, straight on to the visit and then taken straight back.

Long Lartin is geared up to long-term prisoners, and Frank got permission to have the visit in the solicitors' room with the screws sitting outside. There was a meal laid on for me and everything there. I'd arrived with mobs of screws, and they said I was to have it in the solicitors' room. But I said I wasn't going in because I thought there'd be this tiny cubicle with screws either side of us, and I wanted it in the proper visiting room where there'd be a bit of privacy; of course there'd be people all around, but there wouldn't be screws at your elbow. I said I wasn't going on the visit at all if it had to be in this cubicle, so they said, 'All right, have it in the visiting room.' I'd made a big mistake. When Frank was brought in he said, 'Dad, what you done?' He'd had a meal cooked and all. But it was too late to change things . . . Still, it was a lovely visit.

Both David and Patrick I saw in prison as well. Patrick was brought to see me at Canterbury, Cardiff and Winson Green in Birmingham. He was doing time for a security van when he got eleven years. David was sent to Wandsworth when he was doing seven when I was in the punishment block and Patrick, who was there as well – both of them was allowed to come on exercise with me on our own. No other prisoners were with us. I was in my carpet slippers, which I'd been wearing for years.

Frank's done three, four, five years and a twelve months. The three years was for a post office van; four when he was nicked for Bank of America in Davies Street in the West End which got done in both 1974 and 1975. The first time was a bit of a disaster, when more or less everything went wrong that could go wrong. They got in sweet all right, but they couldn't open the vault. They'd been given information by an electrician, Stephen Buckley, who worked in the bank. But when they got in, they found the drills couldn't get through the metals and the bits all broke off. Then there was someone outside, so they dropped the whole thing and went back for another go the next year. This time, quite by chance, the electrician had seen the combination locks on the vaults. No one in the bank had sussed that he'd put up the SP in the first place, and he was still employed there. There was some really heavy bird handed out. Peter Colson got a twenty-one and Leonard Wilde – although I never knew him as anything except Johnny the Bosch – got twenty-three.[1] Tony Gervaise was another who got a long stretch, and a bit after that he became a supergrass. The electrician Buckley copped it and gave evidence against all the rest; he got a six. Frank was lucky. He wasn't amongst the original ones who got nicked and he went to France. While he was there, he paid a very senior copper a lot of money to make sure he wasn't verballed up when he got arrested. Buckley had said Frank was only on the second one.

Frank was lucky. He'd never met the electrician, so the man couldn't say his name. What Buckley did say was that 'Tom Smith and John Brown, and I heard that Frankie Fraser was on it.' The gear had gone into the shop of a fellow called Jeffries who had a fruiterer's in the South Lambeth Road and who wasn't on the robbery. He also said my boy was on it. By the time Frank came back Jeffries wouldn't come and give evidence, and what the electrician said wasn't evidence. He had it slung out at the magistrates' court. All the others had been sentenced.

It was also said that Frank was on both the Williams & Glyn's Bank robbery in 1977 and the one at the *Daily Mirror* in March 1978, when a security guard got killed and the team got away with around £200,000. They didn't call George Copley 'The

---

[1]Johnny the Bosch was regarded as one of the great key-smiths of the English Underworld. 'John could watch a screw put a key in a lock and, with his photographic memory, go away and a few days later run up a duplicate in the prison workshop. He was not always spot on: he always made three slightly different duplicates. One invariably worked.' (Patrick Meehan, *Innocent Villain*, pp.63–4.)

Colonel' for nothing. It all went wrong for the pros when it was discovered that he had managed to tape some interviews and they didn't agree with the police version. When George was in prison on remand, he had either the big wad of depositions or a book hollowed out with a tape recorder got in to him. He had it with him when the officers interviewed him, and when they gave evidence about what was said it wasn't on the tapes. A copper had gone and made an offer that if he pleaded guilty and made a statement about some London detectives being corrupt, all he would get was five years. The people on those two robberies were meant to have paid over £80,000 in bribes to other coppers for getting bail. There were two other robberies they put against my boy and George Copley, and because of the tapes they couldn't proceed on those either. No one ever got convicted. In fact the only unlucky one on the whole thing was Alan Roberts, who got shot accidentally by his partner John Hilton when they were doing a jeweller in 1978; Hilton buried him on a railway line.[2]

It was when the police came to arrest Frank for those robberies that they found some tom behind a false wall in his house, and that's how he got a five, but it was better than going down on a blag. I'm glad to say that he's retired now. He's been a worker and he's looked after his money.

The Copleys were another family like the Brindles. All bits of them all over, and none as closely related as you might think. The other branch of the family was 'Cadillac Johnny' Copley whose real name was Edwin. He was killed when he smashed his car in a chase over Tower Bridge. His girl-friend, Fluffy, took up with George Porritt and there was a real family bust-up over it. There was a row in the Manor House Club near Wrotham and a whole crowd came round to the Porritt home. George Porritt, who was keen on weapons and had a whole

---

[2]Hilton, who had been sentenced to life imprisonment in 1963 for his part in the murder of a man during the Co-op dairy raid in Mitcham, received life imprisonment in September 1991. At the time of shooting Roberts and the jeweller, Leo Grunhut, Hilton was on licence. He was finally caught in a raid on another jewellers in Burlington Gardens, Piccadilly. He was 62 at the time.

arsenal in his bedroom, opened fire and killed his step-father by mistake. He was sentenced to death, but it got knocked down to manslaughter on appeal and he was given a ten. He was in Durham with me at one time. George then married Sheila, who was the daughter of Abe Tobias from Blackpool, and she went down in a raid in Manchester with Albert Redding from the East End. She had a baby-minder while she was driving on the wage snatch, and stupidly went and paid the girl with some of the stolen money. She got five years for that. She was a great friend to Eva when my sister was in the nick over the Torture trial case.

Cadillac Johnny's sister, Gladys, had an affair with John Parry, my friend, and she had a son named Gordon by him. Johnny then married a girl called Kitty Clarke. Although they hadn't been together for years when Johnny Parry died – or Gladys, maybe the other way about – the other one died twenty-four hours later. Gordon Parry, the boy, was one of the ones nicked for the Brinks-Mat receiving and went down. I'd have hoped Kitty could have helped Gordon more by saying all the money he had come from his father, but she didn't.

The Copleys had been a bit unlucky in the late 1940s when they were nicked on a tie-up which was, in fact, nothing to do with them, and one of my great pals had done. They were with Cyril Clark at the time. Cyril and Johnny Copley got eighteen strokes of the birch and eight years penal servitude each, and another brother got five. Cyril Clark, who was no relation to Kitty, married Gladys Copley. He was mixed up in the Hanratty case somehow.[3]

---

[3]The Hanratty case has been one of the *causes célèbres* over the last forty-five years. Hanratty was convicted of the killing of Michael Gregsten on 22 August 1961. The prosecution's case was that he had come across Gregsten and Valerie Storey, who were having an affair, whilst they were parked in a beauty spot in Dorney Reach. He had forced Gregsten to drive through the Home Counties before shooting him on the A6 and then raping and shooting Miss Storey. She identified him and there was dubious supporting evidence. Hanratty called a patently false alibi before saying he had been in Rhyl at the time of the shooting. He was hanged on 4 April 1962, since which time there has been a sustained campaign to show not only that he was innocent but that another named man was the murderer.

I was in the chokey in Durham with James Hanratty when he was doing four years' corrective training, and I've always thought he was innocent of the Gregsten murder. I've always said this, that it wouldn't have been in him. There's no doubt that there was a lot of sympathy for the girl who was raped and shot, and quite rightly so, but she'd already made one wrong ID. I think nowadays perhaps she'd have had a harder time in the witness box, but then again it might have antagonised the jury. When I went down in the Parkhurst case, if I'd let Mr Shindler defend me he'd have been rougher on the screws – but it might have upset people and I'd have been worse off. That's the trouble, you can't tell until it's over.

My son David got Borstal and come out when he was about 19. Then he got seven years over a security van in 1970. The brief George Shindler prosecuted him, and my solicitors wanted him to defend me in the Parkhurst riot. Mr Shindler rang up the prison from his chambers because he thought I ought to know and I said, regretfully, that I couldn't see my way clear to having a man who'd done my son. He explained how barristers prosecute one day and defend the next, and it means nothing to them; they try equally for everyone. But I couldn't bring myself to have him. David's next was fourteen years for a tie-up robbery of an Arab and an airline chief, but it was a ready-eye and the law was on them. On appeal the sentence got dropped to eleven. That was in 1984.

His last thing was sheer misfortune. He got caught up in the middle between a crooked copper and a grass who's tried to row himself out at the expense of anyone he's ever seen. The grass said that David had been dealing in cannabis, and what was worse he said it was on my behalf. There wasn't a shred of evidence against me. No copper ever came round to question me even though I was living not a mile away from where David got nicked. The grass was called Kevin Cressey and John Donald, the copper, was deputed to mind him after he said he'd help out. Cressey'd been found with about 55 kilos of cannabis, and he kept giving Donald money to stay out on bail and to get hold of one of his files. I think Cressey was willing to put up £40,000 to get the drugs destroyed. When it didn't go according to plan, Cressey went to the BBC and was filmed having a talk with Donald. David had known Cressey and because of this he got caught up with the whole thing. He was nicked at the beginning of September 1992 and eventually he got bail. The charges were dropped at the magistrates' court and he went to live in Spain. Then he had another bit of bad luck. He was in a car which belonged to another man, and it was a ringer. There was a gun in the motor as well. David was arrested, and he was found not guilty, but whilst he was in custody, lo and behold, they decided to re-open things and had him arrested over there, and he was in prison there for years before they got him back here. He was in Belmarsh for another couple of years, then he went on trial in September of last year. He must have been in custody one way and another for four years before he ever set foot in the Old Bailey.

I went to see him while he was in prison in Madrid. It was a pleasure. There was the usual security but after that I was locked in a cell with him – bed, shower, toilet, armchair. If a woman come, all they asked was she bring her own sheets. There was no peeping through the spyhole either, we were completely isolated. At the end of the three hours there was a knock on the door and it was over. We was searched on the way out as well and funnily there was no tea or coffee, but over the forty years I've been in prison I've never had a visit nowhere near as good. We should copy it.

When the case finally did get to court, David didn't call any witnesses. It didn't seem there was no need to – it was so weak, the case against him, there was really nothing to answer. They'd really mullered the pros's case[4]. The judge sent the jury out on the Thursday and we expected them to come straight back and chuck it out. They'd only been out about ten minutes, and they come back and asked for a blackboard with the names of the police on it. Then they went out for about four hours and then the judge, she sent them out overnight. That's when I started to worry.

If you haven't got a good case, then for the jury to go out overnight that's great; but if you've a good case, it's not so good. I thought two hours would be about right. Then when they were out all Friday I knew things were going wrong, and in the end he got an eight. Cressey, the grass, got a four to add to the seven he was already doing, and I can't say I'm sorry. The copper, John Donald, pleaded guilty half-way through his own trial, which took place a while back, and got an eight.

When I started, the prosecution used to get the last word summing up if you give evidence and called witnesses, but they changed that in the 1960s. Now the English system seems fair, but all that happens is the judge sums up a bit more against you than he would have done. He's a bit fiercer in his summing-up. The jury's left with his words; they're the ones ringing in their ears. I only wish the English courts had someone like that Boston judge in that Louise Woodward baby case. He was brave in the legal sense. He give the right verdict. If anything, he was 100 per cent with the girl.[5]

Some of the family has done really well. Jamie Brindle, Eva's son, is a lovely boy. He's a credit to Eva and his dad.

---

[4]To muller means to destroy and can be used as in, 'He mullered the prosecution evidence' or more simply, 'He mullered a plate of bacon and eggs.' The verb does not appear in any dictionary of criminal slang, but probably comes from South London. It is used by Shirley Pitts in her *Gone Shopping*.

[5]In November 1997 Louise Woodward, a 19-year-old English au pair, stood trial for the murder in Boston, Mass. of Matthew Eappen. After certain counts had been withdrawn from the consideration of the jury by her lawyers she was convicted of second-degree murder, which meant a minimum sentence of fifteen years before she could apply for parole. There was a campaign in the English press for her release and the trial judge, as is possible in Massachusetts, quashed the conviction, substituted one of manslaughter and ordered her to be released with time served.

He had that good amateur boxer Johnny Cheshire helping him as a trainer, when he had the Henry Cooper gym in the Old Kent Road. That heavyweight who became world champion and lost to Lennox Lewis, Henry Akawainde, trained down there. Marilyn was very good. She got hold of some old boxing photos like the last night at Harringay with Eric Boon and Freddie Mills and Bruce Woodcock, and we gave them to Jamie.

The other one who's done really well has been Jimmy Fraser, my brother's oldest. He got done twice and was innocent both times. The first time was with Challenor, the bent copper in Soho who fitted him up, and he did fifteen months; and the second when he pleaded guilty at the end of the Torture trial so he could be let out there and then. He has the Tin Pan Alley Club now, but before that he bought the A. & R. off Ronnie Knight when Ronnie was having that bit of bother over the Zomparelli killing.[6] Funnily, of all the people I knew, I never knew Ronnie Knight that well.

As for Patrick, he got three months very young, then much later he got six years in the case where Greville Starkey, the jockey, gave evidence. By that time Patrick had already done an eleven for a security van.

At the end of the 1980s he became involved with a fellow called James Laming and a couple of Peruvians called Black. What happened was that this René Black fancied himself as a show-jumper, and his brother wanted to be a racing-car driver,

---

[6]The Artists and Repertoire Club in the Charing Cross Road passed through a number of hands – or perhaps faces is a better word. Ronnie Knight was acquitted of the murder of Tony Zomparelli who had earlier received four years for killing David Knight (Ronnie's brother) at the Latin Quarter night-club. The evidence against Knight and Nicky Gerard was that of a potential supergrass Maxie Piggott. David Knight had been badly beaten in a fight in Islington and on 7 May 1970 Ronnie Knight had taken him to the Latin Quarter to ask for an explanation when fighting broke out and Zomparelli stabbed him. Piggott alleged that Knight had paid him and Nicky Gerard to kill Zomparelli, who was shot at the Golden Goose Amusement Arcade in Soho on 4 September 1974. Both were acquitted. Knight, the one-time husband of the actress Barbara Windsor, later went to Spain after the Security Express robbery for which his brother John received twenty-two years. He later returned to England and served five years for dishonestly handling part of the proceeds.

but the thing René was best at was being a grass. He'd got caught trying to bring in a load of cocaine, and to get himself a lighter sentence when he came up at Southwark in 1990 he said Laming was his distributor and that Patrick was involved with him as well. I'm glad to say it didn't help him all that much, because he got fifteen and the judge confiscated £1.5 million.

Laming's defence was a good one, I'll give him that. He said he wasn't dealing with Black and his cocaine, but was trying to work a swindle in the horse-racing. He'd devised an ultrasonic gun which – if you pointed it at a horse and fired – would cause it to swerve or stumble. Greville Starkey had come off at the front of the field in the King's Stand Stakes at Ascot, and this Laming was saying that proved it worked. He got Starkey to let him try it out in a paddock with Starkey's little girl up on a pony, and it worked again. The jury wouldn't have it though, and Laming got a nine and Patrick had a six. He got chucked from the conspiracy.

Whilst all this was going on Laming's partner, John Lane, got shot in the back. Lane had been nicked along with Laming at his Holborn flat when there was the swoop, but he'd been let go. Then Lane's great friend Lionel Webb got shot as well. He'd been dealing drugs out of his office somewhere in North London, and they found that his safe was stuffed with them.

I'm pleased to say Patrick's called it a day now as well.

As I said before, my youngest, Francis Jnr, did really well at school and sport. He was never in a day's trouble. I don't know what sociologists make of it, but three of them never saw me when they were kids and they all got into real trouble, while the fourth had me whisked away when he was still young and he never did.

Between the others, they've got a lot of bird. A couple of the grandchildren who are brothers have kept the flag flying; they got a bit of bird early on, but it has put them right off. Out of eleven grandchildren, they're the only two who've ever got in bother and not serious bother at that. Let the side down really. The oldest grandchild will be twenty-seven, and I've got one great-granddaughter. I'm back in touch with the family properly and see them whenever I can.

Eleven

When I come out of doing the sentence for the counterfeit coins I used to go down my nephew Jimmy's the Tin Pan Alley Club and there, quite by chance, I met Marilyn, the daughter of Tommy Wisbey. From there on the rest is history, because we've been together almost from that moment. Sometimes I think she's what keeps me young. She's a wonderful girl, got a really good voice and a bundle of personality, and she wants to write her own memoirs. She's been enough places, known enough people and done enough things to be able to write them as well, so what follows is something like a trailer for them.

I've got a first-class criminal pedigree. My dad is Tommy Wisbey, one of the Great Train Robbers, and my godfather is Freddie Foreman who was acquitted of the Curtain Road Security Depot robbery[1] but did ten years for helping clean up after the Jack 'The Hat' McVitie shooting. Our families used to go on holidays now and again together. My mum used to tell us stories when Greg Foreman and I were

[1] The Great Bank Note raid took place over the Easter Bank Holiday 1983 when the headquarters of Security Express were raided and £7 million was stolen. Allen Opiola was arrested and turned Queen's Evidence. He received three years and three months. Ronnie Knight's brother, John, received twenty-two years for the robbery, as did Terry Perkins. James Knight received eight years for dishonest handling and William Hickson who had once been accidentally shot by 'Colonel' George Copley, was sentenced to six years. Foreman received nine years also for dishonest handling of part of the proceeds.

179

babies about when Mum and Dad and Fred and his wife Maureen were all young. When Fred was away over the McVitie thing I used to go and work in Maureen's pub, the Prince of Wales in Lant Street.

Before the Train we were living on the Elmington estate in Camberwell. Dad was a bookmaker. He'd only ever had one conviction, and that was when he got three months over a load of LP records.

The weekend of the Train was August Bank Holiday 1963. I was eight at the time and my sister, Lorraine, was fifteen months younger. Mum was told to take us down to my Nan's chalet in Leysdown. It was the in-place for working-class people on the Isle of Sheppey. There were amusements and a funfair; things like that. Dad was skint and gave my mum his last £20.

He didn't tell her it was the Train as such, but he said he had to disappear for the weekend. Mum knew something was up. Apparently he'd been telling her he was going on 'a big one'. There'd also been a lot more of his friends coming round to the flat. Lorraine and I had been told not to go to our toy cupboard, which was behind an armchair in the living room

I remember on the Friday and Saturday at Leysdown I kept walking past a novelty shop which sold kids' toys and games and tricks, and I kept crying because there was a nurse's uniform I wanted and my Mum told me she couldn't afford it. She told me later she was saying under her breath, 'Wait until Tuesday,' but if I heard I didn't understand. Those first four days we had to make do with sausage, beans and chips, but from the Tuesday on we had fillet steak. Mum would just load up the trolley in the supermarket. Dad had come down the early hours of Tuesday morning and he gave Mum £500 in an empty John Player cigarette packet. I never saw him that night and he went away for a bit to Spain. After that I kept asking where Daddy was and Mum said, 'He's joined the Army.'

I don't remember the police coming round, but I know Mum was upset afterwards because she'd left a postcard from Dad on the mantelpiece which he'd sent from Callafel. She told them she was finished with him and he'd gone off with a younger woman, but they never believed her.

Then when things died down he came back, until one day it was on the radio that he'd been nicked. All he'd done was gone down the betting shop he had then. When they were captured I remember all their photos in the *Evening News*, with noughts and noughts across the page giving the estimated value of what they'd had. Mum took the paper away from me and said, 'Don't worry,' but of course I did. Mum didn't take me to the trial; she thought he'd only get 10–15 years, which was pretty stiff in itself. Once he'd been found guilty Daddy hadn't wanted her to go for the sentencing, and she was hoovering the stairs when the news come through. Gill Hussey, whose husband Jim was also on the Train, was with us and she shouted up, 'They've got thirty years,' and Mum thought it meant the total for all of them. When she heard it was just Daddy, she fell down the rest of the stairs.

There was an empty feeling when Daddy got sent away. Of course we knew it was likely; Mum had prepared us. I was more concerned about her really, but I think it's true what they say – if they've got one good parent children can knuckle down in a situation, and we just got on with it.

Over the years she took me and Lorraine visiting to see Dad, and we had to take time off school. I remember meeting Violet and Charlie Kray Snr and Harry Roberts' mum, Dolly. She was a lovely woman. Harry got life for shooting those police in Shepherd's Bush, and he's done over thirty years now. I think that's more than long enough and he should be released.[2] The visits for the first year were closed with a pane of glass between, and then there was a small cell-like room with a ledge with Dad across from us and screws on either side. That went on for about two years, and then there were open visits. The majority of the time we went on our own, but sometimes we went with Dad's brothers or his Mum and Dad, always by train. We'd get up early in the morning, say 6 a.m., and leave to go to Durham, Hull, wherever. The visits would be over by 4, and then we'd get the train back. We'd get home 11, 12 o'clock at night. It was a long day. Mum only missed two visits in twelve and a half years.

Once we went up to Durham in the snow. I'd been given a jigsaw from Harrods, and in the hurry changing trains I dropped it on the platform and Mum wouldn't let me pick it up in case we missed the connection. When we got to Durham, we were ten minutes early for the visit and it was snowing heavily. Mum knocked on the gate, and when a screw opened it he said we was early and we had to wait outside. Mum knew there would be a fire in the waiting room, but we just stood there with her coat pulled round us, huddled together in a blizzard, till the time come and they let us in.

I took Daddy a toy casino game once, but the screws wouldn't let me give it to him. They said I had to get written permission. Mum said that although it was my birthday I wanted Daddy to have a present, but it made

[2]In November 1958 Harry Roberts attacked and robbed a 79-year-old man who died a year and three days after the incident. Under the existing law, a murder charge could not be brought, and Roberts received seven years for manslaughter. After his release he teamed up with John Duddy and John Witney to carry out a series of small-time robberies. In June 1966 they were on their way either to steal a car to facilitate another robbery or to rob a rent collector – accounts vary – when they were stopped by the police because the car they were driving had an out-of-date tax disc. Roberts shot and killed the two police officers who were questioning him. The third officer was shot by John Duddy, who was himself the son of a police officer; he died in prison. The third member, John Witney, was released in 1992. Caught after a long manhunt, Roberts received life imprisonment; campaigns for his release have been steadily opposed by the police.

no difference. We never bothered to write to the Governor about the toy casino.

Some of the screws were decent but a lot of them, they used to make their own rules up. Prison Governors have a lot to put up with, because the men that are underneath them are the ones who really run the prisons and the P.O.s make their own rules to suit themselves.

What Mum and Lorraine and me hated is what still goes on today. A woman maybe has two kids; she has to go on public transport and she travels all the way to see her husband or son, and she's not been notified they've been moved. There's no reason for it, especially now when there's all these computers inside the prison service. They could easily let the people know.

During the twelve years Dad was away, I would think this happened about six times. You wouldn't know until you got there that they'd moved him in the early hours of the morning, and they wouldn't tell them where they was going either. After Ronnie Biggs escaped, they locked them all up twenty-three hours a day and Daddy got on the roof at Leicester to protest about the conditions, which were already bad but even worse after the escape. That's when Dad lost some of his remission and he got bread and water for his trouble.

A bit ago we went to see Frank's grandson Paul, Patrick's boy, who was in Belmarsh on remand. We were queuing up to get in, and there was a coloured woman with a little boy and she was told her son had been moved to somewhere from Belmarsh, and they'd never told her. It's maybe not so bad if you live fairly local, but even then it's a strain and a struggle; but when you've gone all the way North and find he's been moved, it's just not right. Frank mentioned this to the prison chaplain, who happened to be in the reception area. He said surely in this day and age it doesn't need to go on.

Then there was a time when Dad was in Leicester and

he asked Frank if he would pour the tea out as, 'Renée's coming up with the two girls.' Frank said to me, 'You know you've got the best Dad in the world.' I said, 'You don't need to tell me. I know I have.' It was the first time I ever met Frank.

Mum always said I'd end up with one of Daddy's friends. I told her I wish you'd said I'd end up with a rich solicitor.

At primary school, before the Train, I used to like drama and I was picked to play the second lead in *West Side Story*. Afterwards, except for visiting Daddy we never missed a day of school. Looking back, school plays a major role in growing young people from the age of kindergarten to the age of seventeen. It does prove a little bit that the environment of the school can help bring kids up right.

I never got much help after the Train. Neighbours would draw back the curtains and there'd be whispering. It was always in the back of my mind that Dad was away. Because of the high media attention I used to say 'Wisbey' in a soft tone if I had to give me name to anybody. If I put my hand up in class I would never be picked. I wanted to be a prefect, but my impression was that I wasn't made one because of the stigma.

I just never got picked for anything any more, except by one teacher who was Polish and she taught us English at Westwood School for Girls in Upper Norwood. She had a lot of sympathy for me. Before Westwood we went to a private school, because Dad had put a bit of his money away, and we had a year there. Neither of us liked it there. I used to play up and be a bit of a comedienne, making the other kids laugh, pulling funny faces and imitating the teachers behind their backs. But I did love the private school drama class.

I was smacked across the hands with a blackboard ruler for the mimicking. It was the maths teacher. Me and Ronnie Oliffe's daughter, Christine, were sitting in the back row, repeating everything he said after him. When the teacher said the children repeating me are to stand up, the kids in front turned round and give the game away. We had to come to the front and got five strokes on each hand.

Funnily enough, quite a few people in the private school were the children of 'faces', so we weren't isolated. There was the odd remark made in the playground. Once my sister was in a group playing in a ring with the usual questioning. 'What does your dad do?' And the answers came postman, painter and so on. When it got to Lorraine she said, 'He's a train robber and he's fucking handsome.'

The first time I ever sung in public, it was at a party given by Charlie and Eddie Richardson when I was 6. They had a warehouse in Addington Square and they did a lot of charity work for the kids, and they arranged old people's coach trips to Southend. I got up and sang, 'If I knew you were coming I'd have baked a cake.' In a way they got me started.

Of course I knew all the families from round the Elephant, but a different generation from the ones Frank knew. Olive Cornell was a really nice person. You'd never hear her moan. I admired her when she went round to the Krays; that took a lot of courage. She had cancer and died about five years ago. I grew up with her son Billy and Rayner, her daughter. I know Frank went, but I didn't go to Ronnie's funeral. It was out of respect for Olive and George and the children. I remember seeing George on the corner of Southampton Way when he was into scrap metal with Eddie and Charlie. It was near where me and my sister went to get our sweets. I was about 12, and dying to be a teenager so I'd buy stockings instead of sweets.

When I was 18 I trained to be a croupier at the Knightsbridge Sporting Club. I got my gaming licence and then I decided to try and get a job at the Playboy, but they refused my licence – I think due to my name and because of Dad. Then the Playboy went and lost their own licence. It was ironic, but that was the end of me as a croupier.

I grew up in my teens with Peter and Mickey Hennessey. They came in our pub – Mum owned it while Dad was away – the Alliance in Peckham in Sumner Road, and I used to go to Harry Hayward's pub the Harp of Erin in Deptford. The Sansoms were also great friends. One of the troubles with them is that they all seem to have the same Christian names, generation after generation, so it's very difficult to know who you're talking about!

Terry Jnr[3], who was a cousin of Kenny Sansom the footballer, used to go out with my sister. His dad Freddie died in Hull prison where he was doing time for a jump-up robbery. He got put away with Mark Owens, who was on the Parkhurst riot with my Frank. I was 17 or 18 at the time. I didn't really know the full strength of it then, but I thought he died of an epileptic fit. Later I learned it was because of the beatings he'd had.

Then I started going out with Michael Corbert, who played for Charlton Reserves when Theo Foley was the manager. His father had very bad eyes, and although he could actually see a bit he was known as 'Blind Tom' Corbert. He had a good voice. He died only a couple of years ago.

It was Guy Fawkes night 1971 and Roger Cordery – who was the first from the Train to be released – knew Jonathan King, and he sent a couple of guys from the recording label to hear me sing at the Chinbrook pub in Grove Park. I was getting quite well known locally at the

---

[3]In January 1961 his uncle Terry Sansom Snr was charged with the murder of James Hawney, who received a fractured skull when £9,000 was stolen from a London Transport bus transporting wages. The evidence was that of identifying witnesses, and in April that year after the trial judge warned of the dangers of such evidence Sansom was acquitted along with another man who had been charged with being an accessory.

time, singing ballads. After I'd done the numbers, they went off and the rest of us left to go on to my uncle's. Me and Mum went in one car, and my sister got in with Terry and Michael and two cousins of ours. I said we'd meet them up at Upper Norwood. They said they'd drop my cousin off, but on the way they hit a lamp-post when they skidded on some leaves at Nunhead Road. Michael, who was driving, died instantly; my sister was in intensive care in King's College with brain and chest injuries. The other three survived, though one of my cousins had plates in his leg and head afterwards.

I was working as a junior secretary for *Weekend Magazine* then. The editor was David Hill, and he was very good. He volunteered if I needed a car to go and visit Lorraine, gave me time off work, and we both got a lot of support from our jobs.

My Dad was allowed to visit her from Parkhurst, but he wasn't allowed out for the funeral. She lived just two weeks, and she died on 19 November. Lorraine was working as a junior secretary for the *Daily Express* editor, and they sent a really nice wreath. Dad got just ten minutes with Mum when he came to the hospital.

Ronnie Biggs' wife, Charmian, sent a lovely letter to Mum and me. Her boy Nicky had been killed in a road accident as well.

The authorities had allowed Myra Hindley out for a day's walk across Hampstead Heath about that time, but Dad wasn't allowed out. I wrote to the *Evening News* complaining it was all wrong, and then I went on television and was interviewed by Eamonn Andrews who had a programme about 6 o'clock. That solicitor Victor Lissack was on the show saying that because my dad was top security he shouldn't be out. I'd written prior to that to the Home Secretary, Reginald Maudling, but it did no good. There was Myra Hindley who helped to murder all them little children being allowed out, yet all my dad had done was rob the money. Terry Jnr died just a year after my sister; he'd been heartbroken. His body was found in the Thames off the Embankment; it was never clear whether he fell or slipped or what.

For a time I sort of went into a decline, and so did my Mum. She badly wanted another child to replace Lorraine, and she knew she'd be too old by the time Daddy came out. She even wrote to the Home Secretary to ask if she could have a conjugal visit, but of course she got knocked back. Another prisoner's wife, not from the Train, had been knocked back a couple of years earlier, and they weren't going to do my Mum and Dad no favours. All through their sentences the Train robbers were of media interest, and after Lorraine died we were human interest news. The reporter from the *News of the World* approached Mum and, in a way, words were really put a bit into her mouth. But there again, it helped publicise the outrageous sentences of thirty years because the visit wasn't permitted. When I was 19, I fell pregnant. I didn't want to get married at that time but I wanted to have a baby, and I said to my Mum, 'The baby I'm having will be for you and Daddy.' My Jonathan was wanted. His dad was the first man I really fell in love with. Jonathan was wanted for all of us. I had him when I was 20 and that's what he was, a much wanted baby. When he was born, all the screw done was put a bit of paper under Dad's cell door which read, 'By the way, your daughter's had a little boy.'

The very first time I went to America, I was 22. I'd met an American guy who was over here and he told me he owned a Christmas tree farm. When he went back to America he kept writing, and he invited me out and met me at San Francisco airport. I'd left Jonathan with my Mum and I went for six weeks. The idea was we should tour the States together. I thought we'd be living in luxury hotels, but no such luck; what he had was a small camper van. He didn't seem to have any money to go with it either, because I was spending for everything. I soon ditched him at Fort Worth, packed my stuff and left. Then I went on to Florida on pot luck before coming home.

I think it was just before then that Mum got the Trafalgar pub in Islington. This was just before Dad came out in 1976, and I was working there full-time and singing when I could get the work. When Mum and Dad went for a holiday to America after he came out, they left me in charge, but Dad rang up his friend Alfie Gerard to help me out if there was any trouble and there was. I let it go the first couple of nights but there was a father and son causing trouble. I was going out with Jimmy Wooder's nephew, Eddie, at the time and they were digging him out across the bar and winding him up, and they knocked him about a bit later on. The third night they were still being aggressive, and I rang Alf who came straight over. He just got hold of the younger one, held him up and said, 'Don't upset my pal's daughter when he's on holiday.' Alf looked like that American actor James Cagney, but far bigger. He had this restaurant over Southwark Park Road, and his conger eel and mash with parsley sauce was blinding.

He was a real old-fashioned gentleman like his mates Jerry Callaghan and Ruby Sparks. When I was young, Ruby used to sell nice gold chains in the City Club in the City Road where I used to help out. I wasn't earning a lot, and I couldn't afford a particular chain I fell in love with and which Ruby wanted £40 for, but he went and knocked £20 off it for me.

I had my 21st birthday party at the Leigham Court in Streatham, and some bastard rang up and said there was a bomb in the hotel just because he hadn't been invited. Shirley Pitts got me my dress; my hair was red at the time, and it was an oyster-pink ball gown. She hoisted it for me and sold it ever so cheap. I think I only had to pay her the cab money.

Now I was getting bored in London, so when an English gypsy called Kelly who had a hotel in Palm Springs came up and offered me a job I jumped at it. He'd heard me singing in the pub, and he wanted someone to manage a restaurant he was opening. He said he'd get me a work permit and green card, but it never materialised and so I was an illegal immigrant.

Kelly had changed his mind because he'd employed two Canadians in the bar-restaurant and they ended up stealing all his kitchen equipment and having him over for about $30,000. I stayed over there, green card or not, and I used to sing in restaurants and bars if I could get work. One of them was Pattie-z, and Frank Sinatra sometimes went there where I met his valet-cum-housekeeper 'Greek' Arturo. Sinatra once bought a $3,000 hearing aid for him. Later Dad, Mum and I met Sinatra in Rancho Mirage just outside Palm Springs.

It was while I was there I had a really nasty time in Los Angeles, where I was working as a waitress. I met this man and went out with him, then I went back to his place for coffee and it was a really bad experience. I said I wanted to ring my friend and I asked where the phone was. He said, 'Through that door,' and as I opened it he hit me on the head with a hammer and then he started to try and strangle me. He got me on the bed and I fought with him, rolling over the bed and the floor. My acrylic nails and my own nails came off trying to scratch his eyes out.

Then suddenly he stopped. I didn't scream and I just talked to him, calming him down, saying I wouldn't go to the police and he should just talk to me. Finally I said we'd go out for a drink. By this time my face was swelled up like a football and anyone who saw us in a bar would know something had happened, but he went along with it. Once we was in the car he made me drive him from San Fernando to Long Beach, which was about 60 miles away. I noticed a few police cars and I was thinking of pulling over to them when he said to pull over and we went into a gas station. He got out and I locked his door; then when he was away I rang my friend and she said wait by the phone box, lock the car doors, and she would phone the police and they would come for me.

I ended up in hospital. I had stitches in my mouth and my skull was badly bruised. I took a good beating; in fact, I was very lucky to be alive. I gave a full description of him to the police and I was taken to the Los Angeles Police Department. It turned out he was wanted for three bad assaults in three different states. They told me his name was Tony Wade. They were pleased I came forward and gave a very good description. They said he was apparently a homosexual woman-hater, an ex-Vietnam veteran. I've no idea if he was ever caught or what happened to him. After that I packed up and went back to Palm Springs, and I never heard. To be honest I don't think he was homosexual, just a maniac woman-hater.

I also sang at the Ingleside Inn with a Jewish piano player called Joe. It was there I met an ex-police chief of Mexico City, Arturo Durazo Moreno. He was so handsome; he would have been in his early fifties, and he looked a ringer for Anthony Quinn. He lived up in Bel Air and he used to come down every weekend to see me. He was very kind, a lovely man. I didn't realise he was hookey until there was a two-page article about him in the *You* magazine which comes with the *Mail on Sunday*. The paper said he had $380 million of American money but he didn't give any of it to me. What he did give me though was a great big gold medal from the Mexico City police and a beautiful 50-peso gold coin. Thank God for pawnshops. It's been in and out for years!

Then we came to Europe for a tour, first class all the way. We toured all over Sweden, Germany, Denmark and ended up in Marbella. I was hoping to introduce him to my godfather Fred, but I couldn't get hold of him. I only

stayed at the Marbella Beach Club a weekend. I thought
we'd be staying longer, then I said to Arturo that I wanted
to go and visit my family and he said come over for my
birthday on 3 January. This would be early December.
It was the year the Brinks-Mat went off, which was the
reason he never made it to London. He thought quite
wrongly that my Dad was involved, and because he was
in exile he didn't want to get mixed up. That was the last I
saw of him. I left him at Malaga airport and I never heard
another word, but I heard from a friend in Beverly Hills
that he was doing time in a Mexican jail. He had been
finally caught in Puerto Rico, and the Mexican authorities
had wanted to shoot him but he ended up doing time. I sent
a letter to a prison in Mexico, but it was returned. I was
very disappointed; I'd love to meet him again, though.[4]

When I never heard from Arturo, I decided not to go
back to California and I just left a BMW and apartment
over there. Back home I opened a flower stall in Covent
Garden just by the Colonnades; it's called My Fair Lady.
That's when I was asked to present the Queen and the
Duke with a bunch of flowers because they was opening
Jubilee Hall. The top man, a Mr Turner from the Covent
Garden team, was from Aylesbury of all places. He asked
me to do it; I didn't say who I was, though.

Little did he know! The press would have made a field

---

[4]Arturo Durazo Moreno was Mexico City's police chief from 1976 to 1982.
During his time as Chief of Police he had earned approximately $200 a month,
on which salary he managed his opulent lifestyle including a string of racehorses.
It was estimated that during his tenure as police chief he had paid $7.8 million into
bank accounts in Canada and San Diego. When questioned about his wealth, he
admitted to having other sources of income.

Wanted for extortion and illegal possession of weapons, he was on the run
for two years. When in 1984 his wife had been traced to a house in Montreal,
she said her husband and 22-year-old son were in Paris. He was finally captured
in Puerto Rico in 1984 and extradited from the United States to Mexico on
31 March 1986. Moreno, who was alleged to have headed a drug ring, had
been a childhood friend of the former President Jose Lopez Portillo. Back in
Mexico, Moreno's cell in prison was said to have been as lavishly furnished
as his mansion in Zihuatenejo. Sentenced to 25 years, he was released in 1992
at the age of 70. He was said to have rejoined his wife in California.

day of it. I was told she wouldn't talk to me, and all I had to do was curtsey and say, 'Happy Birthday, Ma'am.' But she did speak, asking me who I was. I looked left to right, thinking she's talking to someone else, but when I realised it was to me I was so gobsmacked that through nerves I just blurted out, 'You loaned my Dad some money once.'

I got married in 1987, but it was a great mistake. His stag night and my hen night was the night of the hurricane, 16 October. The marriage didn't last much longer than the storm itself. He was a jeweller from South London, a very straight man and very boring. I just felt I wanted to get married because I was being left on the shelf. The family came to the wedding. If they're disappointed in me, they don't say much; they let me get on with things. Sometimes I think I'm the black sheep.

Then in 1988 I started going with Albert Moffat, from Glasgow. He was a shoplifter really. His proper claim to fame was that he was the first man to cut Dennis Nilsen – he did it in the Scrubs. He was prosecuted but it was slung out. He said he'd been repelling Nilsen's homosexual advances, and when he done so Nilsen took a piece of metal to him. He gone and called him a big poof as well. Albert was only 21 when that happened.[5]

I was expecting Albert's baby, but we'd split up and I wasn't going to have it, so I went to see the doctors at University College Hospital about a termination. I was feeling very tired when I got back to the flat and I was having a lie-down when the police sledge-hammered the door down; I was arrested and charged with possessing drugs which were found in my flat. I got questioned and

[5]Dennis Nilsen lured a series of young men to his flat in Muswell Hill, a north London suburb, in the early 1980s and killed them, cooking parts of their bodies and disposing of the remainder in the drains. He was arrested in 1983 after neighbours complained of the smell. Found guilty on a 10–2 majority after the defence argued that he was incapable of forming the intent to murder, he was sentenced to life imprisonment with a recommendation he serve not less than 25 years. He should not be confused with Donald Neilson, the so-called Black Panther.

so did Mum, but neither of us would say anything. We were both charged, along with my Dad and with Jimmy Hussey who was on the Train with him.

I was in Holloway for two weeks. I was put in a mother-and-baby unit and the food was terrible. I began to worry that I'd go over the time for a termination, and kept asking the doctors what was happening about my booking for the hospital because I was afraid if they didn't do something I'd have to be pregnant. They kept me waiting to give me an appointment for the UCH to go in the last week it was safe.

I was woken at 4 in the morning to go to UCH. I didn't have nothing to eat or drink of course, and my operation didn't take place until 2 in the afternoon. I was kept in handcuffs and the screws who were with me wanted to come into the operating theatre, but the doctors wouldn't stand for it. When I came round I was really hungry, and there they were sat with their sandwiches. One of them said, 'You don't mind us eating, do you?' I said, 'No, don't worry, I'll be eating a decent meal in a minute' – meaning hospital food, not the disgusting stuff you got in Holloway. And I did get one. Then once I was properly awake, it was into a mini-cab and back to the prison.

Albert done a really decent thing. He heard I was in trouble and came forward to say the drugs were his. It took a man to do that. They weren't his, of course, and the police didn't believe him but they charged him all the same. After two weeks in Holloway I was given bail. I had to keep reporting twice a week, and it was a whole year before the charges were dropped against me and I was completely free. Daddy got ten years and Jimmy Hussey had eight; both of them pleaded to possession. But it was a liberty holding me and my Mum as hostages to get Daddy and Jimmy to plead. Albert got done for wasting police time. I never saw him again until this year when I bumped into him in the Tin Pan.

By the time the case was finished Albert was gone, and the people who I thought might have been supportive didn't want to know because of the stigma of drugs, even though I was innocent. The other thing was, it left me terribly in debt. No one would give me credit for the flower stall. They all thought that next minute I'd be sent away and their money would have gone bang, so once I was out it took some time to get it all back.

After that I met Giacomo Pavanelli, who I called James, through Albert Moffat. He was doing four years over some promissory notes on South American banks. By then I'd finished with Albert and I was writing to James, so when he had some home leave he came and stayed with me and then he overstayed and wouldn't go back to prison. We ended up going to Italy together, and after I came back the next thing I knew he'd persuaded me to let him have £25,000, saying he was starting up a business. Then he wrote to Daddy saying he was sorry about everything but the chemistry between him and me wasn't right, though the money was safe. Of course it wasn't. When I met Frank, I asked him if he knew anyone in Italy and he made a phone call and someone went round to James's house in Turin, but all that was sent to me was £1,000 and he's still floating around the world somewhere on my money.

I got made bankrupt about then; £19,000 was all it was, and that and a bit more went to Pavanelli. Fortunately they couldn't take my flat; I'd bought it when the council offered it, and as I couldn't sell it for five years the trustee in bankruptcy couldn't get it off me. It's worked out that the original £20,000 has doubled and the costs and everything now come to £40,000, so I'm being forced to sell the flat. It seems amazing that you go bust for something and then with lawyers' fees and so on it ends up costing you twice as much. I think the bankruptcy laws should be changed, and I'm trying to take it further.

It was then I started to frequent the Tin Pan Alley wine bar in Denmark Street off the Charing Cross Road. In the old days it was an old-fashioned after-hours drinker, but when people no longer wanted their feet to be stuck to the carpet it went up-market and became a smart wine bar. In fact I'd met my husband in there. It was run by Frank's nephew Jimmy Fraser and Frank Jnr. They knew who I was, of course; I'd known them since I was 18, when they used to come and drink in the Alliance when my mother owned it. In fact I knew Frank's other sons, David and Patrick, much better. David is so handsome. He and the other Fraser boys all took after their Dad. They are real gentlemen – and so has Frank been. He's never laid so much as a finger on me, not even when I've steamed into him something rotten.

Jimmy and Frank Jnr used to take care of me when I went to the Tin Pan. If I was drinking too much they would make sure I was put in a taxi to get home.

In fact, it was in the Tin Pan that I met Frank. He was courting a woman Val at the time, but I didn't know that then and he was on his own that night. I was singing 'Crazy' to a record, and he called me over and asked if I was taking the piss out of him. 'I've been certified three times,' he said. I wasn't going to be intimidated. I said, 'Do you know whose daughter I am?' That's when we got talking. He asked how Dad was, and I asked if he wanted to come and see him. He was in Parkhurst at the time. Dad had mentioned him over the years of course, and I'd met him in Leicester all those years before. Frank came to the Island and made a nice day of it. I'd forgotten to tell him to bring some ID, and when we got to the gate a younger officer said he wouldn't be able to let him in. But then a senior screw came up and said, 'I know who he is. I can vouch for him.' He remembered him from years earlier.

I'd brought some smoked salmon sandwiches from Marks and Spencers and a bottle of champagne, and we made a good day out of a bad day. He took me out to dinner, wined and dined me and at the end of it he just moved in. He never went back to Val from that day on. He was still married to Doreen, but he hadn't been living with her for some time. I wouldn't want Doreen to think I was the woman who took Frank off her.

I found him a very interesting and honourable man. He told me he was writing a book, and I asked how far he'd got with it. He said he'd nearly finished, and I said he should get it done properly by a lawyer because he could be taken to the cleaners otherwise. He had a bit of trouble with someone who wanted to do the book with him, and then a bit after that he was shot. I wanted Frank and me to get a club. We'd been out all day drinking and we went into Turnmills to show him what it was like. The shooting happened as we were leaving. So we never got a club.[6]

He was in Bart's Hospital for a few days, and when Frank and I left we couldn't stop laughing because as we were going there was a board saying, 'Francis Fraser Ward.' I said, 'They've even got a ward named after you. That was quick.'

After the shooting, I didn't want to stay here in this flat and so we moved away for a few months. In the meantime Alan Stanton, a friend of Johnny Bindon, loaned us a villa in Gozo. Alan caught a lung disease from pigeon shit on the landings in Maidstone prison – it was caked up in the roof – but his widow came to Frank's 70th birthday party and sat at our table. I was reading *Gangland* while we was over there and I said, why not give this author a call, and Frank said, 'I already know him. He's defended me.'

Jack Adams is the nephew of Georgie Cornell and he gave me the opportunity to record that Sinatra number

---

[6]In August 1992 Fraser was shot outside Turnmills nightclub near Clerkenwell Green, where he had been with Marilyn Wisbey in the early hours of the morning. The cause has never been satisfactorily established. Fraser maintained from the start that it was the police. Some journalists said that it was because he had upset a local family. (For a fuller account see *Mad Frank*, pp.217–18).

'You and Me'. It's a lovely song from the Triology album. It was used for the BBC Underworld programme which came out the same time as the book. Frank's gone on to do films and in his latest, *Table Five*, I sing at the start and I've got a small part.

I'm keeping up with my singing. I went to a posh wedding recently with my friend Pat, who's the daughter of Johnny who did the jeweller's in Victoria all those years ago with Frank. She knew the bride's mum and dad because Linda and her brother used to play with her two boys in Blackheath. Linda's dad is the chairman of a big public company. Because it was out in the country near Oxford, Pat's son didn't want to take time off from work to go to the wedding, and she asked if I'd like to go with her. I'd rate it as one of the best weddings I've ever been to. Having seen *Four Weddings and a Funeral*, to me it was a wedding very similar to that – all professional people, and it was an experience for me to meet the other side. We sat on the table with the butler and the gardener and later I met some interesting people.

One of the caterers and I got talking, and he phoned me a couple of weeks later and says he's got some singing lined up. It may be he just wants to get in my pants, I don't know. Since I've been with Frank, I've met such a lot of people who are time-wasters and would-be star fuckers.

When Frank does a show, sometimes I sing as well. He does about one a month, and so I organise him for it. I'm doing computer studies at the moment, and then I'm going on work placement. I don't know if my age is against me, but there's whole areas I can go into – legal secretary, receptionist. I'd like to get into the film world even if I'm just making the tea and doing the typing, just to get the experience, going on a screen-writing course hoping to write a film about my life.

Frank's very controversial, and viewers like people like

that. James Whale used to have a show 'Whale-On' late at night, and when he had Frank on he got such a good response and was so pleased with the way Frank and I looked on television, that his researchers asked us if we would like to do another on Central. So when he's on a television chat programme, I often go with him as well.

It's funny how you get these coincidences. When Dad came out after the Train, he got nicked again because of a girl, Zenith Meer (Tina). He was held on remand for fifteen months over stealing American Express cards before he was acquitted and got fined for receiving. Tina was given a new life in Spain by American Express. What had happened was Billy Gentry, who used to be in love with the shoplifter Shirley Pitts (the one who got my dress for me) used to take Tina with him to the stations where he was stealing mailbags. Then he started to knock her about, or go out with other women, and she was upset and went to the railway police and exposed what he was doing. She went and named about thirty people.

In the court before the trials she was wearing all the best clothes, and Billy'd bought her a Mercedes. By the time she came to give evidence, she didn't come in no smart clothes, wore no make-up and made out she was in ill-health. She made it look as though she was one poor cow. Billy Gentry got nine years, and Louis Mendy – who was related to Ambrose Mendy, the boxing promoter – was another she named; he got a few months. Philly Jacobs, who'd been in the Dixon case, got five years. My Dad was in Court 2 and Peter Sutcliffe was in Court 1 at the same time. When I looked through the doors, Sutcliffe just looked like a clerk.

Little did I know when I went on the James Whale show that the topic would be women visiting killers in prison. That was on Central Television in Birmingham. Sarah Lester was on the podium. Frank and I were in the audience, but questions were asked of us. Olive

Smelt, a woman who survived Sutcliffe's attack, was in the audience. When Whale asked me my opinion of the woman visiting Sutcliffe, I replied how dare she visit a man who's murdered all these women; prison's too good for the likes of Sutcliffe, Brady, Neilson. They should all be twenty feet under. I said you should be with them; you're nothing but a perverted, kinky C U N T. I never said the word, I just spelled it out, but I was in a terrible temper. I got very loud applause. After the show, Olive and her husband came up in the Green Room and thanked me for speaking up, and she showed me the two-inch dent in her head. The side of my hand slotted in to it. She was a straight woman, not a prostitute or anything; she just lived in the same area and had the bad luck to meet Sutcliffe when he was out one night. What surprised me and Frank was the way she said her husband got questioned as if he'd done it to her – the ordeal he went through.

There was a tall, lanky psychiatrist there that night and I'd got a hardback copy of *Mad Frank* I was carrying. He said, 'Oh, he's got a book out.' I said, 'And he's been certified three times.' He seemed to be showing airs and graces and he said, 'And what were you certified as?' Frank wasn't having any and said, 'A psychiatrist.' But others you can have a laugh with. When I had a hysterectomy I was under one of the top consultants in Homerton Hospital. When he came to give me my release, Frank was visiting me. The scar had healed perfectly; I was really pleased with it and how well I felt. Frank said, 'You've made such a good job of the stitching you could have been on my firm all them years ago,' and the consultant burst out laughing.

The book has really opened our eyes to a lot of things. I've been with Frank six years, and he's amazed me that after he spent all those years in prison, the things he's done since. I think I ought to get some credit, though. Since he's been with me he's not been back inside.

Sometimes I think my family would prefer me to be with someone more my own age, but since I'm so complicated maybe he's the only one who'll put up with me. It's a shame we can't turn the clock back and wave a magic wand so we were nearer in ages. Then if he'd met me he wouldn't have gone through all that. If he'd had just one good tickle and I'd been with him, I'd have put it to some good use in a business, but as they say, better late than never.

Twelve

People always ask you what you were doing on such and such a day. I remember the day War broke out. I was living at home. It wasn't any big thing, but the siren went for an air raid. The arches right opposite our little houses were where people could go as an air-raid shelter. I was playing football in the street and I wouldn't go in. Then sheepishly they all filed out after a while. It was a false alarm.

I was on the run when Kennedy died in November 1963. I was in Brighton. I shouldn't have been, but I was getting bored in the stow in up-market Chelsea Bill had got for me. I'd been on the run about four months then and things were getting better over the trouble I was in with Harry Rogers. I was coming up to London once a week. I'd get my exercise. I was very disciplined; I didn't smoke or drink much, so things like that didn't worry me and I stayed out of harm. People were all helping me and it wouldn't be fair to abuse what they were doing for me.

In a year or so people will start asking when did you hear about Diana. I didn't know about that until much later in the day, since I didn't get the papers until very late. We'd been out for a drink and got home late. I sometimes wonder about all those people queuing up for nine hours to write a poem in the book. I wonder if they'd go and spend nine hours with their old Nan or Auntie who hasn't had a visitor in the old people's home since God knows when, but it's not fashionable to say things like that.

To this day, no one's ever come to see me about Jimmy Moody who got shot in the Royal Oak. He was the fourth one to get killed out of those that were in Mr Smith's that night Dickie Hart was shot, and I got off his murder despite Henry Botton grassing me. Then Peter Hennessey was stabbed, like I said, and then Botton himself got shot at his home one night. Then there was Jimmy. That was over a row with some of the Brindles. Despite Eva marrying Jimmy, there are dozens of Brindles all over South London who are no relations of mine. Well, they are somewhere along the line but it's a bit like Smith or Patel as a name in South London. So's Fraser. When Marilyn and me went to my nephew Jimmy's wedding reception at the Savoy, the toastmaster seemed to be calling out Mr and Mrs Fraser for about fifteen minutes on end before he even reached us. Sometimes I think everyone's related to everyone else. Take an example: Marilyn's mother's cousin, David, married Georgie Brindle's daughter.

Jimmy Moody had been working for Peter Daley who had a pub off the Walworth Road. Peter Daley's father was Patsy Daley, and he lived underneath me when I was in Mason Street. His uncle Peter was married to the woman they called 'Dartmoor Annie', who had a paper stall at Waterloo on the corner of Alaska Street and could be relied on for a handout as people came off the train after they'd been released. The family had it for years. It was Annie and Peter who bought gear from me when I was young. I think Annie only did one bit of bird and that was quite late on – sometime in the 1950s for receiving a fur coat.

Patsy Daley and his wife Emmie were nice, but they let booze get the upper hand. He was a drunken fighter and did eighteen months; worked a swell, steamed into the law. I think he got nicked with Eva when a load of gear had gone in his flat and he got her out of it. They'd took it round to Patsy's as a stow. Eva was out of the game by then and was just trying to do a good turn. Peter was the one who had helped Eva and me when we was very young over the cigarette machine. I'd have been about 10 at the time, and she'd be that year older.

Patsy did a bit of bird but, no disrespect, he wasn't a good thief. In the big fog of 1952, I think it was, a real pea-souper, Patsy went and smashed a window and got caught. It was late at night and it was just like the black-out only worse, you literally couldn't see your hand in front of your face but still he got caught. That was his last.

But the police did come to see me about Donald Urquhart, the millionaire who got killed in Marylebone High Street in January 1992 when he was walking along with his girl-friend after they'd been out for dinner, and also about a labourer, Tommy Roche, who was shot near Heathrow. They were both shot by people off the back of a motorbike.

The police came from out of nowhere. A 7 o'clock call; rang the buzzer, and there they were with a warrant. We let them in; we'd nothing to hide or anything and they searched the house. There's searches and searches. You can have one where they lift the corner of the carpet, and then you can have one where they take the wallpaper off – and they don't put it back. On a scale of one to ten, this was about a six. They went down to the garage as well. They found nothing because there was nothing to find, but they took my phone books and I never got them back. At first they gave us the fanny that it was drugs, and then they said they were Murder Squad. Once they'd gone, I got on the phone to my solicitor and he checked things out. They really were from a Murder Squad. My solicitor rang up and they said if we wanted the books back to come over to West Drayton. We said, No. Why should we go miles to get something which they took? They could have posted them. What authority did they have to take them anyway? It was a diabolical liberty. That was the first and only time I've been spun since I went to prison over the coins.

Of course, after I'd been spun I took an interest in the whole thing.[1] Funnily, Urquhart lived in Welbeck Mansions, the same block of flats Bert Wilkins – Joe's uncle and Bert Marsh's great mate – did before he moved to Brighton.

It turned out one of the men involved had been paid £2,000 for a four-month surveillance on the property dealer, tapping his telephone, following him to Spain and spending up to five hours a day watching his flat in Welbeck Mansions. The man who actually did the hit doesn't seem to have been that professional from what I read.

He'd made calls from his mobile to Urquhart's ex-directory number, and he'd been seen at Elstree golf club which Urquhart owned. Then his car got clamped near the flat, and if that wasn't enough a parking ticket was put on a van he used while it was outside the flat. There was a witness who said within a matter of hours of the killing the man was celebrating in a bar, punching a friend's arm and repeating, 'I've done it. I've done it.' He'd apparently got £20,000 for the killing, which wasn't bad. They never found out who made the contract, though. The papers said he was either in Spain, or he was a brief who'd gone to America. I never knew any of them. It wasn't meant to be over drugs, just a business dispute of some sort.

I didn't know Tommy Roche either, although apparently he'd worked with the Twins when he was young. There's so many like to say that. He got done in June that same year in a lay-by near London Airport. The papers said he'd once been Urquhart's minder and it was a drug deal. No one ever got charged over him. I think they thought I might have been the pillion rider; but I'd have been 69 at the time and, though I'm still game, there are limits.

There's nothing really new. I read the other day how a prisoner found a parrot in his cell. Oddly enough, a similar thing happened to me when I was in Hull. I was on a wing with a sort of ledge outside, and one night around 2 a.m. I heard

---

[1] In December 1994 Graeme West was jailed for life, and on 10 February 1995 his assistant Geoffrey Heath received a five-year sentence after pleading guilty to conspiracy to murder Urquhart.

a tapping at the window. I thought that's good, it's someone come to get me out. I'd only done about seven years; this was in the winter of 1972. But it was a screw with a little canary which had escaped. It was raining, and he asked if I could keep it as he couldn't alert another screw. I kept it in the bed with me that night and gave it to a cleaner next morning. I never kipped at all, I was so concerned. If it had died on me, it would have put me in a bad light.

The story went round the prison saying Frank had a bird in his bed all night. It turned out the canary belonged to Roy Hall, who'd been sentenced with me in the Torture trial, and he was really happy to get it back. The bird died a fortnight later when it flew into a bowl of water and drowned.

It's funny how there are some coincidences. Years ago when I'd been in Bristol nick, I helped out a black man. I went there in about October-November 1974 and left in June 1975, and in that time I was charged with assaulting three or more prison officers. I had a really bad time in there. When I went there first of all, it was just after the IRA bombing occurred when all those people were killed in the pub in Birmingham. Now there were IRA prisoners in Bristol, and the screws tried to mix it for them and get me to do them: 'Them dogs here.' 'Terrible, look at them, Fraser.' But I wouldn't, I was friendly with them. With my record I wasn't the most popular anyway, but this just escalated it. Then I was down in the punishment cells when they were knocking a black man about. It was just unlucky for the prison officers that I was unlocked at the time and I went to his aid. I just ended up getting knocked about myself, but he appreciated it and I forgot all about it.

Then last year Marilyn wrote the lyrics for a song and Gareth Bowen, who's the black singer Tricky's keyboard player, did the music. A bit later he sent us an invite to go to the Shepherds Bush Empire where they were playing. Tricky said he'd love to meet me and invited us to go to his dressing-room before the show and have a drink. We had our photos took, then he asked us to come on the stage and said could he introduce me.

It was a packed show. I spoke and told them an anecdote and they loved it. Afterwards we went for a drink and then out to a club; that's when Tricky told me the man I'd helped had been his uncle, and I was proud and pleased it had a nice happy ending. Me, Charlie Richardson and Freddie Foreman have all done a record with him; it came out the end of November last year.

That man in Bristol was one of the few black men I ever had anything to do with in prison in the early days. The only black I knew in the 1940s or even earlier was a big man from Soho; he was half a Johnson. The only other was from Ceylon – a seaman who'd jumped ship and kept on coming in to be deported.

At the beginning the odd one or two you saw, you hardly had any association with in the sense of the word, but by the time I come out in 1989, well, I suppose they were on equal ratio or even a bit more. I always got on well with the blacks. I never saw troubles with other prisoners, but then I was behind me door most of the time anyway. It was all of us united against the screws. They would try and make life that bit more difficult for the blacks, and that's why they loved us. The screws – deep down they're far right, otherwise they wouldn't be screws. The old screws, if Hitler come to power now they'd love him. They'd swear blind it wasn't true, but anyone would tell you the same.

One thing I've been all my life, and that's an Arsenal fan. Sometimes I get invited by a friend who's got a box where there's food and drink to spare, but it's no good. I can't sit down; I keep pacing around the back of the box, and they're all yelling at me to come and watch the match. I'm not game enough even to watch them on telly. I can't bear seeing them beaten. I sit with the radio on and if the oppo. gets in our penalty area I switch it off so I don't hear the dreadful word, 'Goal.'

It was with my Arsenal friend that I ran into Jimmy Andrews' daughter. He was with me when Jack McVitie did the screws in Exeter, and we were all sentenced to have the birch. He's the one Georgie Cornell was visiting in hospital the night he stopped for a drink at the Blind Beggar and Ronnie shot him. Jimmy had cancer by then; he'd also had a bit of his leg shot off in some dispute. Anyway this girl come up, said her father was one of my best mates. Of course I didn't recognise her; she hadn't hardly been born when I started my twenty years. I had been to Jimmy's wedding, then years later his widow married Reggie's first wife's brother, Frankie Shay. Jimmy Andrews' daughter married Tony Adams, the Arsenal player.

In fact I got sent a questionnaire the other day. It was being sent to celebrities who were Arsenal fans. One of the questions was, who did I think was the best player, and I wrote down Ian Wright; and as for the worst, I wrote down 'None.' Arsenal's always been good to me too. Before the Richardson case I used to take my youngest, Francis, to the Arsenal boys' coaching. Dennis Evans, who was the youth team coach in those days, knew me very well.

He was the first but not the only man to do what he did. There's a famous clock opposite the North Bank end, and the players can see it and know how much time's left. It was gone the ninety minutes when a wag in the crowd blew the whistle. Dennis, who was left back, had the ball at the time and just kicked it into his own goal. Two seconds after that the referee blows for full time.

I'd lent Dennis some money which he'd paid me back when he was 35 – the age Arsenal players used to get a hand-out. Now when he had my boy up for coaching, Francis was meant to have already played for his local team which he hadn't; he was only 8, and he had to be 9 for that. I think he had to be 10 or 11 to get into the Arsenal coaching and all. I may have got him into the scheme because I knew Dennis, but Francis had to pull his weight. It did him a lot of good and, like I say, he went on to play for Sussex Schools and then for Brighton & Hove Albion. He might have been really top class if he hadn't done his knee. I'd fetch my boy up from Brighton once or twice a week and, of course, I'd stay with him. I took my brother Jimmy's boy, Robert, along as well. He was 15, and could really play. Arsenal were very impressed with him, but with me getting nicked they couldn't go no more and nothing happened.

Dennis give evidence for me at the Torture trial to say I was with my son at the training when a prosecution witness said I was somewhere doing villainy. Dennis was right and it was the truth, but it was good of him to get involved. A lot of people wouldn't have done. After Arsenal won the youth cup, he went to South Africa.

Talking about the Torture trial, not long after I came out after that twenty years, Charlie Richardson and I went to see Rupert Deen who told us he'd been the foreman of the jury at our trial. Charlie had come out twelve months before me and had already met him, and I was introduced to him at one of Frank Warren's boxing shows when he was with Nigel Dempster. In fact I met him a few times, once when he was with that amateur jockey, Sir William Piggot-Brown. His flat was down Pimlico-Chelsea way and Charlie and I went there a few times. We asked if he would come forward and say he thought us innocent, but he wouldn't. We never offered him no money, of course. We were just trying to show what a travesty the whole thing had been. After all, the chief prosecution witnesses was running a long-firm fraud just round the corner all through the trial and they was meant to be under a police guard.

We was also saying how it must have influenced the jury to be told they wasn't going to a hotel overnight but to sleep on camp beds in the Old Bailey, and he didn't knock us down. If they had the facilities they have now for juries who stay out a long time, then it could have been another matter. He was a very engaging man, very friendly, and he did say how he thought we could have been innocent but that was as far as he'd go.

His uncle was Sir Henri Deterding of Shell Transport. He'd retired and gone to live in Germany just before the war. He died in 1939 and there was a big service over there. Funnily

Lawton, our judge, had been in the fascists too; he'd been the parliamentary candidate for them in Hammersmith North in 1934.

Of course I still keep in touch with people. We don't see so much of Freddie Foreman as we'd like, only films and benefits, although Marilyn went to his book launch at the Café Royal and said it was a really good do. Someone out of the past, though, is Donald Hume. He came to do the electrics in our garage about three years ago. Marilyn couldn't believe who he was. She said he looked more like a solicitor.[2]

Another man I bumped into the other day was Tony Reuter. He's a bit younger than me, came from a good family at the Elephant. People remember his brother Peter helping Eddie Richardson fight off the Dunne family and their friends at the Locarno in Streatham in the 1950s. Tony was known as the King of the Teddy Boys and he got religion; he was converted by Billy Graham at one of his revival meetings at Earl's Court. Of course it was all a bit for the papers and, if it wasn't, the conversion didn't last because I saw him round Charlie Richardson's. Unless he was trying to convert Charlie!

Roy James, who was on the Train, phoned Marilyn in the seconds after he'd shot his father-in-law; he was so emotionally upset. He knew Marilyn through Tommy of course. Roy was separated from his wife; he gave her every penny he could for the children, and he was having a hard time.

Roy was the gamest of the game, and tragically he's been the youngest of the Train lot to die. He'd been a good racing driver before the Train – the equivalent of Formula Three nowadays – and he's been up there racing with the best of his generation. He'd had a lot of help from Jack Brabham, who sold him a car

[2]Brian Donald Hume (b.1918) murdered car dealer and receiver Stanley Setty in October 1949, disposing of his body by dumping it from a plane over Essex Marshes. After the jury disagreed, he pleaded guilty to being an accessory and received twelve years. He was released on 1 February 1958 and immediately confessed to the *People*. On 30 January 1959 he shot and killed a taxi driver, Arthur Maag, who tried to detain him after he had robbed the Gewerbe Bank in Zurich. During his first sentence Hume's wife Cynthia married the crusading, if dubious, reporter Duncan Webb.

which he smashed up first or second drive. Brabham was really pissed with him and told him he'd be better off driving saloon cars, but he stuck to it. He got his licence suspended for a bit though. Afterwards when he came back – what was it, twelve years later? – things had changed and of course his reactions weren't the same, so he was really out of it. Still, give him credit, he gave it a go. I spoke to Stirling Moss once, saying if I'd been on a raid I'd have had Roy as first driver and him as a reserve, and the police would never have got me. Stirling cracked up.

Roy got chucked when he was on a VAT charge with Charlie Wilson at the Old Bailey in 1984. The jury had a disagreement over Charlie, and when it came to the retrial he paid the Customs £400,000 and they let him off. Roy had a nice little jewellery business and he got married to one of his assistants, a girl named Anthea whose father worked in a bank.

We used to see him and have a drink with him here and there. Then one day he rang Marilyn, as I said. What had happened was, he'd been having trouble with Anthea. They'd got separated or even divorced, and he was in trouble over paying her £150,000 as a settlement. He thought her father had been advising her – he hadn't as it turned out – and one afternoon when they brought the kids back after a day's outing he went and shot her father and gave her a pistol whipping. He was really besotted by Anthea. Couldn't do too much – bought her a horse, paid for her to have a nose job – but what he didn't realise was that times had changed. Things were different from when he went in and he'd never been married before, so it was extra hard.

I shouted, 'Get out, get out now!' down the phone. If he wasn't there when the police came, then it might still be possible to do something. Then when he told me he'd phoned the police, I didn't know if it was safe to speak over his phone so I rushed out for a phone box. You know how it is – if you want a phone there's always someone in them. By the time I found one it must have been a policewoman who answered.

She said, 'Who is it?' and I just put the receiver down. We went to visit him quite a lot on remand. He got six years which I suppose, all in all, wasn't bad. But when he came out he had a heart bypass and really he wasn't the same person.

Roy never smoked and he didn't really drink. He kept supremely fit; he was the last man I'd ever thought would have heart trouble. If he hadn't have been such a good thief he'd have been a very good professional footballer; he was with QPR as a boy. The criminal world's gain and the football world's loss.

There was a really good turn-out for the funeral. He was the fifth of the Train robbers to go. Charlie Wilson's widow was there, and Tommy and Renée Wisbey and me and Marilyn. Jimmy Hussey and Bruce Reynolds, of course, and Bobby Welch on sticks after the operations he had while he was in the nick. Gordon Goody wasn't there, although he'd intended to come. He'd fallen off a roof, in Mojacar in Spain where he lives, the day before and, when he hit the ground, a pot from the roof also fell and hit him as well. He was there two and a half hours before anyone found him. He didn't break anything, but he was too bruised to travel. Jimmy White, who was the oldest on the Train and who used to have a greasy spoon round Old Street, he wasn't there; he's just sort of dropped out.

Buster Edwards went before Roy: topped himself. I was at the Old Bailey in about 1992 when a friend of mine, Brian Perry, was on bail in the Brinks-Mat receiving case. I knew him through other people and I was asked to be a sort of minder for him, so I'd go over in the dinner hour and have a meal with him. It was a nice summer's day and we went into Ozzie's café in Ludgate Hill. He walked back the other side of the road and I was on the opposite side on my way home. All of a sudden I see Brian beckoning me and I went over to a little crowd. He was pointing over my shoulder; I turned round and there was Buster Edwards. I said, 'Hello, Buster.' 'Hello, Frank.' 'What are you doing here?' 'I'm a witness.' I said, 'Well done, for the defence, good boy.' I never suspected that he was going to say, 'No, for the prosecution.' I said, 'You dirty bastard, get out of it.'

Later I heard he was a witness in the case of the Taylor sisters who were acquitted of killing that Alison Shaughnessy.[3] Next day I made it my business to buy nearly every newspaper, and it was in just one of them about him giving evidence. Like all cases of domestic murder, the nearest and dearest are always the first to be interviewed and the husband had said that at the time of the murder on a Friday he always bought flowers from Buster's flower stall. He went to see Buster and told him and Buster said, 'Quite right, you do.' To Buster's credit here, when the police see him he told the truth: that the man was a very good customer and did buy the flowers.

Then when the sisters were nicked for murder the police approached Buster and asked him to be a prosecution witness, to say about the husband having an alibi and buying the flowers.

[3] At about 6 p.m. on Monday, 3 June 1991, Alison Shaughnessy was stabbed to death in her flat in Battersea. She had been struck fifty-four times. Police inquiries focused on 22-year-old Michelle Taylor, a former girl-friend of John Shaughnessy who had continued his relationship with her after his marriage. Their affair had ended in the autumn of 1990, some three months after Shaughnessy's marriage to Alison. Michelle Taylor remained good friends with both the Shaughnessys. The motive, the police believed, was jealousy and the elimination of a rival.

Michelle Taylor was able to produce an alibi. She had been working in her job as an accounts clerk at a private health clinic in Lambeth Road, South London with John, who worked as a gardener. There was no scientific evidence to link either of the sisters to the killing. No spot of blood could be found on the clothing of either of them. A doctor said he had seen two girls running from the flat at the time of the murder, but he failed to pick out either of the sisters at an identification parade. There were five sets of unidentified fingerprints in the flat and there was some evidence that jewellery had been stolen. The defence was able to show that it was possible Alison had not arrived home until after 6 p.m. that day. What helped to convict both sisters was the alarming press coverage of the affair John had with Michelle. The girls were convicted and sentenced to life imprisonment.

On 11 June 1993 the Court of Appeal released the girls, quashing their convictions which were ruled to be unsafe and unsatisfactory. The press coverage of the trial, described as 'unremitting, extensive, sensational, inaccurate and misleading', had, said Lord Justice McCowan, 'created a real risk of prejudice'. There was also an evidential problem. The Crown's eyewitness, Dr Michael Unsworth, had also made another statement, not disclosed to the defence, in which he had said that one of the girls he had seen fleeing from the flat was black.

That's when Buster should have said, 'On your bike,' but he didn't. He shouldn't have got involved.

I didn't see him again until sometime later when people from the film world were showing an interest in making a film. Marilyn said to go and see Buster. I said I didn't want to see him, but as he'd been down this road she persuaded me. The first thing I said was that I took nothing back, and he said he understood. I said, 'Right, I've now come for some information and advice.' I told him about the possible film and asked if he'd found it a good or a bad road. He said it was a bad road and all he'd got was £5,000. The film rights of the book had run out, plus he got another £12,000 from the *Sun*. That was the last time I saw him. He was a very lovely character, but above anyone he knew the rules and regulations and should have stuck to them. I never went to his funeral because of it.

Another person who's gone is Albie Woods – a good man, a good friend of Bobby Welch. When Ronnie shot Georgie Cornell in the Blind Beggar, Albie was there and he had the sense to pick up all the glasses so there was no question of fingerprints. They had him on an ID parade, but he never picked anyone out. He was with Eva when they did her for conspiracy for trying to get Bennie Coulson to tell the truth in the Torture trial, when I got ten years. Albie got two years. Marilyn and me went down to see him in a hospice in Sydenham. Flo Sutton – who he'd lived with for years, but by then they'd split up – was in the same hospice. Cancer had them both, and they died within a fortnight of each other.

A funny thing happened while we was with Albie. We were joking, saying if Flo could come up from her room we could have a race with me pushing her and Marilyn pushing Albie, when the nurse came in and said she'd seen me before. I said she hadn't but she said yes, she was sure. 'You were seeing Gary when he died in the same bed.' This was Charlie Kray's son who had been in the hospice a few months earlier. I don't think she realised Albie could hear and I sort of hustled her away. Funnily, I hadn't been to see Gary, so there's someone who looks a lot like me about.

A few months ago I saw Patsy Fleming who escaped with Alfie Hinds. He's had a triple bypass and he was fine, but Dido Frett, who got seven years in the Carter case, had the bypass and he died. Ray Rosa died of a heart attack several years ago when opening a window and, of course, his brother Jack was killed in the early 1960s. He had a bent brief with him and his last words were said to be, 'It wasn't me driving.'[4]

I was talking to Johnny Macdonald, who was caught in the Rotherhithe tunnel when I got away in 1945, and he says Tommy Jenkins (Harry Boy's brother) is still alive and living in Rotherhithe. He got eight years for the Binney death, then in 1953 he got five when he was nicked with Nobby Saunders who got life for shooting at a copper after a jeweller's in Peckham Rye. Tommy was with me in Portland in 1941. I don't think we were a great advertisement for the Borstal training system.

Some of the people with me in the Parkhurst riot trial have gone, and I've lost touch with some more. It's hard to think it was nearly thirty years ago. The judge is dead; so is the brief I had, Don Harvey, and so is George Shindler. Timmy Noonan died in Cork and Eva went over for his funeral. He'd had a massive heart attack while he was in Liverpool prison, but he'd still managed to do a screw there. Mark Owens has never been nicked since; Martin Frape got another two years at Leicester, and he hasn't been in since. Mickey Andrews was another who never got into no more trouble. Blythe went out with Eva's daughter Shirley for a time, but they've split up and I don't know what's happened to him. Andy Anderson disappeared into the King's Cross mob. In October I saw Tony Peterson got four years for possession of amphetamines. The Court of Appeal had quashed a murder charge against him when he was in Parkhurst with me after Melford Stevenson, who

[4]In this context brief means a driving licence, but it can mean a variety of things, amongst others a lawyer, a bank note, a warrant of arrest, a memorandum or note, a railway ticket or even a character reference.

was the judge in the Kray case, misdirected the jury.[5] This time Peterson was done with Tony Knightley and a couple of others over a laboratory in Norfolk.

Some people you have to lose touch with, even if it breaks your heart. One of them was Johnny Hasse, a Liverpool kid. When I first knew him, he was doing three years in Strangeways with me. There was also a guy, Roy Grantham, who'd done a screw with a can of boiling tea and who more or less called everyone from every prison in his defence. We were brought from all over the country to give evidence for him. Grantham came in with eight years for his bird, and then he got a bit more over the can of water.

He did about eleven years in total, and when he was released he teamed up with Johnny Hasse. Hasse then gets a tip that Grantham's got six months for drunken driving and, while he's doing it, he's going supergrass up in the North. This would be in the 1980s. Johnny was appealing against his three years and he won his appeal, but now he knew he was going to be nicked by Grantham. Through him, Johnny got fourteen years over some post office vans. I went to see him at Long Lartin and Marilyn sang when we went to his daughter's wedding. Later he got on the roof at Bristol and put up a banner proclaiming himself as being innocent. I was down the punishment block, or I'd have been out there with him.

Then Johnny finished his fourteen and got nicked again, this time for drugs on the docks in Liverpool in the early 1990s, and got eighteen years for a lot of heroin in a thing they called the Turkish Connection up in Liverpool. Blow me, within a year of his sentence he and another man, Paul Bennett, are out on the streets. He, of all people, has gone hookey. The judge had always wanted them to be released early, and he wrote to the Home Secretary. Apparently the long sentence was just to make it look good to the others whilst Hasse was in prison so he didn't have to go with the other grasses on Rule 43. He was released in September 1996, and a couple of weeks later he rang me up to say would I and Marilyn go to his wedding. I said, 'No, on your bike.' He said 'You calling me a grass?' and I said, 'Yes, I am.' It broke my heart because I liked him so much: 'I'm not having nothing to do with you.'[6]

While Hasse was on remand for the eighteen years, a gun was found in the top security wing and there was a suggestion in the press that it had been brought in for a man who'd done a couple of tax inspectors in Stockport. That wasn't the case. Anyway, not too long ago a London brief got in touch with me to say would I get hold of Johnny Hasse and get him to come clean and say he'd been in collusion with the law over bringing it into the nick. I said I wouldn't even think of talking to him. First, it would be a waste of time; and second, the next thing you'd find yourself up on a conspiracy to pervert with a man like that.

Until just recently, Marilyn and I lived in Islington in a small flat with Danny her dog. He's a Lhaso Apso and Gina Lollobrigida bought his litter sister, so he's well connected. She got him from Harrods – bought, not nicked – and I've been the one who takes him for a walk in a morning.

One thing I had with me all through my long prison stretch was a St Christopher medal given to me by my wife Doreen. You must fight for little things, and one thing I wouldn't let them take off me was the medal. In those days – 1960s – you couldn't even have a watch. It was just as well I never let them have it because when they came to give me back my property in 1985 there was no sign of my watch or the very nice cuff-links or a decent pen I had.

Two years ago I lost the medal. A link in the chain must have broken and it slipped down and out of my trouser leg and I never noticed. Or maybe it just fell off when I bent down.

---

[6]In 1972 Hasse received seven years for his part in a series of raids on post offices. In 1980 he was acquitted of attempted murder after a rival, Tony Murray, failed to attend court after being shot in the leg with a pump-action shotgun. In 1982 he received fourteen years for post-office van robberies, and in 1995 he received eighteen years for the Turkish Connection case.

Anyway, I noticed when I went to take it off before I went to bed. I searched everywhere, I retraced my steps for that day and there was no sign of it. I was really upset.

A week or so later Danny and me were down by St James's Church, opposite the post office in Upper Street. A lot of leaves and rubbish had blown in the gutter because the shop next door had been empty for months if not years. Where there's a bit of dirt dogs like to have a jimmy, so Danny just sort of jumped down off the pavement and nosed about and there was my medal. Fancy it being just by the church of all places!

I used to have him on a lead before he had his nuts off a bit late in life. He was getting a bit of a handful: wouldn't come when he was called, off all over the place. I thought of doing his nuts myself, but then I thought it would be better to take him to the vet. If he had been on a lead I'd never have seen the medal. I'd have just given a yank and said, 'Come on, Danny.' I wouldn't walk him as far as that now. You don't need to now he's 15 years old.

Marilyn and me moved back across the water to New Cross just a bit before Christmas, and it's funny how many old faces there are. One of the first I ran into was Mickey Collins. He lives just opposite. He was doing a few months when Jack Duval who'd given evidence against us at the Torture trial was up again a few years later – this time with Brian Mottram – over a long firm. He was telling me the other day that when Duval went to court one day he left his wig behind in the cell and him and Brian Clifford, who was known as 'Little Legs' because he was so small, put ketchup in it.

Mickey's doing well, but Brian's dead now. He was shot when some people burst into his house, pushed his wife aside and went up and did him while he was in bed. No one was ever done for it I heard.

Although I say it, my first book was a success. It was really that and the television series *Underworld* which changed things around for me. I was in four of the *Underworld* programmes out of the six, more than anyone else, and the last one was at my 70th birthday party in Lancashire. That was what really got me going. I have to say it was luck they both came out together. That producer Lorraine Hegarty, and Frank Simmonds who did the programme with her, asked me months before the book came out. Frank knew Marilyn's cousin. The writer Martin Short asked me to go in his programme on ITV called *Gangsters* which was shown in the South East but I said no, partly because I'd already said yes to Lorraine but more because he'd wrote a book strenuously in that copper Martin Lundy's favour. I couldn't stand for that.[7]

Just about the first thing happened was the vicar of the Methodist Chapel in the City Road saw me on television, and he went into the bookshop round the corner from me at the Angel where the book was on display and asked how he could get in touch with me. They told him that I come in fairly regular to sign copies, so when I next popped in I found he'd left a letter there to give me.

So I phoned him and met him and he told me that they have sort of seasons of services at lunchtime when they have famous people who come and talk about their lives. When I say famous it included Margaret Thatcher, everybody. I said, 'Yes' of course, and I turned up and done it and it was headlines, TV, radio and newspapers. A couple of hymns to start, and then he asked about my life. He told me later that I had the biggest crowd they had after Margaret Thatcher. He invited me back and I did it again, and that went down just as well.

After the vicar I was really up and running, TV, radio, all over the country, here and in Ireland, magazines, even the Internet which led to offers for me to appear on stage. So I took one of the offers up and appeared at the Brick Lane Music Hall, which had a history of having literally every famous actor and actress appearing over the years. It went down so good I had to go back and do another one. Then I went to the Edinburgh

[7]Martin Lundy has been one of the most controversial police officers in recent decades. Considerable resources went into an effort to establish a case against him but failed.

Festival and did a week. Last year I went back because they were putting on the play *Gangster One*, and after it I went on stage and talked about my life. It should have been half an hour but it was more like an hour and a half. It was the biggest audience. I was billed as specially appearing.

I've been in two films. One of them, *Hard Men*, is in the top ten most popular videos, and I've got another couple of parts lined up for 1998. It's just catapulted. Whether I like it or not I've become a celebrity, and I'm not grumbling. I can suffer that. Before, I was a celebrity, but in a different way through being in and out of prison over one or two famous cases and for my violence in prison. Now I am a celebrity both because of all that and the show business side of it, and it has got quite interesting and very enjoyable.

Bruce Reynolds' son Nick is a sculptor and he's done a cast of my face. If you've never had one done, what happens is straws get put up your nose and your face is covered with clay. The only way to breathe is through the straws. It was a good job he took it off when he did because, if you've had your nose broken a couple of times like I have, it's very difficult to breathe. If you were in difficulty you had to tap with your hands, but there's no way I would do that. Fortunately they could see my knuckles were going white; so they took it off and I looked more like a Red Indian in a strait-jacket. This was eighteen months or so ago at his studio down near Turnmills near where I was shot. Indeed, TV filmed me outside Turnmills with my cast. Nick's giving me one and he'll sell the rest.

Funny things happen. I did a show down the East End and it was so popular that I was asked to do it again for a few nights at the Jermyn Street Theatre off Piccadilly. A woman called Tina Cave went to see me and laughed so much her waters broke and she had to go straight to hospital. She's called the baby partly after me – Billy Jordan Frank Fraser Cave. She's asked me to be his godfather as well, and of course I've agreed. The magazine that wrote it up also went and got hold of Kathleen, the mother of my first three boys, for a comment. She don't like me even now. 'He wasn't such a good father – he was always in and out of prison. These days he always makes a fool of himself – but I never found him that funny when I was with him,' she said. I hope they didn't give her more than a couple of quid for slagging me off.[8]

When I try to earn something honestly, there's always people who don't think I should. Take my coach tours. Peter Luff, the Conservative M.P. for Mid-Worcestershire, said to scrap the tour because it was 'real exploitation of personal misery and suffering'. It was in all the papers, but fortunately no one took any notice of him. I do it most Saturdays, showing people places of interest round the East End and answering questions about my life and whether I think prison does any good, and what changes there should be made. It ends up on the river, and there's a lunch when I have an informal chat with them.

Now I'm working hard getting an honest living some people don't like it, even though I've paid my price. People still go off instead of clapping their hands and saying, 'Well done.' I'm over 70, and no one would employ me after all those years in prison. How could I get a straight job at my age? What do they want me to do? When footballers and policemen and politicians retire they write their books, but people don't go off about them.

On the other hand, I got a surprising number of letters after the book; people saying they'd been inside with me and so on and will I send them photos. I try to reply to every one. One of the most surprising was Trevor Rook, who was the youngest Mayor of Lincoln. He got in touch through the publishers and invited Marilyn and me up to stay with him and his wife for a weekend. They couldn't have been kinder. He asked if he could have his photo took with me outside Lincoln prison. The screws ran out to say they couldn't take photos on prison property, but when they saw who it was they ran back saying it was all right.

[8]*EVA*, 30 April 1997.

One of the things that has happened is that minor villains want to say they've worked with me or gone up against me. There was an article in a Belfast paper that a man had ridden with me to Ronnie Kray's funeral, but he did nothing of the sort. Then the next week or so, another man gave a story to the same paper saying that in the late 1940s I'd gone and shot a Belfast hard man called Paddy Joe McKee – according to the story, known as 'Silver' because of his blond hair. Apparently he'd been a street fighter and enforcer in the markets there.[9] It said I'd been running a pitch-and-toss game in the Edgware Road, Paddington for the Richardson brothers; that it was a game worth about £1,500 and McKee had decided to take it over. He'd stripped off ready to fight me and I'd gone and shot him twice; he'd had to go to the Royal Free Hospital. I don't know why they took him there. If he'd had to go to hospital, he'd have gone to St Mary's. That's how straight the story was. I wrote complaining.

It's all rubbish. I never met McKee in my life to my knowledge, and for a start I never ran a pitch-and-toss game. You could see them before the War, but they took place mostly up in the North and in Wales and sometimes at the races. What used to happen is that there would be a ring and a ringmaster would spin half-crowns in the air, and the betting was whether three or more would fall heads or tails. Big money could change hands, but it was never popular in London. Crown and Anchor was more popular here; you could see that being played at the racecourses and outside the dog tracks. It was a con, of course. The punter never had any chance of winning, whereas with a pitch-and-toss ring he really did. In Crown and Anchor there was a board.

The next thing that was rubbish about the story was that I was running the game for the Richardsons. I didn't meet them for another ten years, and I know Charlie was a good businessman but he'd have only been 15 at the end of the 1940s. If anyone

[9]Martin O' Hagan, 'The Day Silver McKee's fists couldn't match "Mad" Frankie's Gun in *Sunday World*, 3 August 1997.

ran the Edgware Road end of things at that time, I'd have to admit it was Jack Spot; certainly it wasn't Charlie and Eddie Richardson. But I suppose it makes a good story for them, and some of them get a few quid from the papers.

Everyone wants to have been in on something. The prison officers who want to say they were in the dock guarding the Krays or Charlie and me or the Train; if this was true, the dock would have to have been three times the length of The Mall.

When Marilyn and her Mum and Dad were at Newbury doing the catering, some man at the bar said he'd been in the nick with the Train Robbers and Tommy was standing just by. Renée Wisbey asked, 'Tom, was you away with that fellow?' and Tommy said, 'Never seen him in my life.' People just like to be associated with top villains.

Shirley Pitts says in her book that I had the Astor with Verdi. I wish I had done. It was Billy Hill who had it at the start; he put the money up for Bertie Green who made it what it was, and then he repaid Billy. Verdi was just the manager and an act himself in addition to the cabaret; he had a good voice. Later, he went off and opened a bar in Covent Garden. That isn't to say I didn't carry a good deal of clout in the Astor because of my association with Billy, but own it – never. In fact I never saved my money. Just before the twenty I did straight, I was just beginning to get moving. Another two or three years I'd have been comfortable, and even begun to think of retiring. Eddie Richardson and I had the machines and they were a good straight business. Over the years I'd had some big touches, but I never thought of putting it away safe. It was come and spend. I wasn't greedy, I was very good-hearted. What I had put away before the Mr Smith's Club shooting dribbled away over the years I was inside. Everyone had to live.

Things could have been different if it hadn't have been for Mr Smith's. If we hadn't been in custody when George Cornell got shot, there would have been war then. It would have been difficult because I knew the Twins both before and more than I knew Charlie and Eddie. They were awfully good to Eva.

But it would have had to be done. Of course, if we hadn't been in custody it probably wouldn't have happened, but if it had that shooting of George really wouldn't have been allowed to pass.

I think the Twins were a bit jealous. We had the machines and the long-firms and the blue films racket George Cornell had. Charlie had five scrap-metal yards and contracts with the Ministry of Works, a perlite mine in South Africa and the car parking at Heathrow, and our standing was really much higher.

We all could and should have got together really. They wanted to get together because it was better business for them; but they didn't go about it the right way, and we had all our people to look after so it wasn't easy. There'd be about forty in all, but some would be part-time. You'd only have to get permission if it affected the standing or business. We'd see our workers and give them the respect. It would be mutual. Will this affect you in any way at all if we do such and such? We'd ask them whether they were full or a quarter part-time. Criminally, we had been thieves and done quite a lot of bird. The Twins were thieves' ponces and would muscle straight in if they ever had an opportunity. But, to be fair, they could do a lot of good for a lot of people. But there was nothing like the enmity the media has made out. It's just good reading.

For my opinion, not knocking Reggie, I thought Ronnie was the more honest. Whatever he said he meant, whereas Reggie might fiddle and fumble about. But then again when I saw Ronnie in the Grave Maurice a bit before Mr Smith's and he marked my card, he never said who was causing trouble. I know now it was James Taggart, the one who went to the copper MacArthur and had us all nicked, and Ronnie must have known or could have found out. I think they knew a bit more than they let on, and maybe they were happy to see us go. They could have done more to help us when we were nicked as well.

If the positions had been reversed, I know I would have

tried very hard for them and been able to help them. Some of the prosecution witnesses – they could have been bumped into. I'd have gone flat out if it had been reversed, if only because I don't like grasses. I'd have felt a traitor if I hadn't. I know that once when I was in prison with Johnny Carter I did him, but that wasn't like the troubles Charlie and Eddie had with the Twins; this was a long-standing family feud and it had to be done. It had been running too long just to let it go.

Naturally, since I wrote the first book there's been a lot of deaths and funerals. Billy Howard would have been in his element if he'd been alive to see them.

Ronnie Kray's one who's gone of course. He married twice while in Broadmoor, to which he had been sent and where, apparently, he had enjoyed most of his creature comforts. He died suddenly of a heart attack on 17 March 1995. He had been a very heavy smoker. His funeral, in traditional East End style with six plumed black horses, was said to have cost £10,000.

Reggie rang me up from Maidstone to ask me to be a pall-bearer and naturally I agreed. I was honoured. Then Marilyn said, 'Who are the others?' I rang up Charlie Kray and he said I'd be with Ginger Dennis, who got done for Jack Spot with me, Johnny Nash and Freddie Foreman. They're all six foot and more, and I'm half their size so to speak. It would have looked disrespectful having the coffin at a tilt like that. So regretfully I turned it down. Reggie wanted me to sit right behind him at the funeral and walk at his right shoulder when he come out of the church, and I was pleased to.

I went into English's the undertakers to pay my last respects – Reggie was already there – just before the coffin was closed. German TV filmed me outside just before I went in. They had a car laid on and I went all the way to the cemetery. There was a church service at St Matthews.

People tried to get in the car with me, and Alex Steene – the boxing promotor who died last year – jumped in. The crowds were running up, shaking hands through the windows. At times the cars were going so slow that kids was running alongside the ones Reggie and I was in, pushing pieces of paper through the windows asking for autographs. One man even pushed in a £50 note for me to sign. When I gave it back, I said if my poor mother could be seeing this she'd never forgive me handing back fifty quid to someone. This went on all the way from St Matthews to Chingford. The crowds were unbelievable.

I had thought Noller Knowles' funeral in 1950 was very, very big, and Jimmy Brindle's certainly was. Billy Blythe's was big, and Cassandra of the *Daily Mirror* wrote it up saying all about how the gangsters were in early 1957. Billy was something special; he cut the copper Peter Vibart and got three years for it in 1945. Vibart'd fitted up a pal of his and so he did him. He was a boozer and he was crooked, same as Tommy Butler was. In fact he was in a boozer when Billy did him. But compared to even these, Ronnie's funeral was massive. Winston Churchill would have been proud of it. I told German TV it was bigger than Churchill's, and they loved it, and I really think it was.

A terrible thing happened though. It turned out Ronnie's brain had been removed by a Home Office pathologist and it wasn't returned for some months, so there had to be a second funeral arranged. Reggie's never been able to accept the inquest verdict, and he's been trying to arrange an inquiry into his brother's death ever since.

It was just after that Charlie Kray got nicked. He was 69 and his son – poor Gary, who'd had serious educational problems throughout his life – had just died of cancer at the age of 44. Charles had been released in 1975 from his ten-year sentence for assisting in the disposal of the body of Jack McVitie, and from then on had done things like selling cutlery at the Ideal Home Exhibition and managing a pop group. He had also been the consultant on *The Krays*. He was as innocent of the charge over Jack as he is of the 12 years he's doing now. He would be the last person you would ask to dispose of a body; he wouldn't have the bottle – and I mean that in a nice way. He was charged with conspiracy to sell cocaine worth £39 million to undercover officers. I don't mean it unkindly, but he was making a living trading off the family name rather than making a living for himself. He'd had a hard time paying for Gary's funeral.

The police version was that he was still deeply involved in the Underworld, and that he had been investigated on at least three occasions to do with amphetamines, counterfeit videos and fake coins. Charlie never had neither a bank account nor a credit card, and he never claimed benefit. This, said the police, showed that he was still deep into things.

The police in the case were recruited from provincial forces and at Charlie's 70th birthday party he had been introduced to 'Jack', an undercover officer posing as a businessman dealing in drugs. In subsequent taped conversations, he offered to supply 5 kilos of 92 per cent pure cocaine every fortnight for up to two years. The price was to be £31,500 a kilo. If the deal had gone ahead, the pros said Charlie and his associates would have grossed £8 million. His defence was that he was stringing the purchasers along in the hope of conning money from them.

This was the fourth time I'd given evidence for other people, and it doesn't seem to have done any of them any good. The first was for the Twins, when really it was a show, a gesture. The second time was for real when I gave evidence for the kid in Birmingham who was doing life; it wasn't at his murder trial, but something later. Then I give evidence for that Roy Grantham. Charlie was the fourth; I'm sorry to say he got the 12 years.

Robin McGibbon, who'd wanted to write my first book with me, got in touch and asked if I would give evidence and I said, 'Yes, of course.' He then asked if I could give my phone number to Ralph Haemms. One of his clerks got in touch and then Ralph said he wanted to do the interview himself; he was the solicitor from the days of the Kray trial. I went to Peckham Rye and he told me he'd got my boy David a not guilty years ago. I thought that was a good sign. This time he had Jonathan Goldberg as the brief. Goldberg had defended one of my sons some time ago as well, so I knew who he was.

He had me down to his chambers in the Temple so he could see what evidence I was going to give.

I said to Haeems and Mr Goldberg that I wasn't sure it was a good idea to have me give evidence. With my convictions, was it wise? They said it was. They said it was an exceptional case and there were exceptional circumstances; that getting it from me was getting it from the horse's mouth that he never was nor had been a rascal, and that he wouldn't have the nerve. So I said OK.

What I should have said at his trial was to prove what a fool Charlie was. Patsy Manning had unknowingly introduced him to undercover cops. There was no problem in saying, 'This is Tom, this is Dick and this is Harry,' and having a chat, but once Charlie'd started talking serious what he should have said is, 'What's your surname?' 'Can't tell you.' 'Who do you know?' Any *bona fide* villain would ask. It just shows you what an idiot Charlie was. And if you're dealing in something serious like a robbery or anything, then if the man can't put up names of people he's worked with or won't tell you his name you know the score – and it's, 'On your bike, get back to your local police station.' You are brought up automatically to ask questions and protect yourself; it's instilled in you from the time you're 10 years old. Charlie simply didn't have a clue about life – that's how simple he was. I thought that was the most important bit of all.

When I give evidence at Charlie's trial, I was asked why I hadn't mentioned him in my book when Ronnie and Reggie were getting so many mentions, and I answered the truth. I said it was because he wasn't a villain and so he wasn't worth mentioning. That I hadn't because he was a nothing. He was just poor old Charlie who got dragged into things.

There was some jokes and laughs when I said it was the first time I was going to leave a court a free man. I did, and I didn't enjoy it. I enjoyed it in the sense I tried to help someone, but also it was sadness to see Charlie in the position he was – a lamb led to the slaughter. I wouldn't take a penny expenses from the court, although I was entitled to as a witness. It didn't seem right.

Robin McGibbon's not too popular at the minute. There was a do at the Carlton pub in Peckham where they collected £1,400-plus to help pay private investigators to see what they could find out about the coppers who'd first approached Charlie. Marilyn went on my behalf. There was also another £1,400 that David Vaughan, the son of the comedian Norman Vaughan, had collected while the trial was taking place. The investigators did well, and they managed to trace the woman who had slept with one of the coppers.

Now it's turned out the investigators hadn't yet been paid. Judy, Charlie's friend, had a lot of exes [expenses] during the trial, and she had to keep going to see Charlie in Belmarsh and leaving money for him because you can't take anything in nowadays. Robin McGibbon went and told Charlie about the non-payment of the investigators. There was nothing Charlie could do about it in Long Lartin, and it was just winding him up. So Judy sent Robin a terrible letter; he showed it to me and I told him that I thought he'd been foolish telling Charlie because he wasn't going to sling Judy to the wolves.

There's an appeal going for Charlie, and a series of benefits, so by the time this book comes out maybe with luck he'll be out with it. People tried to get Reggie to give evidence on his brother's behalf, but he said it would be a circus if he did and it wouldn't do Charlie any good, and I think he was right. Things have turned out a bit better for Reggie now. In July he married Roberta Jones in Maidstone prison. She's a nice decent woman and with her background she should be able to help get him parole. I really do hope he'll be out soon.

I was on television with the M.P. Teddy Taylor and he was fuming because I was saying how I attacked the hangman Albert Pierrepoint when he was going to hang Derek Bentley. A bit ago I read in the *News of the World* that he was worried about a man he knew, Peter Bleach, who was alleged to be supplying arms to the Hindus in India and was likely to be topped over there if he gets a guilty. I wonder if Taylor'd mind if I chinned the hangman when he was going to do his mate.

There was also some talk at the time of trying to get this man Bleach sprung, using the man who kidnapped Ronnie Biggs in Brazil. I don't know if anything came of it, but I do know a top comedian stuck the money up for Biggs' kidnapping. There must have been a lot of money put up. If the plot had succeeded and they'd delivered him outside the gates at Wandsworth the hype would have been amazing. The man could have come forward and said how he'd done his duty. Imagine if they had succeeded! He must have thought that in the long run the publicity would be worth it, but, thank God, it never got that far.[10]

I was very pleased when I heard the government got knocked back when they tried to get Biggs extradited in 1997. They had me on a couple of radio shows when the decision was announced, and I said on Liberty Radio that one of the government's platforms in getting elected was they were going to be tough on crime and Jack Straw did this as window-dressing, making it look as though he was being tough. The government out there was happy with him and our government knew full well it would fail, but they could sling their hands in the air and say, 'We tried, we done our best.' Clever move; if I'd been Home Secretary I'd have done the same.

Biggs was a lovely man but he was never top class, and I mean that nicely. I knew him in prison mostly when he was doing bits of bird in the 1950s. It's not knocking him, but he wasn't anything. He and his wife, Charmian, were nicked for breaking into a sports pavilion in the West Country. He somehow got her a fiver when they was in the dock together,

---

[10]Biggs escaped from Wandsworth prison on 8 July 1965 along with Eric Flowers, from South London, Robert Anderson who was with Fraser in the Parkhurst riot, and Anthony Jenkins who was also known as Patrick Doyle. It was thought by the police that Biggs was being held by what they called the Flowers Mob for his money. This was nonsense, and in fact Flowers went to Australia where he was recaptured.

but when she went back to the women's wing in the Exeter nick she was searched and she got bread and water for smuggling it in. I was there in Exeter, and it was when Jimmy Andrews and me done the Governor and got the cat ordered.

Marilyn saw an advert in the *Evening Standard* for a café in Islington – a little cubicle on a landing in the market just round the corner from our flat. Pierrepoint Row of all names. It gave me all the more urge to get it. It was £2,000 deposit, so when you turned it in you got your money back. The man sold it as a market bar and we did our best, but it didn't turn out well. The rent was £150 a week, but there was really only two days' trading when the market was open and you could make your dough. We'd got a little bit of the money and we were so keen to do something to look after our little bit of wedge. Marilyn cooked all the soups and I carried them round at half-three in the morning. I wouldn't have minded if there'd been anyone there to eat them.

It was damp as well, but we tried hard. In that time we'd been on TV, radio, and in the papers. It must have had half a million pounds' worth of publicity. We had a free gallery show, but we still couldn't make a go of it. One of the few punters was a screw from Hull who was down with his wife. He told me who he was and said, 'If I'd known it was your caff, I wouldn't have come in.' I said, 'If I'd known who you were I'd have pissed in your tea.' We sold some copies of the book there. In fact, I think we sold more books than sandwiches. It lasted about three months and then we had a right struggle to get our deposit back, but I did. Sometimes it pays to be known as 'Mad'. Since we turned it in in January 1995, there's been six lots of other people had it.

The last job I did wasn't really hookey at all, but it could have turned out wrong in a big way. A couple of years ago, maybe more, there was a guy who'd been turned over by another fellow and he asked me and a friend if we could help him get his dough back. I said, 'Of course,' and the fellow went round. The idea was for him to ask nicely for the money and then, if the man wouldn't hand it over or make proper arrangements, for us to explain things. Of course, what happened was there was a set-up. The man who'd had my friend over, he'd blown up the law.

I was in the back of a parked car somewhere over the water and the driver says, 'Frank, there's someone behind. Lock the doors.' I did mine in the back and leaned over and did the passenger side, and my friend was away. It was a ready-eye. He did magnificent. We were chased by untold cars; they rammed him and he rammed them back.

We got away and dropped the motor, still south of the river in the best possible spot and conveniently near to a block of flats where we knew some people lived. What was best was, it had a sort of underground car park and the car couldn't be seen from the air. They'd had a helicopter out and all. We got the lift up and, blimey, there was no one in. We couldn't kick the door in, in case someone came out from opposite and called the law. So we knocked on some other flats, and there was no answer there either. We couldn't really be sitting on the steps in case the coppers got round to searching. So we come down thinking how we were going to move next, and our luck turned. The wife of the man we knew came in with her kids and took us up to the flat. Ten minutes later the man himself comes in, and he's telling us about a chase he'd seen about half an hour before. I said, 'That was us,' and we all burst out laughing. It was a great chase. Say the flat we got to had been in Islington, then we lost the coppers at Mount Pleasant and we'd been chased from Waterloo Bridge. Eight in the evening, fairly light, and fortunately in the part of London where we actually were there wasn't that much traffic about.

With that I got in touch with some Italian friends up in the North. They didn't hesitate. Come straight up, they said. I moved from that flat to a good friend who come and collected me. I slung a toothbrush in a bag and caught the train. Someone had handed me the ticket and I didn't have to hang around. They were waiting the other end and they put me up. I think it was the wise thing to do. We weren't sure if the police knew who me and the driver actually were. We'd been in a straight car, but by then the geezer whose motor it was had made a statement saying it had been stolen after he'd left it parked.

If I'd stayed down South, I wouldn't know exactly who was who – and anyway the third man in our party had been nicked. You had to keep away out of sight of course, not put yourself about, otherwise it's not fair to the people who are minding you.

I stayed away for about seven months. By the end I was coming backwards and forwards, and throughout the time friends were having a word to tell the man to drop it out. The one who got nicked and the others was able to do a bit of business and once he was found not guilty that was really it, so I came back down South full time. That was really the last bit of excitement I had, although of course I still get offers. Much as I dislike that Nipper Read, he may be right when he says the only thing that stops professional criminals is when their legs give out.

Sixty, forty, even twenty years ago we were told that fingerprint evidence was infallible. Now we know that it's not quite as solid as it was thought to be. It's all a question of how you take the dabs off the surface and then match them. You can get discrepancies. The same thing seems to have happened with DNA testing. It's good that it's caught a lot of rapists and child molesters, but in sixty years' time will some scientist come up with something which will dispute it? I'm worried when one body of scientists comes up with something which is infallible, then years later another body comes up and says, 'No, it isn't. *This* is what's infallible.' What's happened to all the poor people who've been convicted in the meanwhile?

What would I have done if I hadn't become a criminal? People might think that the fame itself following the book has made it worthwhile, but it isn't just that. To be fair, nothing could compare with the excitement I've had, daft as it may sound, of doing the crimes over the years. The sheer adrenalin of a success; I couldn't have changed it and I wouldn't have wanted to. I suppose I could have become a solicitor and helped innocent people and as many guilty people as I could to get acquitted. Seriously, though, what would I have wound up as? A bus driver? Even if I'd come out after all them years and written no books or had no fame, I wouldn't have liked to be a bus driver who goes straight on by when an elderly lady puts her hand out late at night at a request, and he splashes her and all. Bus drivers exist who do that. Always have, always will, and I might have been one of them.

Crime, it's been a risky life but it's been a good life. I'm not grumbling. In fact I'm in the pink.

Bibliographical Notes

There have been independent accounts of many of the incidents and characters referred to in this book. In more or less historical order, the career of Cammie Grizzard is documented in Christmas Humphreys' *The Great Pearl Robbery of 1913* (1929, London, Heinemann). There are a number of files at the Public Records Office on that case and on the Sabinis and other racecourse gangs of the 1920s and 1930s, including MEPO/3/366. Edward Hart's biography of Darby Sabini, *Britain's Godfather* (1993, London, True Crime Library) is heavily reliant on the not-always-accurate recollections of George Sewell. He has also used pseudonyms and, to make matters even more difficult, has juxtaposed events.

The Dartmoor Mutiny has been covered from various points of view, notably by the Rev. H. Baden Ball, *Prison was my Parish* (1956, Heineman); Dr Guy Richmond, *Prison Doctor* (1975, BC Nunaga) and in Ruby Sparks, *Burglar to the Nobility* (1961, Arthur Barker), which of course also deals with his career generally. W.F.R. Macarthy, *Walls Have Mouths* (1936, Victor Gollancz), is the most dispassionate. On the subject of prison riots, Alistair Miller was the Governor at the time of the Parkhurst riot in which Fraser took part. His memoir is *Inside, Outside* (1976, London, Queensgate). There is a compilation of prison writings in Paul Priestley's *Jail Journeys; The English Prison Experience 1918–1900* (1989, Routledge). J.P. Bean's *Over the Wall* (1994, London, Headline) recounts the escapes of Ruby Sparks, Patrick Meehan, Alfie Hinds, Jimmy Moody and Sydney Draper amongst a number of others. Details of Ruby Sparks' career and particularly his escape from Dartmoor, along with the machinations of Lilian Goldstein, can also be found in the files at the Public Record Office at Kew MEPO 3/503. Rather disappointingly, the file relating to Alf Hinds Snr and the Portsmouth bank robbery contains little on the robbery but a great deal on the efforts to trace the lost notes.

Rafael Samuels' account of the life of Arthur Harding, and the Underworld after the turn of the century to the 1930s is in the seminal *East End Underworld* (1981, London, Routledge & Kegan Paul). There is an account of the life of the fire-raiser Leopold Harris by William Charles Crocker in *Far from Humdrum* (1967, London, Hutchinson). Frank Owen's *The Eddie Chapman Story* (1953, London, Allan Wingate) takes the safe-breaker's career only to the end of the Second World War and so has no account of his subsequent life and times with Billy Hill.

For an overall survey of London's gangland from the turn of the century there is James Morton's *Gangland* (1992, London, Little, Brown); Duncan Campbell's *The Underworld* (1994, London, BBC Books) and Robert Murphy's *Smash and Grab* (1993, London, Faber & Faber), which last includes an account of the Spot-Hill relationship from the Spot point of view.

Both men wrote their own memoirs. Billy Hill's *Boss of Britain's Underworld* (1955, London, The Naldrett Press) is confusing in that there are many pseudonyms. For example, the Black family is the White family and Spot is referred to as Benny the Kid. Spot's own version of the gospel is by the American pulp novelist Hank Janson who wrote *Jack Spot: Man of a Thousand Cuts* (1958, London, Alexander Moring Ltd).

While there is a mention of 'Italian Jock' in Sammy Samuels' *Among the Soho Sinners* (1970, London, Robert Hale), this should not necessarily be taken to refer to Albert Dimes' brother, Victor 'Italian Jock' Dimeo, who was a much older and more powerful figure at the time. Assuming it is he, there is no other record of Victor Dimeo having only one leg. However, in the book there are a number of references to Billy Hill and clubs he owned. Shifty Burke's *Peterman* (1966, London, Arthur Barker) uses pseudonyms; Spot appears as King Solly and Burke hides his own identity by saying he received seven years for the London Airport bullion robbery, a sentence which none of the participants actually collected.

Jimmy O'Connor's account of his conviction for murder and the part played by George Sewell – the father, not the present-day actor – is in *The Eleventh Commandment* (1976, St Peter Port, Guernsey, Seagull). Curiously, the case is not mentioned in the investigating officer's memoirs: Arthur Thorp, *Calling Scotland Yard* (1954, London, Allan Wingate).

There have been a number of books on the Hanratty case, the best known of which is Paul Foot, *Who Killed Hanratty?* (1971, London, Jonathan Cape).

Alfie Hinds' version of the Maples robbery is contained in his autobiography *Contempt of Court* (1966, London, The Bodley Head). It is not necessarily a correct one. The better view in the Underworld is that he committed the robbery but that Sparks did fabricate the evidence against him. There have been many books on the Great Train Robbery including Peta Fordham, *The Robbers' Tale* (1965, London, Hodder & Stoughton); Piers Paul Read, *The Train Robbers* (1978, London, Hodder & Stoughton) and Bruce Reynolds, *The Autobiography of a Thief* (1995, London, Bantam Press). Robert Parker's *Rough Justice* (1981, London, Fontana) is the definitive version of the story of Charlie Richardson and his brother Eddie.

The best of the books on the Krays is John Pearson's *Profession of Violence* whilst Leonard' Read's *Nipper* (1990, London, Little, Brown) is an account of his tracking the twins. Leslie Payne wrote a relatively unbiased view from inside the firm in *The Brotherhood* (1973, London, Michael Joseph). Eric Mason's account of those years is in *The Inside Story* (1994, London, Pan Books) whilst Tony Lambrianou wrote

Inside the Firm (1991, London, Smith Gryphon). Reg Kray wrote a small book *Villains We Have Known* (1993, Leeds, N.K. Publications), which contains a number of vignettes of the Twins' contemporary criminals.

There is an entertaining little account of the fight between police officers in the Albion public house in Laurie Taylor's *In the Underworld* (1985, London, Unwin Paperbacks). Jack Slipper, *Slipper of the Yard* (1981, London, Sidgwick & Jackson) has accounts of the Great Train Robbery as well as the shooting of the police by Harry Roberts and the robbery in Glasgow by Fraser's schoolfriend's son Billy Murray and others. The tale of the supergrass Don Barrett and David Croke can be found in Liz Mills, *Crimewatch* (1995, London, Penguin). Supergrasses generally are dealt with in James Morton's *Supergrasses and Informers* (1995, London, Little, Brown). John Ball, Lewis Chester and Roy Perrott look at the machinations of Bertie Smalls and the bank robberies of the 1960s in *Cops and Robbers* (1979, London, Penguin). The Earl Mountbatten *Report of the Inquiry into Prison Escapes and Security* (1966, London, HMSO) examines the escapes of Frank Mitchell, Charlie Wilson and Ronnie Biggs as well as the one by John McVicar and Billy Gentry.

Joe Beltrami gives an account of Meehan and the Ross case in *A Deadly Innocence* (1989, Edinburgh, Mainstream).

The story of Shirley Pitts and her brother Adgie is in Lorraine Gamman's *Gone Shopping* (1996, London, Signet). Again, in some cases names have been changed. The Billy B. referred to is Billy Benstead and her brother, Charles, who quarrelled with the Goodwin family to the cost of both of them, is called Eddie.

The Brinks-Mat case is the subject of Andrew Hogg, Jim McDougall and Robin Morgan's *Bullion* (1988, London, Penguin).

Ronnie Biggs' account of his escape from Wandsworth and his journeys are in his *Odd Man Out* (1994, London, Bloomsbury).

Patrick Meehan, in *Innocent Villain* (1978, London, Pan Books) is another who uses pseudonyms. In his story Arthur Thompson, the Glasgow gangleader and friend of Fraser, becomes McTampson. Meehan's lawyer Joe Beltrami wrote the account of the efforts to free him in *A Deadly Innocence* (1989, Edinburgh, Mainstream).

In Ronnie Knight's *Black Knight* (1990, London, Century), there is a short account of the 1983 Security Express raid after which his brother John received 22 years, and Freddie Foreman nine, for dishonest handling of part of the proceeds. Foreman's own book is *Respect* (1997, London, Century).

A number of the incidents referred to briefly in this book can be found in more detail in Frank Fraser's earlier book *Mad Frank* (1994, London, Little Brown).

Index

MAD FRANK
Memoirs of a Life of Crime

Frankie Fraser as told to James Morton

Mad Frank is Frankie Fraser's own extraordinary story – the truth about the legendary villain who for fifty years was a key figure in Britain's underworld. A peer of the Krays and the Richardsons, arguably as influential and certainly as dangerous, Fraser has served over forty years in prisons and mental institutions for his various crimes.

Mad Frank – a man who has been at the cutting edge of crime in this country, and who took the time to sharpen it while he was there.

'A pivotal figure in any history of England's gangland . . . a harrowing book' *Sunday Times*

'Fascinating . . . a chilling account of a truly dangerous person' *Daily Express*

'Unputdownable' *Independent*

'An amazing account of the workings of criminal families in Britain' *Sunday Telegraph*

EAST END GANGLAND

James Morton

Murder. Extortion. Vice. Drugs. From the immigrant gangs of the early 20th century to the Kray twins and after, nowhere in Britain is as synonymous with organised crime as London's East End. Now, in this fascinating and revealing book, James Morton, author of *Gangland* and *Gangland International*, looks back at the crimes and the criminals that have given the area its legendary reputation.

Impeccably researched, *East End Gangland* offers both absorbing detail and informed overview, chronicling those who may have lived beyond the law, but never broke the unwritten rules of the underworld.

Praise for James Morton's Gangland books:

'Fascinating' *Sunday Telegraph*

'. . . teems with lively information about dozens of great gangs and gangsters of the century' *The Times*

SUPERGRASSES AND INFORMERS

James Morton

Some do it for money, some because they are scared for their lives, some because they are going straight, and some have found religion. They are as old as history. They break the underworld's code of silence, turning against their own kind. And they are essential to any criminal investigation.

In *Supergrasses and Informers*, leading crime expert James Morton unravels the tangled history of the key players: characters such as 'Bertie' Smalls, the original supergrass, and his successor, 'King Squealer' Maurice O'Mahoney; double agent Roy Garner, and the one who got away, Nikolaus Chrastny; Joe Valachi, the first of the great post-war Mafia informers, and Leslie Payne, the Krays' *consigliere*.

This is a fascinating and well-documented account of the criminal underworld on both sides of the Atlantic.

Praise for James Morton's Gangland books:

'An essential addition to the library shelf' *Time Out*

SEX, CRIMES AND MISDEMEANOURS

James Morton

Sex and the law have never been easy bedfellows. While there have been outrages and indecencies since time immemorial, the definition of immorality, unacceptable behaviour and what legally constitutes evidence has undergone constant revision through the ages. Taking the nineteenth century as his starting point, James Morton negotiates a moral minefield in this study of sex crime.

From the glamorous to the seedy, *Sex, Crimes and Misdemeanours* charts the evolution of sex in the eyes of the law. The use of case studies lends this broad survey accessibility, focus and depth – taking in both the big names of scandal such as Oscar Wilde, John Profumo and Lorena Bobbitt, as well as those lesser known, though equally significant, like the Brighton Poisoner.

Sometimes shocking, always pertinent, Morton's scope is great, his research exhaustive and this study a compelling tour of the taboos and technicalities of sex law.

Praise for James Morton's Gangland books:

'Faithfully factual, gripping . . . prescribed reading' *Evening Standard*

GANGSTER'S MOLL

Marilyn Wisbey

Marilyn Wisbey grew up alongside some of the most notorious villains of London. She is the daughter of Great Train Robber Tommy Wisbey, the goddaughter of the infamous Freddie Foreman, who was acquitted of the murder of Ginger Marks and convicted of being an accessory to murder with Reggie Kray of Jack 'The Hat' McVitie, and she was a long time friend of Reggie and Charlie Kray. She lived with the legendary 'Mad' Frank Fraser for nine years.

Marilyn has many tales to tell and also examines the role of a 'moll', what she feels about the morals of being one, the glamour and how the public react to her.

Frank, funny and revealing, *Gangster's Moll* is Marilyn Wisbey's remarkable story of a life at the sharp end of London's Gangland, a candid account of a woman's lot in a hard man's world.

Other bestselling Warner titles available by mail:

The prices shown above are correct at time of going to press.
However, the publishers reserve the right to increase prices on covers
from those previously advertised without prior notice.

WARNER BOOKS

WARNER BOOKS
Cash Sales Department, P.O. Box 11, Falmouth, Cornwall, TR10 9EN
Tel: +44 (0) 1326 372400, Fax: +44 (0) 1326 374888
Email: books@barni.avel.co.uk.

POST AND PACKING
Payments can be made as follows: cheque, postal order (payable to
Warner Books) or by credit cards. Do not send cash or currency.

All U.K. Orders	**FREE OF CHARGE**
E.E.C. & Overseas	25% of order value

Name (Block Letters) _____

Address _____

_____

Post/zip code: _____

☐ Please keep me in touch with future Warner publications
☐ I enclose my remittance £ _____
☐ I wish to pay by Visa/Access/Mastercard/Eurocard   Expiry date

